Better Homes and Gardens.

TRADITIONAL AMERICAN CRAFTS

© Copyright 1988 by Meredith Corporation, Des Moines, Iowa.
All Rights Reserved. Printed in the United States of America.
First Edition. Second Printing, 1988.
Library of Congress Catalog Card Number: 87-63206
ISBN: 0-696-01530-7

*T*urn these pages to discover the best of traditional and country crafts and needlework, all beautifully displayed in some of America's finest country inns and historic homes. If you are looking for a spectacular project to use as a focal point for a favorite room, or as a token of affection for a loved one, you'll find it here. The more than 120 time-honored designs and projects represent 21 techniques. Even if you're already an admirer or collector of authentic Americana, you'll find that Traditional American Crafts will deepen your appreciation of the skill and dedication of traditional American artisans.

CONTENTS

AMERICAN CRAFTSMANSHIP

A LIVELY TRADITION

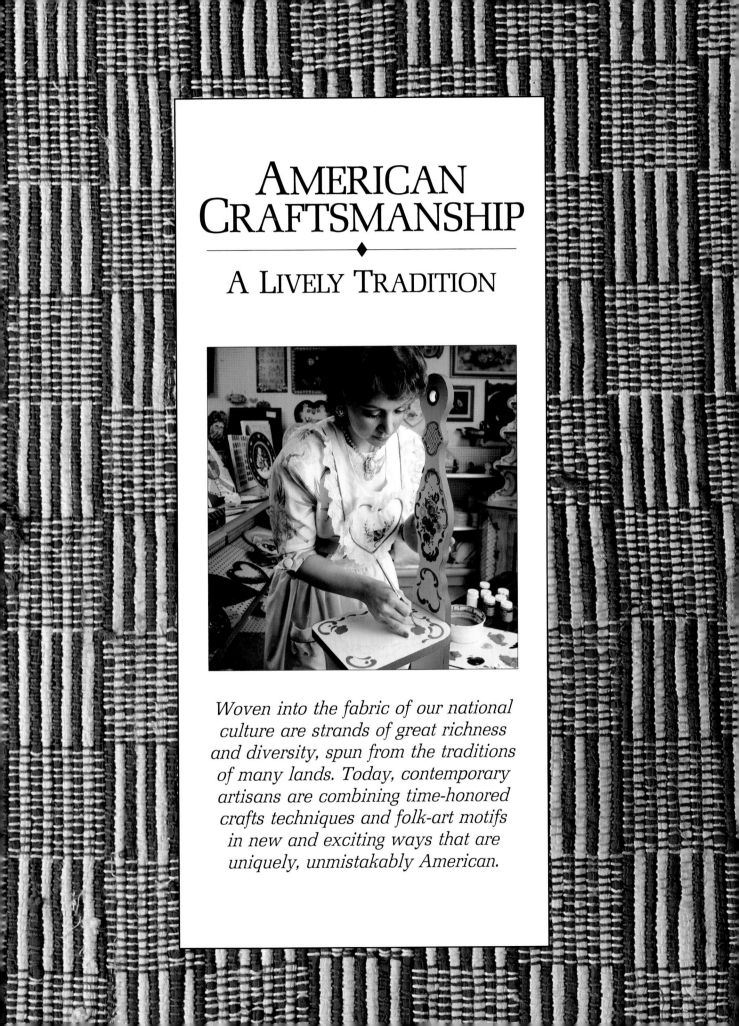

Woven into the fabric of our national culture are strands of great richness and diversity, spun from the traditions of many lands. Today, contemporary artisans are combining time-honored crafts techniques and folk-art motifs in new and exciting ways that are uniquely, unmistakably American.

AMERICAN CRAFTSMANSHIP

Weaver Mary Rust of Alexandria, Virginia, exemplifies that proud blend of personal interest and professional commitment that characterizes many working craftsmen in America today.

Devotees of country-style living, Mary and her architect husband, John, have filled their home with handcrafted items representing three centuries of American artisanry. A few of the pieces are family heirlooms. Others are shop and auction finds.

To this mix, Mary makes her own contribution: beautiful rag rugs, runners, and table mats, *below,* which she weaves on her home loom and on a vintage loom in her antiques shop, The Sow's Ear.

(How-to for woven mats begins on page 93.)

AMERICAN CRAFTSMANSHIP

From their home in the lovely Bluff Creek Valley, near Boone, Iowa, Pam Dennis, Rick Weiss, and their daughter, Deyhdra, bring their unique skills and vision to a long and proud tradition: the making of handcrafted furniture.

A large bog at the rear of their homestead provides an abundant supply of the supple willow twigs and saplings from which they fashion chairs, tables, planters, baskets, and various one-of-a-kind designs.

Pam and Rick spent years developing their willow-working skills. Rick enjoys working with designs that have curves, giving his somewhat rustic pieces (several of which are pictured here) an unexpected grace and sophistication. His chairs, settees, and chaise longues grace many a country porch and sun-room in the area.

Pam, who has a degree in horticulture, bends willow shoots into lyrical baskets, which are often filled with homegrown flowers and herbs from the family garden. Her other specialties include tables and planters, like the handsome design *opposite*. Deyhdra assists where needed, often coming up with her own whimsical creations.

To make the plant stand, turn to page 200.

AMERICAN CRAFTSMANSHIP

In early American homes, furniture was often painted to camouflage plain-looking wood or to accent special details. Today, Pennsylvania folk artist Ivan Barnett, *opposite,* takes a more light-hearted approach. Each piece of his unique furniture is painted in a combination of bright, bold colors—turquoise, magenta, orange, yellow, and royal blue.

Working out of his Lancaster County studio, Barnett began by painting cast-off furniture, then moved on to design new pieces. Many of Barnett's designs, like the fanciful mirror, *below,* are embellished with his signature appliqués— painted metal cutouts in traditional folk-art shapes. (How-to begins on page 181.)

AMERICAN CRAFTSMANSHIP

Minnesota artists Jill Fitzhenry and Nancy Jefferson have developed an individual approach to painted furniture. Drawing on the influence of the colorful floral patterns of Bavarian folk art, the two friends established a thriving crafts enterprise teaching decorative folk-art painting and creating custom designs.

Originally paired in the Creative Artists' Workshop, *above right,* Jill, *standing,* and Nancy began their crafts careers teaching students how to paint on every sort of surface from wooden furniture and wall plaques to tinware (known as tole painting) and fabric.

Though the patterns and techniques they teach are basically traditional, Nancy and Jill have introduced contemporary materials and added their own special design flourishes.

The author of numerous books and articles on decorative folk-art painting, Jill has recently opened a new shop, Jillybean's Studio, near Minneapolis, where she and Nancy will continue to teach and design in the best tradition of working artists. (Instructions for making the Welcome Sign begin on page 110.)

AMERICAN CRAFTSMANSHIP

Drawing on ideas born during moments of nostalgic reverie, Texas doll maker Judie Tasch has lovingly fashioned an extended family of little friends from fabric and paint.

"All of my dolls are original designs inspired by antiques," she explains. "They are made of cotton cloth, painted in several separate steps, antiqued with a glaze, and then varnished."

Each doll has a winsome, old-fashioned name—Serenity Wisdom (Judie's first cloth doll), Serenity's beau, Adam Pittsfield (a portly country gentleman), and others such as the infants, Cordelia and Constance, *right*. Because her creations are influenced by the work of 19th-century doll makers Ludwig Grenier, Izannah Walker, and Martha Chase, using these gentle, old names for her new dolls seems quite appropriate.

Though Judie began her career creating reproduction porcelain dolls, she was moved by the more pliant and gentle character of those made from cloth. "The porcelains are fragile; you must be very careful," she says. "I much prefer the dolls you can hug, hold, and confide in."

To create your own dolls, turn to page 139.

AMERICAN CRAFTSMANSHIP

One of the oldest and most enduringly popular of American crafts, quilting is traditionally a social activity. Today, as in days gone by, quilting bees offer a welcomed opportunity for friends to visit and swap news as they create something beautiful together.

Gathered around the quilting frame, *opposite,* are four expert stitchers, part of a group of local volunteers who demonstrate their skills at the Living History Farms museum near Des Moines, Iowa. The costumes and setting are vintage 1875, but the quilters' pleasure in plying their needles is very much in the present.

Below is a pillow created in the Dutch Tulip pattern, illustrating the fine, even stitches of a master quilter. (For pattern, turn to page 243.)

COLONIAL CRAFTS

◆

PLAIN AND FANCY

Some colonists arrived in the New World with a comfortable cushion of old-world wealth and resources. Others were obliged to create a new life for themselves from the materials at hand. But rich or poor, all helped to shape the arts and crafts of early America.

COLONIAL CRAFTS

More than 300 years ago, men and women flocked from every corner of the Old World to seek their fortunes in this new one.

Some who came were members of the upper classes of England and Europe, staunch supporters of the colonial powers and diligent conservators of their cultural traditions.

In the domestic arts, this respect for tradition led to literal imitation of the patterns, tastes, and techniques that prevailed "at home." But by the early 1800s, American stitchery began to break free of the stiff, formal patterns of the past, exhibiting a new spontaneity of expression that has been the hallmark of American needlework ever since. Most immigrants, moreover, found that the scarcity of materials and the harsh realities of day-to-day life in a frontier environment demanded swift and creative responses. They quickly developed a finely honed talent for creating something useful—and often quite beautiful—out of whatever materials lay at hand.

In the absence of lavishly embroidered coverlets, the colonial housewife kept her family warm with ingeniously pieced quilts, like these Log Cabin and Pinwheel designs.

COLONIAL CRAFTS

Log Cabin designs like the Barn Raising variation on the bed, *below,* were popular from the early days of the Republic onward. Stitched from simple rectangles cut from old wool clothes, the basic block is easy to piece and can be arranged in a number of pleasing patterns. (Courthouse Steps, Light and Dark,

and Straight Furrow are other Log Cabin designs.)

Both this woolen quilt and the Pinwheel-pattern cradle quilt beside it are true scrap-bag quilts. Each makes thrifty use of many different fabrics, relying on the basic contrast between light and dark shades to sustain the pattern.

Another scrap project, the woven rug beneath

the cradle, makes effective use of felted wool strips salvaged from worn-out blankets and sturdy winter clothing.

There was little leisure time for fancy stitchery on the frontier, but simple cross-stitch samplers, like the one *opposite,* were seen as a practical way of teaching a useful skill.

COLONIAL CRAFTS

Much of every woman's daily life in Colonial America was spent beside the hearth.

In humbler abodes, this often meant staying in a single room that served as kitchen, nursery, and "family room" in one. Here the mistress of the house might spend her evenings spinning and weaving. Perhaps she stored her finished lengths of homespun in a cabinet, like the one *opposite,* embellished with comb-, sponge-, and spatter-painted designs (as were the bowls and baskets) in an effort to give the plain pine wood a semblance of something finer. (For more on painted finishes, turn to page 106.)

The stacks of fabric pictured here have all been rinsed in tan fabric dye—a clever technique for getting new fabrics to match the softer palette of antique textiles.

In the Colonial mansions of Virginia, Maryland, and Massachusetts, the mistress was apt to spend her evenings by the fireside stitching yet another crewelwork cushion. If the fire blazed too brightly, milady's cheeks likely were shielded from the heat by a needlepoint fire screen, like the one shown here.

COLONIAL CRAFTS

In an age before printed needlework patterns of any sort were widely available, favorite embroidery designs were frequently used over and over again and eagerly shared among family and friends. Designs were continually adapted, reinterpreted, and recombined in new and imaginative ways to suit the stitcher's fancy and meet her own particular needs.

Pictured in the room, *right,* are a number of crewelwork accessories based on a single exquisite pattern of carnations and foliage interpreted in several different ways.

Above the bed hangs an embroidered linen mirror frame stitched with a beautiful pattern of blossoms and leaves. The same arrangement of elements is repeated in the doily on the nightstand.

Above, a pair of guest towels sports a simple design of leaves and berries based on a single arc of the overall pattern. (For a closer view of these projects, please turn the page.)

The bed, *right,* is dressed with a handsome quilt in the Dove at the Crossroads pattern. The coverlet boasts particularly fine quilting in a feather-wreath-and-hearts design that suggests it may have been stitched as a wedding quilt.

28

COLONIAL
CRAFTS

Designs on the mirror frame, *opposite,* and the matching doily, *below,* were embroidered in four shades of pink and three shades of green wool yarn on fine linen cloth.

Three simple stitches were used to create these lovely motifs—satin, chain, and stem stitches—but the resulting pattern has the rich texture and subtle shading characteristic of classic crewel embroidery.

On the table, *opposite,* stands a handsome brass lamp with a cut-and-pierced paper shade—yet another interpretation of the carnation pattern found on the embroidered accessories.

Use these designs for a variety of other home furnishings. Embroider a window valance or the edging on a fine wool blanket. Or, cut and pierce a purchased paper window shade.

(Patterns for the projects shown begin on *page 32.*)

INSTRUCTIONS FOR COLONIAL CRAFTS

Crewel Embroidery

Shown on pages 20–21.

MATERIALS
Linen fabric in ecru or yellow
Persian yarn in desired colors
Embroidery hoop
Crewel embroidery needles
Dressmaker's carbon

INSTRUCTIONS
Full-size flowers and leaves from the crewelwork on *pages 20–21* are given *below* and *opposite*. Use these elements to design a chair or bench cover, or to make a pillow. Add or subtract elements as necessary to fit the size and shape of your project.

The antique embroidery on the Chippendale chair seat, *page 21,* was the inspiration for the needlework background, *pages 20–21*. The elements were repeated to fill the required space.

If the chair or bench has an old covering, remove it and use it to determine how much background fabric you will need for upholstery. Center the design and move the basic floral elements around within the allotted space until you achieve a pleasing arrangement.

Transfer the design to your fabric using dressmaker's carbon. Mount the fabric in an embroidery hoop for ease in stitching.

The design on *pages 20–21* was worked in three basic embroidery stitches: chain, satin, and stem or outline stitches (stitch diagrams are given on *page 252*)—with French knots added for flower centers.

Refer to the color photograph on *pages 20–21* for color and stitch guidance. Or, embroider the pattern using your favorite decorative stitches.

When embroidery is completed, remove the fabric from the hoop and press it on the back side.

Stretch the fabric over the padded seat form, or finish the embroidery into a pillow as desired.

Barn Raising Log Cabin Quilt

Shown on pages 22–23.
Finished size: 78¾x78¾ inches

MATERIALS
Approximately 5 yards *each* of light and dark wool, silk, and satin fabric scraps
6½ yards of muslin
5 yards of backing fabric for conventional back
10 yards of bias for binding

CREWEL EMBROIDERY
Full-Size Patterns

32

INSTRUCTIONS

Note: Quilts that are made of fragile fabrics usually are sewn to a muslin square and not hand-quilted. When made from cottons, the blocks usually are pieced without the muslin square and are hand-quilted.

This quilt consists of 196 blocks, each 5⅝ inches square, arranged in 14 rows of 14 blocks each. Each block consists of a 1⅛-inch center square surrounded by 1⅛-inch-wide logs.

Use the diagram, *page 34,* as a guide, and plan the position and color of each block on graph paper.

TO CUT THE PIECES: All cutting measurements include ¼-inch seam allowances. From the muslin, cut 196 squares, *each* 6½ inches square, for block linings.

Cut the light and dark fabrics into 1⅝-inch-wide strips. Construct the blocks, using the appropriate color combinations.

BARN RAISING LOG CABIN QUILT

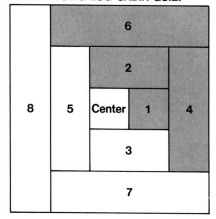

Block Piecing Diagram

TO PIECE ONE BLOCK: The piecing diagram, *above,* is shaded into a dark and a light half. The pieces are numbered to indicate the order in which they should be added to the center square.

Choose a light and a dark fabric for the block. Cut a light strip into the following lengths: 1⅝ inches for the block center, 2¾ inches for piece 3, 3⅞ inches for piece 5, 4¾

inches for piece 7, and 6⅛ inches for piece 8.

Cut a dark strip into the following lengths: 1⅝ inches for piece 1, 2¾ inches for piece 2, 3⅞ inches for piece 4, and 4¾ inches for piece 6.

Pin the *wrong* side of a center square to the center of a muslin square. Pin piece 1 atop the center square with *right* sides facing. Sew along one side of the stacked squares through the muslin lining square. Open out piece 1 and finger-press the seam.

With *right* sides facing, pin piece 2 atop the center square and piece 1. Sew along the long side, sewing through the center square, piece 1, and the muslin square. Open out and finger-press piece 2.

Referring to the diagram, continue to add pieces in numerical order. When all of the pieces have been added, trim the muslin square even with the raw edges of the pieced block. Make 196 log-cabin blocks.

continued

continued from page 33
Colonial Crafts

TO PIECE THE QUILT TOP: Lay out the blocks into 14 rows of blocks with 14 blocks in each row. To create the Barn Raising set, turn the four center blocks so that the light halves are together, forming a square turned on point. Referring to the photograph on *pages 22–23* and the diagram *below,* turn and rearrange the other blocks so that they form light and dark bands around the center light square.

Sew the blocks into 14 rows with 14 blocks in each row. Carefully press all seams open.

TO ADD THE QUILT BACK: Piece the backing fabric to size; baste to quilt top. Tie each block corner to the quilt back, forming the ties on the quilt back. (Follow the general instructions, *opposite,* for tying a quilt.) Bind the edges.

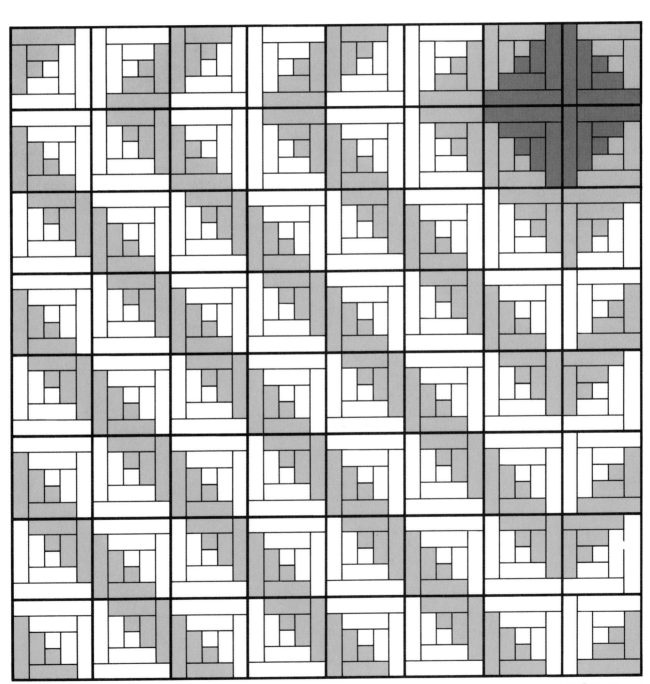

BARN RAISING LOG CABIN QUILT

¼ of Quilt Design

Pinwheel-Pattern Crib Quilt

Shown on pages 22–23 and page 24.
Finished size: 39x45 inches

MATERIALS
1 yard each of light and dark
   calico fabrics in assorted prints
1½ yards of white print fabric for
   sashing and borders
1½ yards backing fabric
1½ yards lightweight batting
5 yards bias binding

TO TIE
A QUILT

Use an embroidery needle
and yarn or floss that either
matches or contrasts with the
quilt top. Use single or
double thread, depending on
the desired effect.

   Pin and baste all layers of
the quilt together (top,
batting—if any—and
backing). Begin at the center
of the quilt and work toward
the edges. Working from the
right side of the quilt, push
the threaded needle through
all of the layers of the quilt
and out the back. Then
reenter from the back, going
through all layers and coming
up ⅛ inch from the point of
entry. Allow 2 inches of
thread at either end of the
stitch and cut. Tie the ends
of the thread in a neat, tight
square knot; trim the ends.

   If you do not want the ties
to show on the front of the
quilt, reverse the procedure
and tie the threads to the
back. (Use this procedure for
the log-cabin quilt, *page 32.*)

INSTRUCTIONS
Quilt consists of thirty 4½-inch pinwheel blocks arranged in five rows
of six blocks each. Blocks are joined
by 2¼-inch-wide sashings and
framed by 2¼-inch-wide borders.
Squares measuring 2¼ inches (one
dark and one light triangle) mark every intersection of the sashing strips
and each corner of the border. Quilt
is bound in plain white bias.

CUTTING INSTRUCTIONS: Make
plastic or cardboard templates for
pattern pieces A and B, *below.*
Trace and cut the following pieces,
*adding ¼-inch seam allowances to
each piece:* 144 triangles (A) from
dark prints and 144 triangles (A)
from light prints. From white print
fabric, cut two pieces 2¾x36 inches
and two pieces 2¾x42 inches for
borders. Cut 49 rectangles (B) from
white print fabric.

TO PIECE ONE BLOCK: Stitch one
light and one dark triangle together
along longest sides to form a square;
make four. Referring to piecing diagram, *below,* stitch four pieced
squares together to form one pinwheel block. Press seams toward
darker fabrics.

   Make a total of 30 pinwheel
blocks.

   Stitch remaining 24 light and 24
dark triangles together to make 24
small squares.

TO PIECE QUILT TOP: Arrange 5
pinwheel blocks in a horizontal row
and slip four white print rectangles
between the blocks. Stitch all blocks
and rectangles together; press
seams toward rectangles. Make a
total of six horizontal rows.

continued

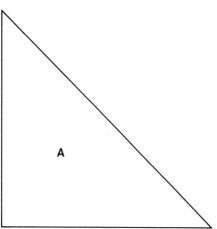

Piecing Diagram

PINWHEEL-PATTERN CRIB QUILT   **Full-Size Finished Pattern**
                                         (Add ¼-inch seam allowances)

35

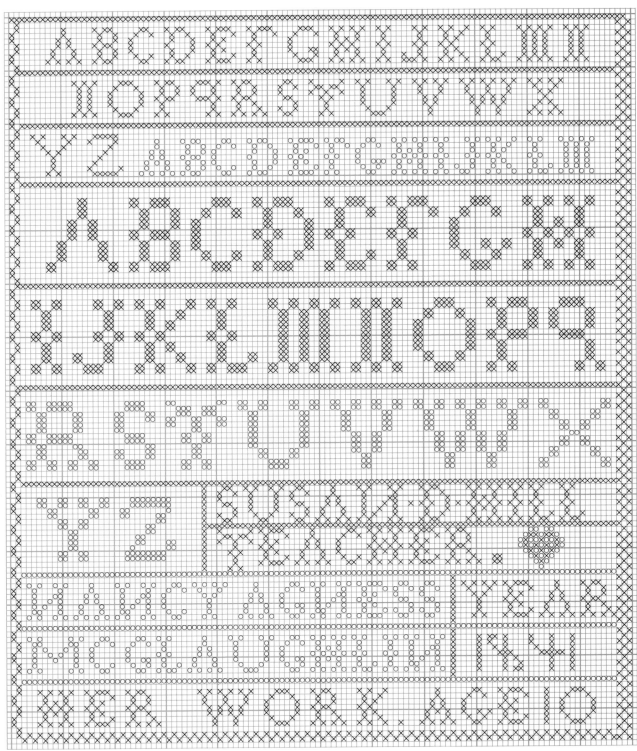

ALPHABET SAMPLER

COLOR KEY
⊠ Blue
⊡ Tan

36

continued from page 35
Colonial Crafts

Lay out five rectangles horizontally and slip a pieced 2¼-inch square between each strip. Stitch the five strips and four squares together end to end; press seams toward rectangles. Make a total of five such sashing strips.

Lay out alternating rows of blocks and sashing strips, following piecing diagram, *page 35*. Stitch rows together; press seams toward sashing strips.

To add the quilt borders, stitch one 2¾x42-inch border strip to each long side of the quilt top (trim length to size, if necessary). Trim a 2¾x36-inch strip to the right length, stitch a small pieced square to each end, and stitch this border to top of quilt. Repeat for bottom border. Press seams toward borders.

TO FINISH QUILT: Complete quilt by cutting and piecing backing fabric to size. Cut batting to size.

Sandwich backing, batting, and pieced top together; pin and baste. Quilt in parallel lines or in quilting pattern of your choice.

To finish, trim edges and batting even and bind with white bias strips.

Alphabet Sampler

Shown on page 25.
Finished size: 8½x9¾ inches, excluding the border of plain fabric

MATERIALS
10½x11¾ inches of 14-count Aida cloth
Embroidery floss in the colors listed on the color key, *opposite*

INSTRUCTIONS
TO PREPARE THE PATTERN: Chart the complete pattern, *opposite*, onto graph paper using marking pens. Or, you may work directly from the pattern.

TO STITCH THE DESIGN: Separate the embroidery floss and use two strands for working the cross-stitches.

Locate the center of the pattern and the center of the fabric; work outward from this point.

Stitch each counted cross-stitch over one thread of fabric.

TO FINISH THE SAMPLER: If necessary, lightly press the stitchery on the back side of the fabric. Frame as desired.

Woven Felt Strip Rug

Shown on page 24.
Finished size: 44½x30½ inches

MATERIALS
50-inch-wide, heavyweight felt in the following colors and amounts: 1 yard gray, ⅓ yard black, ¼ yard each of red, dark and medium brown, tan, dark and light beige
Sharp scissors
Sewing machine

INSTRUCTIONS
All felt strips should be ½ inch wide. Cut 79 gray strips 27 inches long for crosspieces. Cut the following 50-inch-long strips for lengthwise pieces: 22 black, 4 red, 10 gray, 2 dark brown, 2 medium brown, 2 tan, 4 dark beige, and 5 light beige.

Lay out the 79 shorter gray strips side by side on a table and begin to weave the longer strips over and under these cross strips in the following sequence: 6 black, 1 gray, 1 red, 3 gray, 1 dark brown, 1 medium brown, 1 tan, 1 red, 1 gray, 5 black, 2 dark beige, and 5 light beige (center of rug).

Continue weaving to far side of rug: 2 dark beige, 5 black, 1 gray, 1 red, 1 tan, 1 medium brown, 1 dark brown, 3 gray, 1 red, 1 gray, and 6 black.

Begin and end weaving approximately 2½ inches in from edges of

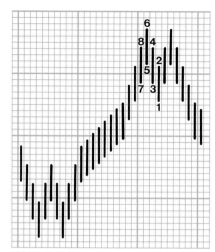

NEEDLEPOINT FIRE SCREEN

crosspieces. Keep strips closely packed together but still lying flat.

When weaving of felt strips is completed, baste and then machine-stitch around the perimeter of the rug, stitching through the center of each outer horizontal and vertical strip to secure the weaving. Trim fringe to approximately 2½ inches wide all around.

Needlepoint Fire Screen

Shown on page 27.

MATERIALS
Number 10 mono needlepoint canvas
Persian wool yarn in the following colors: light, medium, and dark gold; light and medium coral; rust; and dark and medium brown
Needlepoint needles
Needlepoint frame (optional)
Masking tape
Waterproof markers
Purchased fireplace screen

INSTRUCTIONS
The fire screen pictured on *page 27* is an antique frame. The needlework was stitched using two
continued

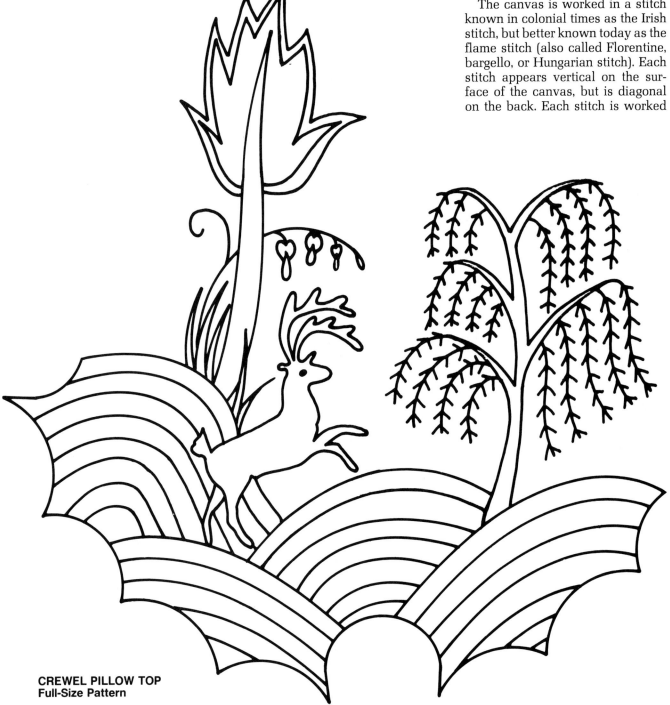

continued from page 37
Colonial Crafts

strands of Persian wool yarn on Number 10 needlepoint canvas. Our finished screen measures approximately 23x21 inches.

To create a similar piece of needlepoint for a fire screen, chair seat, pillow top, etc., follow these simple directions.

The canvas is worked in a stitch known in colonial times as the Irish stitch, but better known today as the flame stitch (also called Florentine, bargello, or Hungarian stitch). Each stitch appears vertical on the surface of the canvas, but is diagonal on the back. Each stitch is worked

CREWEL PILLOW TOP
Full-Size Pattern

over six threads so that the work progresses very quickly.

Cut the canvas at least 2 inches larger all around than the desired size of the finished needlepoint. Bind the canvas edges with masking tape to prevent raveling.

With a waterproof marking pen, carefully mark the center horizontal and vertical threads of the canvas. Working from the center of the canvas outward toward the sides, work the first row of the pattern in rust. (Refer to the stitch and pattern diagram, *page 37*.) Center the first row and use it as a guide for the entire pattern.

Work upward toward the top of the canvas, changing colors from row to row in the following sequence: rust, medium coral, light coral, dark gold, medium gold, light gold, medium brown, and dark brown. Repeat sequence.

Continue to work pattern up toward top and then down toward bottom of canvas until surface is completely stitched.

Remove canvas from the frame; block. Mount finished needlepoint on fire screen, chair seat, or chosen furniture project, or finish for pillow as desired.

Crewel Pillow Top

Shown on page 27.
Finished size: 12x12 inches

MATERIALS
14-inch square of linen and matching square of backing fabric
1½ yards of coral red piping
3-ply Persian wool in the following colors: 3 shades of green (dark, medium, and light), 5 shades of olive, medium and light pink, tan, and brown
Water-erasable pen
12-inch pillow form

INSTRUCTIONS
Enlarge pattern, *opposite,* to size and transfer to center of linen square.

Using a single ply of yarn, embroider the design as follows:

Tree (left): Work the trunk in tan satin stitch. Work foliage in medium green (outer row) and dark green (inside) satin stitch.

Willow: Work trunk in tan satin stitch and fronds in tan feather-stitch.

Bleeding-heart flowers: Work stems in dark green stem stitch, leaves in light and medium green satin stitch, and flower buds in medium pink satin stitch with light pink centers.

Deer: Work body in brown long and short stitches and antlers in tan satin stitch; use dark green French knot for eye.

Hills: Work hills in five shades of olive satin stitch.

When design is completed, block and press on wrong side. Pin and stitch coral red piping to pillow front. With right sides facing, stitch pillow back to pillow front, leaving bottom side open for turning. Turn pillow right side out, press, insert pillow form, and slip-stitch fourth side closed.

Embroidered Guest Towels

Shown on page 28.
Finished size: 18x25 inches

MATERIALS
19x26-inch piece of linen for each towel
Wool yarn or embroidery floss in dark green, medium green, and red
Small embroidery hoop
Needle
Dressmaker's carbon

INSTRUCTIONS
Transfer the full-size motif, *right,* to lower edge of each towel (design runs horizontally with three motifs across the bottom of each towel).

Embroider the ruffled leaves in dark green outline stitch. Work small leaf in medium green satin stitch; work berries in red satin stitch. Press towels gently on wrong side.

Dove at the Crossroads Quilt

Shown on pages 28–29.
Finished size: Approximately 88x88 inches

MATERIALS
6¼ yards of muslin
3 yards of rust fabric
2 yards of dark green fabric
½ yard of red fabric (optional)
8¾ yards of backing fabric
Quilt batting

INSTRUCTIONS
From cardboard or plastic, make templates for the full-size patterns *continued*

EMBROIDERED GUEST TOWELS
Full-Size Pattern

39

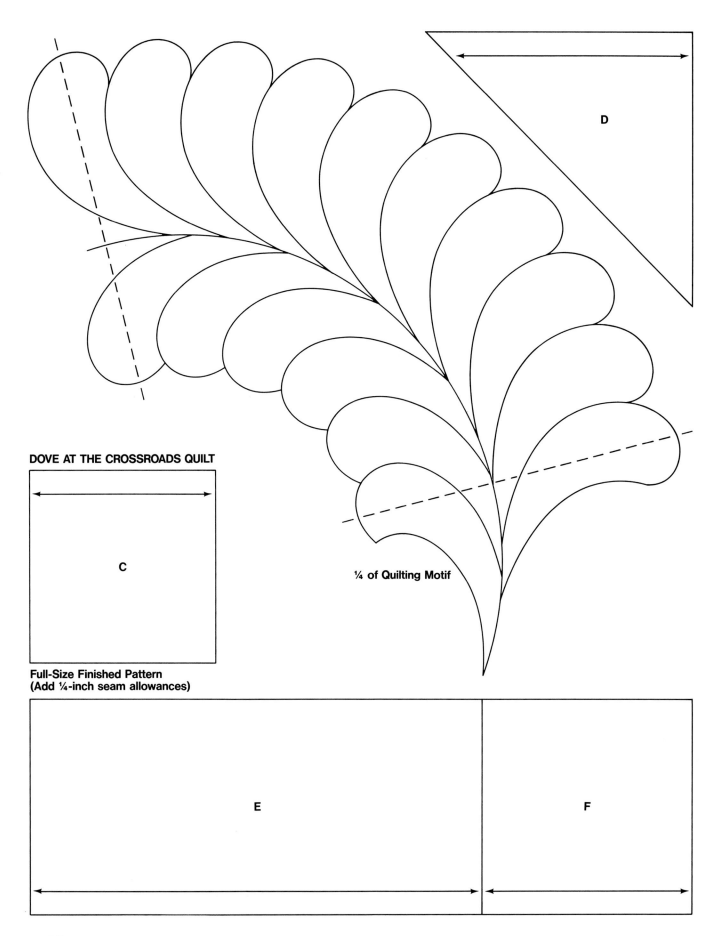

DOVE AT THE CROSSROADS QUILT

C

Full-Size Finished Pattern
(Add ¼-inch seam allowances)

¼ of Quilting Motif

D

E

F

continued from page 39
Colonial Crafts

opposite and *top right*. Patterns *do not* include seam allowances; add ¼-inch-wide seam allowances to pieces before cutting from fabric. Draw a 12-inch square on paper. Make a template from the square.

Cut borders from yardage *before* cutting pieces for patchwork. Measurements for borders *include* seam allowances and are longer than necessary. Trim borders to size when sewing them to completed inner quilt top.

TO CUT FABRIC PIECES: Use the 12-inch-square template to cut 16 squares from the muslin fabric, adding ¼-inch seam allowances.

For triangles, draw a diagonal line between opposite corners of the template used for squares to make two triangles. Through lower section of template, draw a second diagonal in the opposite direction to divide one triangle into two smaller triangles. Cut on drawn lines to make templates for a large and small triangle. Triangles are finished size; add ¼-inch seam allowances when cutting from fabric.

Using the large triangle template, cut 16 triangles from muslin with the long side of the triangle on the straight of the fabric grain. Use the small triangle to cut four corner triangles with the legs of the triangle on the straight of the fabric grain.

From the remaining muslin, cut pieces as follows (the number to cut for one block follows in parentheses): 100 (4) of C and D, 200 (8) of B, and 25 (1) of F.

From the rust fabric, cut four borders, *each* 2x89 inches. Cut other pieces as follows: 200 (8) of A and 100 (4) of E. (*Note:* The antique quilt shown in the photograph on *pages 28–29* has red pieces in place of some rust pieces. Probably the quilt maker ran short of rust fabric and cut red pieces to complete the quilt. To achieve the same look, cut some of the A and E pieces from red fabric and work them in randomly when piecing the blocks.)

From the dark green fabric, cut 200 (8) of A. Cut 11 yards of 1¼-inch-wide bias for the quilt binding.

TO PIECE EACH BLOCK: Referring to block piecing diagram, *middle right,* make four corner units. Sew four pairs of two rust diamonds together, then add a green diamond to the side of each rust diamond to form half of a star. Set a B triangle into the space between each of the rust and green diamonds. Set a C square into the space between the two rust diamonds. Sew a D triangle along the edge of each half star.

Sew a corner unit to opposite sides of an E strip. Repeat for a second E strip. Sew an E strip to opposite sides of an F square to form the center unit of the block.

Sew the strips with the half stars to *opposite* sides of the center unit.

Make 25 pieced blocks.

TO ASSEMBLE THE QUILT TOP: The feathered circle quilting design, *opposite,* is only one-quarter of the total circle. Repeat on tracing paper to complete the circle. Trace the design on each of the plain muslin squares. Draw a heart in the center of each feathered circle and in the four corners of each square. Mark one-half of the circle on the large muslin triangles and one-quarter of the circle on the corner triangles. Mark hearts in open areas on triangle corners.

The quilt top is set diagonally with plain setting squares between the pieced blocks. Lay out the pieced blocks into five rows of five blocks each with the blocks set on point. Place the 16 setting squares in the open spaces between the blocks. Fill in the outer edges with the triangles and corner triangles. Refer to piecing diagram, *bottom right.* Sew the blocks, setting squares, and triangles together in diagonal rows. Join the rows to complete the inner portion of the top.

Add borders to opposite sides of the quilt top; trim borders even with the quilt top. Sew the remaining two borders to the remaining opposite sides and trim.

continued

DOVE AT THE CROSSROADS QUILT

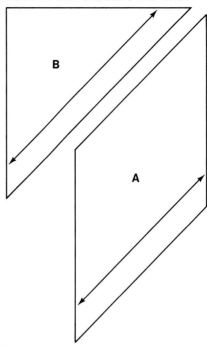

Full-Size Finished Pattern
(Add ¼-inch seam allowances)

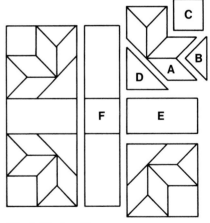

Block Piecing Diagram

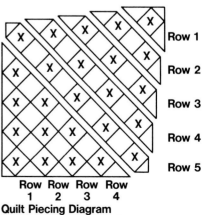

Row 1
Row 2
Row 3
Row 4
Row 5

Row Row Row Row
1   2   3   4

Quilt Piecing Diagram
X denotes pieced block

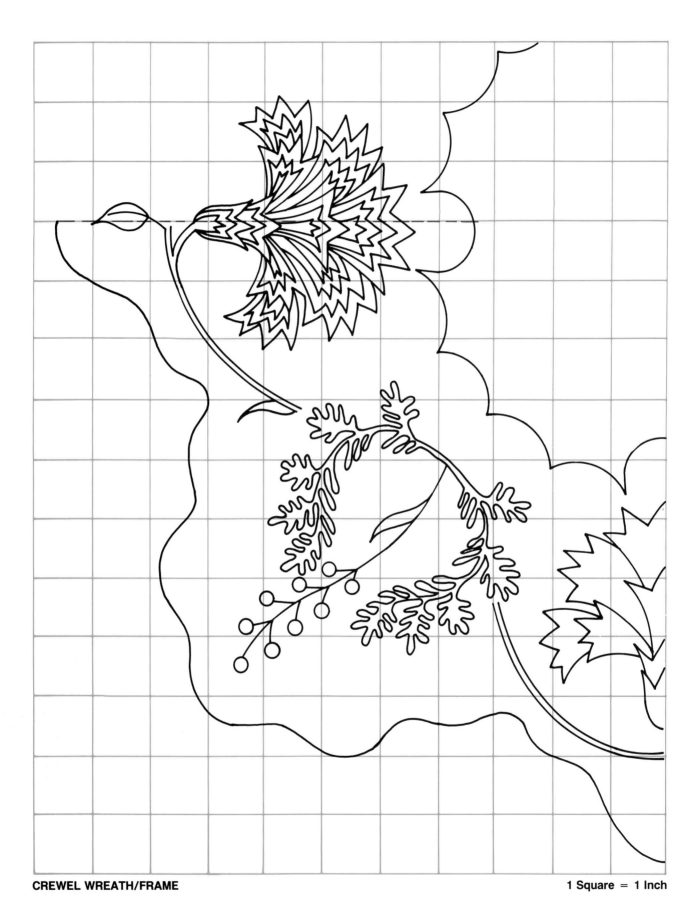

CREWEL WREATH/FRAME

1 Square = 1 Inch

continued from page 41
Colonial Crafts

TO FINISH THE QUILT: Piece the quilt back from the backing fabric. Layer and baste together the quilt top, batting, and back.

Mark a diagonal grid of 1-inch squares on the border.

Quilt the pieced blocks in diagonal lines or as desired. Quilt the marked quilting designs.

When quilting is completed, trim the batting and backing even with the quilt top; round off the corners slightly.

Bind the outer edges of the quilt with green bias. Finished binding on the quilt shown is ⅜ inch wide.

Crewel Wreath/Frame

Shown on page 30.
Finished size: 28½ inches across widest point

MATERIALS
36-inch square of linen
1½ yards of coral fabric for lining and piping
3-ply Persian wool in the following colors: 3 shades of green (dark, medium, and light) for leaves and vines, 4 shades of pink (dark, medium, medium light, light) for blossoms, and coral red for berries
Water-erasable pen
30-inch square of cardboard
Two 30-inch squares of quilt batting
Embroidery hoop and crewel needles
Package or strapping tape
Cording

INSTRUCTIONS
Enlarge pattern, *opposite,* to size, flopping quadrant to complete the design. (*Note:* The two main floral motifs are given full-size, *right.*) Transfer floral design to center of large square of linen with water-erasable pen.

continued

CREWEL WREATH/FRAME
Full-Size Patterns

CREWEL DOILY
Full-Size Patterns

continued from page 43
Colonial Crafts

Stitch diagrams appear on *page 252.* Using a single ply of yarn, embroider design as follows:

Carnations: Work blossoms in four shades of pink (satin stitch), base of blossoms in three shades of green (satin stitch), and stems and vines in dark green (chain stitch outlined with stem stitch).

Berries: Work berries in coral red (satin stitch), stems in dark green (outline stitch), and "wreath" of leaves in dark green (chain stitch).

Single leaves: Work individual leaves in combinations of medium and light green (satin stitch).

Block and press completed design on wrong side.

Trace and cut cardboard wreath shape slightly smaller than outline of design. Cut two layers of quilt batting in the shape of the wreath and glue to cardboard. Machine-stay-stitch along inner and outer outlines of wreath shape on linen. Cut enough bias strips of coral fabric to make about 48 inches of piping. Stitch bias fabric over cording to make piping. Pin and stitch piping around inside border of frame, covering line of stay stitches. (Raw edges of piping should face center of frame.)

With right sides facing, stitch backing fabric to crewel design along piping stitching line. Clip out center of both layers of fabric, leaving a ¼-inch selvage around piping; clip curves. Turn frame right side out and press. Stretch crewel design over batting-covered cardboard shape, clipping seam allowance as necessary to allow design to lie flat. Pull outer edges of stitchery to back of cardboard, trim, and secure in place with strips of tape. Stretch backing fabric over back; pin and glue in place. Trim edges of backing fabric to ¼ inch larger than cardboard shape. Turn under raw edges of backing fabric; slip-stitch to linen.

If desired, use sturdy packing tape to secure picture or 9-inch square mirror behind center opening. Attach ribbon for hanging.

Pierced-Paper Lampshade

Shown on page 30.

MATERIALS

28x40-inch piece of white 80-pound
    watercolor paper
Tracing paper or lightweight
    vellum (from art-supply stores)
Brown kraft paper
Compass and string
Crafts knife
Sharp needle
Green and red watercolors
Small artist's brush
8-inch and 14-inch metal rings
⅝-inch-wide grosgrain ribbon to
    cover rings
Soutache trim (optional)

INSTRUCTIONS

TO MAKE THE LAMPSHADE: Before buying supplies, determine the size of shade and amount of materials needed. The size of the lampshade pattern, known as the arc, is determined by the diameters of shade top and bottom, and the height of the shade.

Make an arc by taking apart an old lampshade and tracing the shape onto watercolor paper.

Determine height and diameter needed; buy rings. Lay out a sheet of brown paper 1 yard long and 1 yard wide, piecing if necessary. Using diagram, *above,* as a guide, draw a line 6 inches from one edge (line A).

Draw line B parallel to first line with distance between the two equal to desired height of the shade.

Draw line C in center of paper. Measure diameter of top ring. Make two dots on line B equal to diameter with line C centered between dots (D and E).

Measure diameter of bottom ring and center two dots (F and G) on line A as for line B. Draw lines through F and D and G and E to cross line C. Lines should meet on line C; mark point H. Place a compass point on H and compass pencil point on D. Draw a curved line through D and E. Repeat for F and G.

Using string, measure the circumference of bottom ring. Lay string on bottom curved line of pattern, cen-

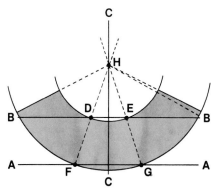

PIERCED-PAPER LAMPSHADE

tering it on line C. Mark ends of string on pattern. Draw lines from these points to H. At one end, add ½ inch for overlap. Cut out shaded area in diagram; check fit by clipping pattern to rings with clothespins. Adjust pattern if necessary.

TO PAINT AND PIERCE SHADE: Trace completed arc onto watercolor paper; cut out. Use one of the full-size carnation and berry designs, *page 43* or *opposite* (a large shade will require the larger pattern); refer to the photograph of the shade on *page 30* for motif placement. For a 10-inch-high shade with 8-inch and 14-inch rings, the design will repeat 4 times. Transfer design to back of arc, taking care to arrange motifs to fit within length of arc.

Using a needle, pierce holes ⅛ inch apart along sides of carnation stem, edges of each carnation petal, berry stem, and berry leaf stems.

With a sharp crafts knife, cut carnation petals, leaves, and berry leaves. *Do not cut out entire leaf.*

Turn arc to front side. Paint designs with watercolors. Use deepest red on bottom edge of petal, graduating color toward center. Turn arc to back side. Sculpt-cut edges of leaves by curling around needle.

Cut tracing paper or vellum to fit arc, allowing for seam. Glue to top edge of arc; glue sides and bottom arc. Press lining in place to eliminate bulges; trim seam. *Use a straight-edge to trim ends of arc.*

Fit top ring in place from center to back of arc. Secure ring with

clothespins. (Clothespins should be right next to each other.)

Secure bottom ring in place in same manner. Check shade for warping. To eliminate warps, reposition rings, working back and forth from top to bottom ring, from center to back, stretching shade paper as if a painter's canvas.

Run a thin line of glue down length of back seam. Clamp seam or press with weights until dry.

Install rings one at a time. Remove top ring, run glue along line left by ring, and resecure with clothespins. Place pieces of waxed paper over edge and under clips to prevent glue seepage. Allow to dry; repeat for bottom ring. Trim excess paper. Cover edges of shade and rings with ribbon. Add soutache trim, if desired.

Crewel Doily

Shown on page 31.
Finished size: 22 inches in diameter

MATERIALS

26-inch squares of linen, backing
    fabric, and iron-on interfacing
Crewel yarns in colors listed for
    frame, *page 43*
Embroidery hoop; crewel needles
Water-erasable pen
Sewing machine and white thread

INSTRUCTIONS

Enlarge pattern, *page 42,* omitting scalloped inside edge. Full-size floral motifs appear *opposite.* Work design with same colors and stitches as mirror frame.

Block finished stitchery with medium-hot iron and damp press cloth. Iron interfacing to back of design.

From backing fabric, cut two pieces, each equal to half of the shaped doily (add ½-inch seam allowances all around). Pin and stitch straight edges together (½-inch seam), leaving 4 inches open in center for turning. Press seam open.

With right sides facing, stitch backing to front around outer edge. Trim seams, clip curves, turn, and slip-stitch opening closed. Topstitch ⅛ inch in from edge.

AMONG FAMILY AND FRIENDS

◆

TOKENS OF CELEBRATION AND REMEMBRANCE

Whether it's a simple crayon drawing from a child or an intricate, cut-paper valentine, cross-stitch memento, or lavishly quilted coverlet, a gift made by hand and offered from the heart is special, unique, and forever cherished.

AMONG FAMILY AND FRIENDS

Among the most distinctive of American folk traditions are the arts and crafts of the Pennsylvania Dutch—a catchall term used to describe the central Europeans (largely of German origin) who settled in what is now Pennsylvania and Delaware during the 17th and 18th centuries.

Handsome paper documents called *fraktur* were created to record, celebrate, sanctify, and certify almost every event and relationship in the lives of community members.

These elegant certificates—of birth, baptism, merit, marriage, and family history—hung on the walls of every home, reinforcing the individual's link with the institutions that were the primary focus of life—church, school, family, and friends.

The modern-day adaptations of traditional fraktur pictured here are pleasing arrangements of calligraphic text, abstract borders, and symbolic figures (birds, hearts, vines, and flowers). Use the designs to frame announcements and pronouncements of your own devising.

Instructions for these heartfelt gifts begin on *page 56.*

Born into this world
March 15, 1837
Sara Jane Portner
daughter of
Paul and Mary
Marietta ~Pennsylvania

48

AMONG FAMILY AND FRIENDS

Another unique folk art introduced to America by immigrants from the German-speaking areas of Europe was the technique known as scherenschnitte. The term derives from the German *schnitte,* meaning to cut, and refers to the lovely, lacy, cut-paper designs produced by the Pennsylvania Dutch and their European counterparts during the late 18th and 19th centuries.

Historical evidence suggests that the craft was originally practiced by men, using small, sharp-bladed knives. But, women quickly adopted this appealing form of decoration as well, using their sharp embroidery scissors to cut out the major design areas, and sewing needles to prick in delicate details.

Perhaps the most endearing examples of scherenschnitte are the *liebsbrief,* or love letters, on which the hearts-and-flowers design, *left,* is based. According to English custom, valentines were only exchanged on February 14, St. Valentine's Day, but handcrafted love notes could be offered by young men to their sweethearts any time during the year. Similar designs were cut and given as birthday gifts or on other special occasions by young and old alike.

Frequently the cut-paper love token was intricately folded and beautifully painted with watercolors or tinted inks. The inscriptions were often lengthy, quaintly phrased, and deeply sentimental. For this reason, the traditional liebsbrief was not intended for public display and would never have been framed or hung in the home—unlike contemporary pieces, proudly exhibited today.

AMONG FAMILY AND FRIENDS

As a symbol of love and affection, and an emblem of courage, honor, and trust, the heart motif has always been a favorite embellishment for the gifts we Americans give to family and friends.

A traditional heart-and-flowers design sparks the crocheted antimacassar, *right,* two hearts frame the pair of Victorian silhouettes, *below,* and another heart shapes the beaded velvet pincushion.

Simple stitchery based on valentine motifs—like the cherub and lovebird, *right*—was considered fashionably romantic in an earlier era and often appeared on boudoir pillows.

The heart-shape trinket and shell-encrusted picture frame, *below,* are seamen's valentines that lovesick sailors fashioned for their landlocked sweethearts during long, lonely voyages to exotic ports.

Even the least romantic of gifts, like the painted game boards, *below,* were often decorated with heart designs betokening the love with which they were crafted and the affection with which they were offered.

AMONG FAMILY AND FRIENDS

Perhaps one of the most desirable tokens of affection in early America was the friendship quilt. These textile autograph "albums" were stitched in dozens of different patterns for hundreds of occasions.

Some were made by a single individual—by a mother for her child, by one friend for another, or by a girl for her sweetheart. Others were created by groups of women to honor a family member or community figure, or as a special gift for neighbors moving far away. Whoever the recipient and whatever the occasion, the friendship quilt was a tangible reminder of time, memories, and affections shared.

Preferred patterns for friendship quilts varied from region to region and changed as new patterns were created. Sometimes a single block and similar fabrics were common throughout a geographic region, as with the New England example shown here. Elsewhere, it was the fashion for each contributor to piece or appliqué a different pattern block, and the squares were then assembled as an album quilt.

Whatever the overall design, each block bore a name, sometimes a date, and usually, a heartfelt

wish (Forget Me Not), or a pretty drawing penned by the maker. Sometimes all of the inscriptions on a quilt were penned by a single hand, usually that of someone noted for her fine calligraphy.

Today, a friendship quilt still offers an unexpected way to commemorate an occasion or celebrate a special friendship.

Love Cross-Stitch

Shown on page 47.
Finished size: Design only measures 1½x3¾ inches (31x85 stitches)

MATERIALS

2½x4¾ inches of perforated paper with 24 holes per inch (available from needlework shops)
Embroidery floss in the colors listed on the color key
Embroidery needle
Frame and matting, or candle screen as shown (available in most needlework shops)

INSTRUCTIONS

Transfer the chart, *below,* to graph paper, or work directly from the one *below.*

Cross-stitch the design on perforated paper using one strand of embroidery floss.

Begin stitching ½ inch in from the left edge and ½ inch up from the bottom of the paper. Take special care to conceal thread ends behind the stitched area. Do not pull stitches tight; the paper will tear.

When the stitchery is completed, frame the design as desired.

Fraktur Birth and House Blessings

Shown on pages 48–49.
Finished sizes: Birth Record measures 5x7 inches, House Blessing measures 7x9 inches

MATERIALS

Good-quality paper such as parchment or watercolor paper
India ink
Calligraphy pen with flat tip
Acrylic paints
Artist's brushes
Pencil

INSTRUCTIONS

Use a light pencil to transfer the full-size patterns, *opposite* and *page 58,* to parchment or watercolor paper.
For the birth record: Outline the checkered border and the dark lines around the border with a black felt-tip marker.

For both projects: Lightly pencil in names and dates. Use india ink and a calligraphy pen to outline the penciled letters and numbers. (Use different size pen points for different lines of lettering to create an interesting effect.)

Use acrylic paints and a fine-tip artist's brush to fill in all design areas. Refer to the photograph on *pages 48–49* for colors, or use your own selection of colors. Paint the light colors and background shapes first; allow the paint to dry. Proceed to the dark colors.

When all paint is thoroughly dry, frame the birth record or house blessing as desired.

continued

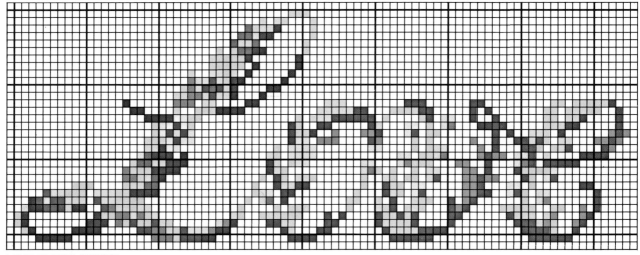

LOVE CROSS-STITCH

COLOR KEY

☐ Yellow (743)   ■ Medium Green (580)   ■ Medium Purple (552)   ☐ Light Pink (604)
■ Rust (400)   ■ Dark Green (895)   ☐ Light Blue (519)   ■ Medium Pink (602)
☐ Light Green (471)   ☐ Light Purple (554)   ■ Medium Blue (517)

FRAKTUR HOUSE BLESSING
Full-Size Pattern

57

continued from page 56
Among Family and Friends

Cut-Paper Valentine

Shown on pages 50–51.
Finished size: 10x12 inches, framed

MATERIALS

10x12-inch piece of colored mat
   board for backing
10x12-inch piece of flat white
   watercolor paper
Watercolors
Fine-tip artist's brushes
Fine-point scissors
Sharp crafts knife
Sharp needle; rubber cement

INSTRUCTIONS

Use a sharp pencil to trace the full-size pattern, *opposite,* onto paper; flop the design to repeat the other half.

Cut out the design, using fine-point scissors and a crafts knife.

From the back (penciled) side of the cut design, make tiny, closely
continued

FRAKTUR BIRTH RECORD **Full-Size Pattern**

CUT-PAPER VALENTINE

Full-Size Pattern

59

continued from page 58
Among Family and Friends

spaced pin pricks along those lines indicated by dots on the pattern.

Turn the cutout to the right side and paint areas of the design with light washes of watercolor. (Refer to the color photograph on *pages 50–51* for color suggestions, or paint using shades of your choice.) Use pen and ink to write the message on the center of the heart.

Mount the cut paper on the mat board using rubber cement; frame as desired.

Heart and Flowers Chair Antimacassar

Shown on page 52.
Finished size: 11½ by 16 inches

MATERIALS
DMC Cébélia crochet cotton, Size 20
No. 10 steel crochet hook

Gauge: With suggested materials, 5 spaces = 1 inch, 6 rows = 1 inch.

INSTRUCTIONS
Starting at wide end, make a chain approximately 18 inches long, taking care not to pull stitches tightly.

Row 1: Dc in 4th ch from hook and in each of next 209 ch. Cut off remaining chain about a half-inch from end; unravel extra sts and weave thread into work. Ch 3, turn.

Row 2: Dc in 2nd dc and in each of next 5 dc (2 blocks made), (ch 2, skip 2 dc, dc in next dc) 66 times, dc in last 5 dc and in top of turning ch. Ch 3, turn.

Row 3: Make 2 blocks at beginning of row as before, (ch 2, dc in next ch) 20 times, 2 dc in next space, dc in next dc, (ch 2, dc in next dc) 24 times, 2 dc in next space, dc in next dc, make 20 more spaces and 2 blocks at end of row. Ch 3, turn.

Continue working filet design as shown on chart, *below,* having all spaces consist of 2 dc with ch-2 be-

tween and blocks composed of 2 dc in place of the ch-2.

At end of *Row 42* do not make ch-3, but instead turn and sl st in last 10 dc just made. Then ch 3 and continue across *Row 43* as shown, ending by not working over last 3 blocks of previous row. Width of remaining rows is decreased in this manner until all 64 rows are completed. Do not break thread at end of last row but go around outside of piece as follows:

Edging: Ch 6, sl st in 3rd st from hook for picot, ch 3, sc in corner of previous row, ch 6, sl st in 3rd st from hook, ch 3, sc in center of remaining blocks of next row. Continue making picot loops in this manner evenly spaced around outside of work. Join and fasten off.

Paper Silhouettes

Shown on page 52.

MATERIALS
White or black medium-weight paper
Tracing paper
Sharp pencil
Black poster paint, acrylics, or india ink
Small, very sharp scissors
White card stock or mat board for mounting

INSTRUCTIONS
Most miniature silhouettes, like the ones shown on *page 52,* were cut freehand by an artist in just a few minutes as he or she studied the subjects' profiles.

For life-size silhouettes, the artists often taped a piece of tracing-weight paper to a sheet of clear glass. They then propped the glass up before their subjects, who were illuminated from behind by candles. The sub-

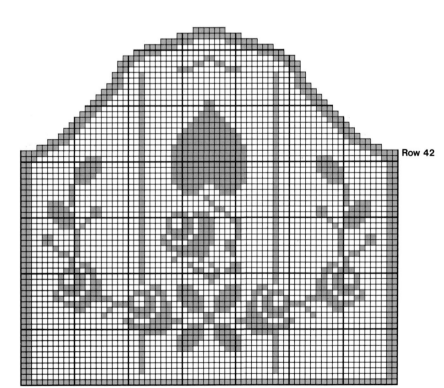

Row 42

HEART AND FLOWERS CHAIR ANTIMACASSAR

jects were urged to sit perfectly still as the artists rapidly traced their profiles onto the paper. The silhouettes were then cut out, painted black, and mounted on white paper for framing.

The simplest way to make a life-size silhouette today is to tape a large sheet of white tracing paper to a wall. Ask the subject to stand in front of the paper with a strong light behind the subject's head. This should cast a good, crisp shadow against the paper. Trace around the shadow with a sharp pencil; transfer the outline to heavy white paper, refining the details such as the curve of the eyebrow, outline of the nose, etc. Paint the silhouette with black poster paint, acrylic paint, or india ink. Mount the silhouette on white paper and frame as desired.

Whether you experiment with the freehand method for making small profiles, or the traced outline technique for life-size silhouettes, practice will definitely improve results.

Beaded Heart Pincushion

Shown on page 52.
Finished size: 4½x5 inches

MATERIALS
Scraps of beige velveteen (heart)
Scraps of muslin (backing)
Glass beads in assorted colors
2 gold sequins
Cording (optional)
Polyester fiberfill

INSTRUCTIONS
Trace two heart outlines from pattern, *right,* onto velveteen for front and back of pincushion. Do not cut out. Trace flower and vine design onto center of one heart; embroider with beads. (Refer to the color photograph on *page 52* for bead and color placement.)

Add sequins where indicated by X on pattern. When beading is completed, cut out velveteen front and back.

Trace two heart outlines onto muslin; cut out. Back each velveteen heart with a muslin heart.

With right sides facing, sew front and back together; leave an opening along one side for turning. Trim seams, clip curves, and turn right side out.

Stuff pincushion with fiberfill; slip-stitch opening closed.

Sew a double row of blue beads around the edge of the heart (see photo, *page 52*).

TO MAKE BEAD LOOPS: String 50 beads in different colors on a strong piece of thread. Attach the thread in a loop shape to one side of the heart. Repeat for the second side and bottom, attaching the thread to the areas indicated by a dot on the pattern. Add a total of two loops at each point.

Add a loop of decorative cording to the top for hanging, if desired.

Pink-Embroidered Miniature Pillows

Shown on page 53.
Finished size: 8x8 inches

MATERIALS
⅓ yard of closely woven white fabric (makes two pillows)
Pink embroidery floss
Polyester fiberfill
Tracing paper
Light-color dressmaker's carbon

INSTRUCTIONS
From white fabric, cut two 10x10-inch squares for each pillow.

continued

BEADED HEART PINCUSHION　　　　　　　　　　　**Full-Size Pattern**

continued from page 61
Among Family and Friends

Transfer the full-size patterns, *left,* onto tracing paper. Center pattern and use dressmaker's carbon to transfer the designs onto pillow-front fabric squares.

Work designs in outline stitch using three strands of embroidery floss. Work the heart on the mailbox in satin stitch. (Stitch diagrams are on *page 252.*)

With right sides facing, pin pillow backs to fronts; baste in place. Machine-stitch around three sides and halfway along the fourth side. Turn the pillows right side out. Stuff with polyester fiberfill. Slip-stitch openings closed.

PINK-EMBROIDERED MINIATURE PILLOWS

Full-Size Pattern

Sailor's Valentine

Shown on page 53.
Finished size: 3¾x3⅛ inches

MATERIALS

Scrap of ¼-inch balsa wood
12-inch strip of ¾-inch-wide, bias-
cut velvet
8 dozen small shells (border)
Assorted shells for decorating
Postcards, photographs, stickers
White plaster or mastic
Crafts glue
Ribbon (hanger)

INSTRUCTIONS

Trace the full-size pattern, *right;* cut shape from balsa wood. Wrap edges of wooden heart with velvet strip; secure fabric to wood with white crafts glue.

Coat one side of the heart with a thin layer of mastic, plaster, or white crafts glue; lay picture, postcard cutout, or sticker in place on the heart. (Refer to the photograph on *page 53* for guidance.)

Using crafts glue, add a small border of shells all around the outer edge of the heart shape, covering the edge of the print you have secured to the middle.

Allow all materials to dry thoroughly; repeat for second side.

Glue a small loop of ribbon at the top of the heart for hanging.

SAILOR'S VALENTINE

Shell Frame

Shown on page 53.
Finished size: 4¾x6¼ inches

MATERIALS

Sturdy cardboard
Copper foil tape
Assorted shells
Plaster, mastic, or white crafts glue
Scrap of clear acrylic film or thin
glass

INSTRUCTIONS

Trace the frame shape, *page 64,* onto heavy cardboard. Cut out the shape; cover the inside and outside edges with strips of copper foil.

Cover the front of the frame with a thin layer of plaster, mastic, or white glue; encrust the surface with shells, arranging them in a pleasing manner. (Refer to the color photograph on *page 53* for suggestions.)

When the frame is completely dry, tape a rectangle of clear plastic film or thin glass behind the center opening. Center the photograph over the opening; back with a rectangle of cardboard taped securely in place.

TO MAKE THE STAND: Cut a wedge-shape piece of cardboard approximately 5½ inches long, 2½ inches wide at the base, and ¾ inch wide at the top.

Score the wedge ¾ inch down from the narrow top end and glue the top to the middle of the back of the frame.

continued

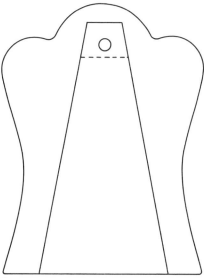

SHELL FRAME BACK

continued from page 63
Among Family and Friends

Painted Checkerboards

Shown on page 53.

MATERIALS

½-inch pine or plywood, cut to
  desired board size
White primer paint
Acrylic paints
Artist's brushes
Tissue or scrap paper
Dressmaker's carbon
Ballpoint pen
Antiquing glaze
Clear polyurethane finish

INSTRUCTIONS

The diagrams on *pages 65* and *66* show the general layout for the two old checkerboards shown on *page 53*. Use these as guidelines for making your own checkerboard design.

Adjust the size of the playing squares to fit the size of your board.

Cut the pine or plywood to the size you want your finished checkerboard to be; sand all surfaces smooth. Prime all surfaces of the wood with white primer paint.

Once the primer is dry, paint an acrylic base coat on all surfaces of the board in a color to fit your decorating needs.

TO PAINT THE DESIGN: Draw the outline of your board on a piece of

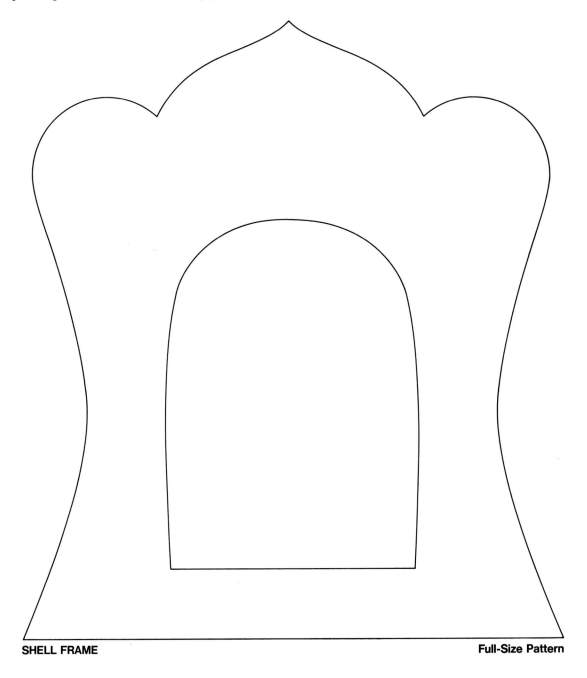

SHELL FRAME

Full-Size Pattern

scrap paper. Sketch the exact placement of squares, hearts, and other motifs. When you have an arrangement that pleases you, use dressmaker's carbon to transfer the design to the painted board.

Use a complementary color of acrylic paint to fill in alternate squares of the checkerboard pattern. (Refer to the photograph, *page 53*.) Fill in heart shapes and other motifs with acrylic paint. Allow all paint to dry.

Cover all painted surfaces with antiquing glaze, following manufacturer's application directions on container. Dry thoroughly. Apply several coats of clear polyurethane finish, allowing ample drying time between coats.

To play the game, use dark and light buttons for checkers.

Chimney Sweep Album Quilt

Shown on pages 54–55.
Finished size: 87¾x99 inches

MATERIALS
6 yards of muslin fabric
Approximately 3 yards of medium-color fabric scraps (predominantly pinks)
Approximately 1½ yards of dark-color fabric scraps (predominantly browns and greens)
9 yards of muslin for the quilt back and binding
Quilt batting
Cardboard or plastic for templates
Fine felt-tip permanent fabric marker (Test any marker on a scrap of muslin to be sure it is permanent on fabric. Pilot's SC-UF ultra-fine-point permanent pen works well.)

continued

PAINTED CHECKERBOARD

continued from page 65
Among Family and Friends

INSTRUCTIONS

The quilt shown in the photograph on *pages 54–55* is made of 64 Chimney Sweep blocks. The quilt is like an autograph album because each block is signed, and frequently includes the signer's hometown and the date signed.

In the main portion of the quilt, the blocks are arranged in eight vertical rows with seven blocks in each row. At the bottom of the friendship quilt a two-block-by-four-block section was added as a drop for the foot of the bed. This arrangement allows the quilt to fit smoothly around the bedposts. All blocks are separated by muslin sashing strips.

TO BEGIN: Make cardboard or plastic templates for the patterns, *opposite.* The patterns are finished

size; add ¼-inch seam allowances when cutting each of the pieces from the fabrics.

From muslin, cut 64 of pattern piece A for the signature squares. Have various people autograph diagonally through the squares using a felt-tip marker that is permanent on fabric. Or, have the people autograph the squares with a pencil and trace over the autographs with a permanent pen. Signers may want to include the date and their address along with their signature. Allow plenty of time to collect all of the signatures and be prepared to send out reminders.

CUTTING INSTRUCTIONS: Cut sashing strips from the muslin. Measurements for the sashing strips include ¼-inch seam allowances. Cut seven vertical strips for the main portion of the quilt, *each* 2¾x80 inches. Cut five vertical strips for

the foot section, *each* 2¾x22 inches. The vertical strips are longer than is needed; trim them to exact length when sewing them to the rows of blocks.

Cut 60 horizontal sashing strips, *each* 2¾x9½ inches.

From the remaining muslin, cut the additional pieces for 64 blocks. (The number to cut for one block is listed first; the number to cut for the entire quilt follows in parentheses.) Cut 8 (512) of piece B and 4 (256) of piece C.

From the assorted medium fabric scraps, cut eight of A, using one of the fabrics for *each* block.

From the assorted dark fabric scraps, cut four of A, using one of the fabrics for *each* block.

TO MAKE ONE BLOCK: Referring to the piecing diagram, *opposite,* lay out the pieces for one block with the signature square in the center. Piece the squares and triangles into diagonal rows; join the rows to complete the block.

Piece 64 Chimney Sweep blocks.

TO SET THE BLOCKS TOGETHER: Sew a 2¾x9½-inch sashing strip to the bottoms of 56 of the blocks. Set aside the remaining eight blocks and four short sashing strips for the foot section of the quilt.

Sew the sashed blocks into eight vertical rows with seven blocks in each row. Measure the length of a row and trim the 80-inch vertical sashing strips to this length. Join the rows together with a sashing strip between each row.

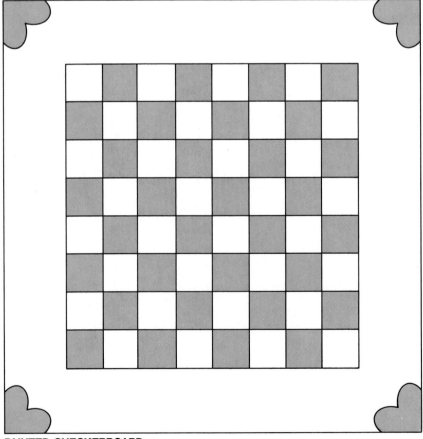

PAINTED CHECKERBOARD

66

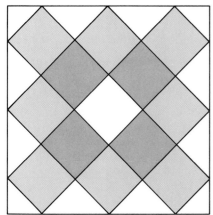

Block Diagram

To make the foot section of the quilt, sew a 2¾x9½-inch sashing strip to the bottoms of four of the remaining blocks. Sew a block to the bottom of each sashing strip to make four vertical rows with two blocks in each row separated by a sashing strip. Measure the length of a row and trim the 22-inch vertical sashing strips to this length. Join the rows together with a sashing strip between each row, and at the beginning and the end of each row. Sew the foot section to the center four blocks at the bottom of the main portion of the quilt.

FINISHING THE QUILT: Piece the backing fabric to make a quilt back at least two inches larger all around than the quilt top. Layer and baste the quilt top, batting, and backing. Quilt as desired.

From the backing fabric scraps, make approximately 12 running yards of 1½-inch-wide bias for the binding. When quilting is completed, trim the quilt back and batting even with the quilt top. Bind the outer edges with bias binding, mitering the inside and outer corners of the binding.

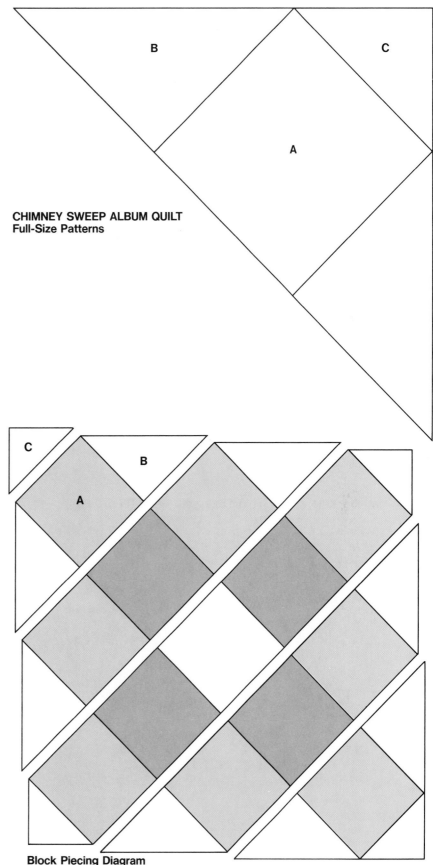

CHIMNEY SWEEP ALBUM QUILT
Full-Size Patterns

Block Piecing Diagram

67

ART UNDERFOOT

◆

RUGS AND FLOOR COVERINGS

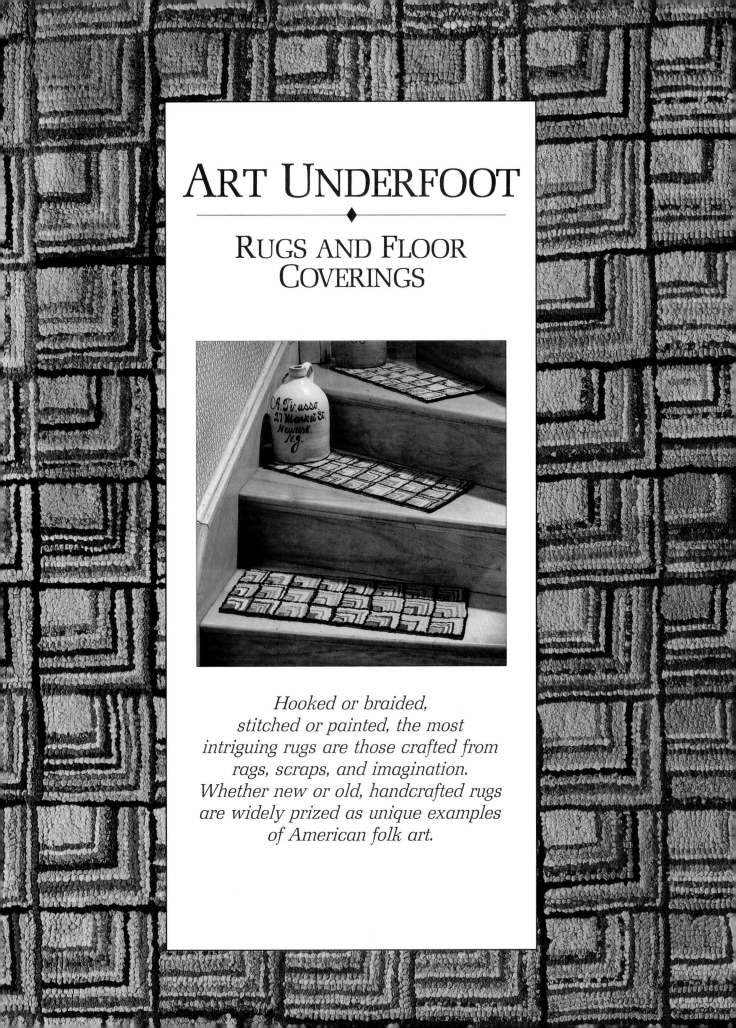

*Hooked or braided,
stitched or painted, the most
intriguing rugs are those crafted from
rags, scraps, and imagination.
Whether new or old, handcrafted rugs
are widely prized as unique examples
of American folk art.*

ART UNDERFOOT

One of the few truly indigenous American folk arts, rug hooking found its beginning in Maine, New Hampshire, and the Canadian Maritime Provinces. Many of the sailors here were as adept as housewives at hooking the narrow loops of woolen fabric through burlap backing to create boldly patterned designs.

By the end of the 19th century, hand-hooked rugs were being made from coast to coast. Active interest in the craft continued well into this century, when Mrs. Adeline Nowell of Wilmington, Delaware, made the two handsome rugs pictured here.

To personalize the eagle design for her grandson Mark, Mrs. Nowell hooked this patriotic motif with scraps of fabric from two generations of family military uniforms—an artful blending of sentiment and craft.

Like her 19th-century predecessors, Mrs. Nowell had to home-dye and cut countless yards of fabric to create her granddaughter Amy's lovely Lily Pad rug, *right*. (Today, precut strips are available through mail-order suppliers.)

Instructions begin on page 82.

Art Underfoot

Because little artistic skill is required to create an appealing pattern, geometric designs have always been popular with rugmakers, who turn again and again to easy-to-draw squares and diamonds when planning a new rug.

The lively diamond pattern cross-stitched on the rug, *center right,* for example, might have been inspired by the geometric Spanish tile designs so popular in this country in the late 18th and early 19th centuries. The colors of the rug date it as a 20th-century creation. (Note that the area between the diamonds is stitched in dozens of colors—an excellent way to use up leftover yarn.)

Other designs were fashioned after familiar old quilt patterns. The Attic Windows rug pattern, *near right,* strongly resembles the Log Cabin quilt design. (Similarities between the quilt and rug patterns are even more apparent in the stair treads on page 69, in which each hooked square has a red center, as did the traditional pieced Log Cabin block.)

Even when you are constrained by straight lines, it's possible to create patterns full of movement. The hooked diamond-pattern rug, *far right,* fairly ripples with waves of color.

72

ART UNDERFOOT

Among the very first homemade coverings to grace American floors were brightly patterned "carpets" painted on scraps of sail canvas. Designs were either applied freehand or stenciled to imitate the richly patterned tiles and imported carpets that had begun to appear in some of the wealthier homes.

Today, painted floorcloths are an easy and inexpensive way to add color, pattern, and warmth to any room. Painted on sturdy artist's canvas and finished with several coats of polyurethane, they warm drafty floors, hold up well under heavy traffic, and can be wiped clean with a damp cloth.

Using original patterns or purchased stencils, you can create designs in any style you like—from authentic Early American to contemporary country, from art deco to op art. Use the same materials and techniques to make wipe-clean place mats for your kitchen.

The floorcloth, *opposite,* was stenciled in colonial shades of red, blue, and green, but the same design could easily be re-created in colors of your choice. (Smaller versions of the tree and border motifs were stenciled onto the companion place mats.)

ART UNDERFOOT

Perhaps the most common of all rag floor coverings—and the simplest to make—is the braided rug. Plaited from narrow strips of fabric, the rugs are sturdy, reversible, and adaptable to almost any size and shape desired. While most 19th-century rugs were round or oval, the rectangular, square, and heart-shape designs were not unknown.

The most durable braided rugs are made of closely woven fabrics, but the same technique can be used to make decorative mats and chair seats using any soft, resilient fabric. The round and oval table mats, *below,* were braided from strips of silk, rayon, and other lightweight dress fabrics popular in the 1930s and '40s.

Crocheted rugs have come into existence more recently. Made from strips of cotton fabrics, they may have evolved as an alternative to traditional woven rag rugs, and become appealing to the 20th-century housewife because her smaller, more crowded home now rarely had space for a floor loom.

The colorful crocheted design, *opposite,* dates from the second quarter of this century.

ART UNDERFOOT

Today we think of rugs only as floor coverings, but up until the early 1800s, most floors in America were bare, and rugs were used only to cover beds, tables, and other items of furniture. (Our word "rug" may derive from an early Scandinavian term meaning a "coarse cloth or coverlet.")

Even after rugs had become a familiar sight on the polished and painted floors of 19th-century American homes, table rugs remained a popular decorative item in many of the more modest homes of the period. In fact, they continued to be made through the 1920s (particularly in New England and the Middle West), though in far fewer numbers than the more familiar hooked and braided floor rugs.

Table rugs generally fall into one of two categories. Most common is the geometric "penny rug"—so-called for its appliquéd design of wool or felt circles layered in graduated sizes. Rarer are the pictorial table rugs, with appliquéd or embroidered designs of flowers, animals, or other motifs.

Typical of the first category are the two penny rugs shown here. The muted earth tones and graceful teardrop border of the larger rug, *right,* are characteristic of earlier penny rugs. The small hexagonal mat, *above,* is a simple but striking arrangement of bright felt pennies appliquéd with contrasting threads.

Art Underfoot

The appliquéd and embroidered table rug, *opposite,* recalls many late 19th-century New England pictorial designs.

Each large black penny is appliquéd with a clover motif consisting of three brightly colored, blanket-stitched petals on an embroidered stem. The pennies, in turn, are appliquéd to a background fabric with more decorative stitching.

The narrow binding is embellished with featherstitching, and at each end of the rug is a scalloped pen-wiper border, named for the pen-wiper-shape pieces with which it is constructed. (Pen wipers were small tongue-shape pieces of flannel or felt sold in precut packets and intended for wiping the excess ink off steel pens.)

On the chest, *below,* is an embroidered pen-wiper rug, boasting a simple picture of a mare and her colt, bordered by four rows of overlapping pen wipes. Each tongue-shape piece is finished with blanket stitching, and the first rows of pen wipes are embroidered with stars of yarn as well. The naive design indicates that this may have been a child's first effort in rugmaking.

General Instructions For Hooked Rugs

Use only wool rug yarn or closely woven wool fabrics that have been cut into narrow strips for rug hooking. Strips should be ¼ to ½ inch wide, depending on weight of fabric. It is easiest to work with strips no more than 12 to 24 inches long.

Hem backing fabric (burlap or hopsack) to prevent raveling. Trace design on right side of background fabric, then mount fabric in rug frame, pattern side up. Make certain that horizontal and vertical threads of the fabric are parallel and perpendicular to the side of the frame.

Work with one hand above the frame, hooking the strips up through the backing fabric. The other hand remains beneath the frame to guide the strips of cloth.

Always hook outlines and pattern motifs first, then fill in the background of the design.

To start hooking a strip of wool, slip hook through backing fabric and pull up the tail end of a wool strip from back to top, so that the tail extends about ½ inch above the surface of the burlap. (Tail will be trimmed later.) Next, about two threads away from the first stitch, slip hook through backing fabric again. Pick up a loop of wool and pull it through the backing, making a loop about ⅜ inch above backing.

Repeat the hook-down-and-pull-up motion, keeping loops a uniform ⅜ inch high, until strip is finished or until line of design is completed. Pull tail end of strip to front of rug so that it can later be trimmed even with hooked pile.

After completing letters and motifs of design, work background, hooking from center of design out toward edges.

When design is finished, remove rug from frame. Trim edges of wool strips on surface to match height of hooked pile. Trim background fabric to within 2 inches of hooked design. Tack raw edges to back of rug.

Apply two coats of liquid latex to back of rug to prevent raveling. Finish edges with 1-inch-wide strips of rug binding.

Attic Windows Hooked Rug

Shown on pages 68–69 and 72–73.
Finished size: 38½x52 inches

MATERIALS

Narrow strips of wool fabric (or rug yarn) in assorted colors: Use dark blues, black, and browns for lattice and beige for corner of each block; use other light and dark colors for remainder of pattern (refer to color photo)
47x61-inch rectangle of burlap or hopsacking for backing
Masking tape
Permanent marker
Rug frame and hooking tool

INSTRUCTIONS

Tape edges of burlap or hopsacking fabric to prevent fraying.

Draw a 38½x52-inch rectangle in the center of the background fabric with permanent marker. Each "window" in the pattern measures 3½x4 inches. Divide the rectangle into 11 rows of 13 window blocks each.

Secure fabric in frame, pattern side up. Outline perimeter of rug and lines of lattice grid with a single row of dark (black, brown, or navy blue) hooking.

For each window block: In lower right-hand corner, hook a beige rectangle 1½ inches high and 6 rows wide. Next, outline left and top sides of this beige rectangle with single rows of hooking, alternating light and dark colors. (Depending on width of wool strips, you should have approximately 11 to 13 strips of color between corner rectangle and lattice.)

When pattern is completed, trim fabric to within 2½ inches of hooked design. Turn fabric under ½ inch, press, and topstitch hem. Turn hem to back of rug, miter corners, press, and slip-stitch in place.

Attic Windows Hooked Stair Treads

Shown on page 69.
Finished size: 10x26¼ inches

MATERIALS

16x32-inch piece of burlap or hopsacking
Narrow strips of wool fabric (or rug yarn) in black (for lattice), red (for corners), and assorted bright colors
Rug frame and hooking tool
Permanent marker
Masking tape

INSTRUCTIONS

Tape burlap or hopsacking fabric edges to prevent fraying.

Sketch a 10x26¼-inch rectangle on center of backing fabric with permanent marker. Divide rectangle into three rows of eight squares each (making twenty-four 3¼-inch windows).

Place fabric in rug frame, pattern side up. Outline perimeter of rug and lattice lines with a single row of black.

Next, in lower left-hand corner of each "window," hook a square of red about ¾ inch high and three rows wide. Then trace top and right sides of this square with successive single rows of bright colors, alternating light and dark shades.

When pattern is completed, trim backing fabric and finish as for Attic Windows Hooked Rug, *left.*

EAGLE HEARTH RUG

1 Square = 3 Inches

Eagle Hearth Rug

Shown on page 70.
Finished size: 36x22 inches

MATERIALS

Narrow strips of closely woven
  woolen fabrics (or rug yarn) in
  navy blue, crimson, and several
  shades of gold
30x44-inch rectangle of burlap or
  hopsacking for backing
Masking tape
Permanent marker
Rug frame
Rug hooking tool

INSTRUCTIONS

Tape edges of backing fabric to prevent fraying.

Enlarge pattern, *above,* to size
and transfer to right side of backing
fabric with permanent marker. Secure fabric in frame, pattern side up,
and hook design.

Refer to the photograph on *page
70* for color distribution.

When design is completed, finish
rug as described under "General Instructions," *opposite.*

Lily Pad
Hooked Rug

Shown on page 71.
*Finished size: Each block measures
12 inches square. Instructions are
for a rug 28x40 inches. For the room-
size rug, join as many squares as
your room dictates.*

MATERIALS

Narrow strips of wool fabric or rug
  yarn in assorted shades of
  green, gold, rust, and brown
36x48-inch rectangle of burlap or
  hopsack for backing
Masking tape
Permanent marker
Rug frame
Rug hooking tool

INSTRUCTIONS

Sketch a 2x3-foot rectangle on the
center of the burlap and divide it
into six 12-inch blocks.

Enlarge both block designs, *page
84,* and transfer to backing fabric
(refer to color photograph on *page
71* for positioning of designs).

Tape edges of burlap and secure
in rug frame, pattern side up. Work
pattern blocks by hooking dividing
lines (deep rust), and leaf and tree
designs first, then filling in background. Add "bubbles" of color (a
few loops of color, surrounded by a
row of gold loops) along the outer
edges of each pattern block. When
pattern blocks are finished, hook a
2-inch-wide border of green around
all four sides of the rug.

Remove rug from frame and finish
as described, *opposite,* under "General Instructions."

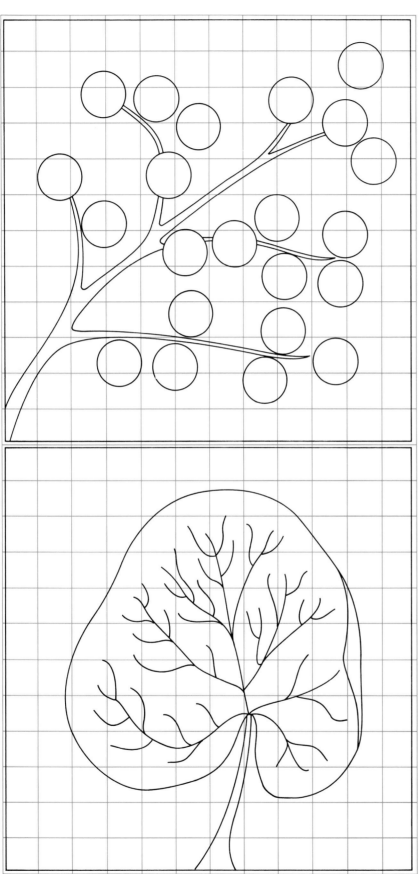

LILY PAD HOOKED RUG

1 Square = 1 Inch

continued from page 83
Art Underfoot

Cross-Stitch Rug
Shown on pages 72–73.
Finished size: 21x32 inches

MATERIALS
27x38-inch rectangle of rug canvas, burlap, or hopsacking
Wool rug yarn in the following colors for diamonds: black, gold, and fuchsia
Scraps of yarn in assorted colors for stripes
Masking tape
Yarn needle
Embroidery hoop (optional)

INSTRUCTIONS
Tape edges of fabric to prevent raveling. Mark center horizontal and vertical threads of fabric or canvas with basting thread or permanent marker.

Insert fabric in embroidery hoop, if desired, and, following diagram, *opposite,* cross-stitch gold, black, and fuchsia diamond designs on background material. Each cross-stitch should cover approximately ¼ square inch.

Next, fill in stripes between diamonds with single vertical rows of cross-stitch in assorted colors (refer to color photo, *pages 72–73,* for placement and color suggestions).

When pattern is completed, block rug and press on wrong side. Trim fabric or canvas to within 2½ inches of stitched design. Turn hem under ½ inch and topstitch. Turn fabric to back of rug, leaving one row of unstitched canvas visible on right side of rug. Miter corners, press hem, and slipstitch fabric to back of rug. With the black yarn, work closely spaced buttonhole stitches all around edges of rug for border.

Diamond Pattern Hooked Rug

Shown on pages 72–73.
Finished size: 25x37 inches

MATERIALS

35x47-inch rectangle of closely
  woven burlap or hopsacking
Narrow strips of wool fabric or rug
  yarn in the following
  colors: black, dark (cherry) red,
  medium (tomato) red, maroon,
  red tweed, and gray tweed
Rug frame and hooking tool
Masking tape
Tracing paper, dressmaker's
  carbon paper
Permanent marker
Latex rug backing liquid (optional)

INSTRUCTIONS

Tape edges of fabric to prevent fraying. Center and trace a 24x36-inch rectangle on fabric, then trace diamonds using the diagram, *lower right, page 86,* inside rectangle. Go over outlines of pattern with permanent marker.

Next, enlarge diamond design, *page 86,* and transfer to center of each diamond outline on rug. Adapt pattern to fit half- and quarter-diamonds around border of rug (refer to color photo, *page 86*).

Place burlap in rug frame, pattern side up, and hook design. Begin by hooking outline of rectangle and all diagonal lines with a single row of black. Also, trace each of the six wavy lines within each diamond with a single row of black.

Next, working from center of each diamond outward, fill in successive rows of pattern (gray tweed in center, followed by maroon, red tweed, cherry red, gray tweed, and tomato red). Fill in outer row of each diamond with tomato red. Use subtle variations of this color scheme for each diamond (refer to color photo, *page 72–73*).

CENTER ROW

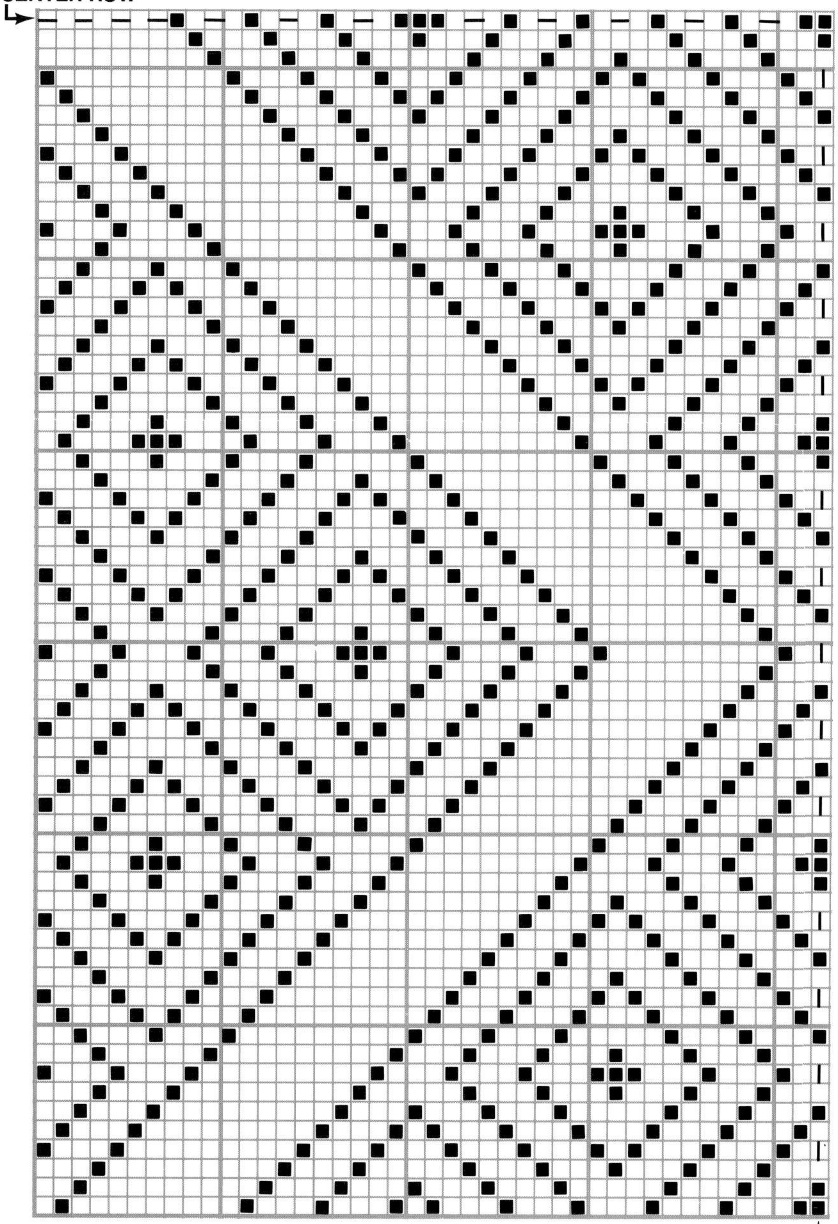

CROSS-STITCH RUG (¼ of pattern)

CENTER ROW

Finish design by hooking four more rows of black around perimeter of rug.

Remove rug from frame, block, press on wrong side. Trim fabric to within 2½ inches of hooked design. Turn under raw edges ½ inch and topstitch. Coat back of hooked design with liquid latex, if desired. When latex is completely dry, turn under hem, miter corners, and slipstitch fabric to back of rug.

continued from page 85
Art Underfoot

Stenciled Floorcloth

Shown on page 74.
Finished size: 30x53 inches

MATERIALS

31x54-inch piece of artist's canvas
Gesso (available at art supply
    stores)
Acrylic paints in white, blue, red,
    and green
Acrylic varnish
Stencil paper
Mat knife
Stencil brushes
Newspapers

INSTRUCTIONS

Round all four corners of canvas rectangle slightly (refer to photograph on *page 74*).

Coat both sides of the canvas with gesso. Allow prepared canvas to dry thoroughly before proceeding. Canvas will shrink slightly.

Apply a base coat of white acrylic to one side of the canvas. Allow the paint to dry.

Use full-size patterns, *opposite* and on *page 88;* cut stencils for each shape.

Stencil house and tree design on floorcloth, positioning motifs as shown in color photograph, *page 74.* Begin by stenciling the red houses, then add the blue chimneys, windows, and doors. Allow the paint to dry thoroughly between colors.

Stencil trees, hearts, and red centers on leaf border. Add blue leaves. When design is complete, protect the cloth with several coats of clear acrylic varnish.

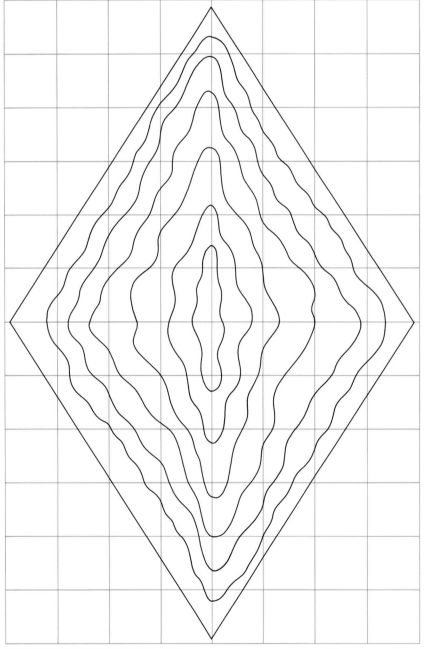

DIAMOND PATTERN HOOKED RUG

1 Square = 1 Inch

DIAMOND PATTERN HOOKED RUG

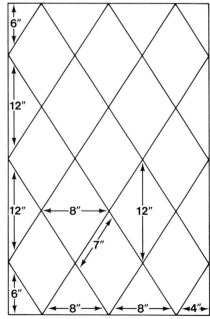

PLACEMENT DIAGRAM

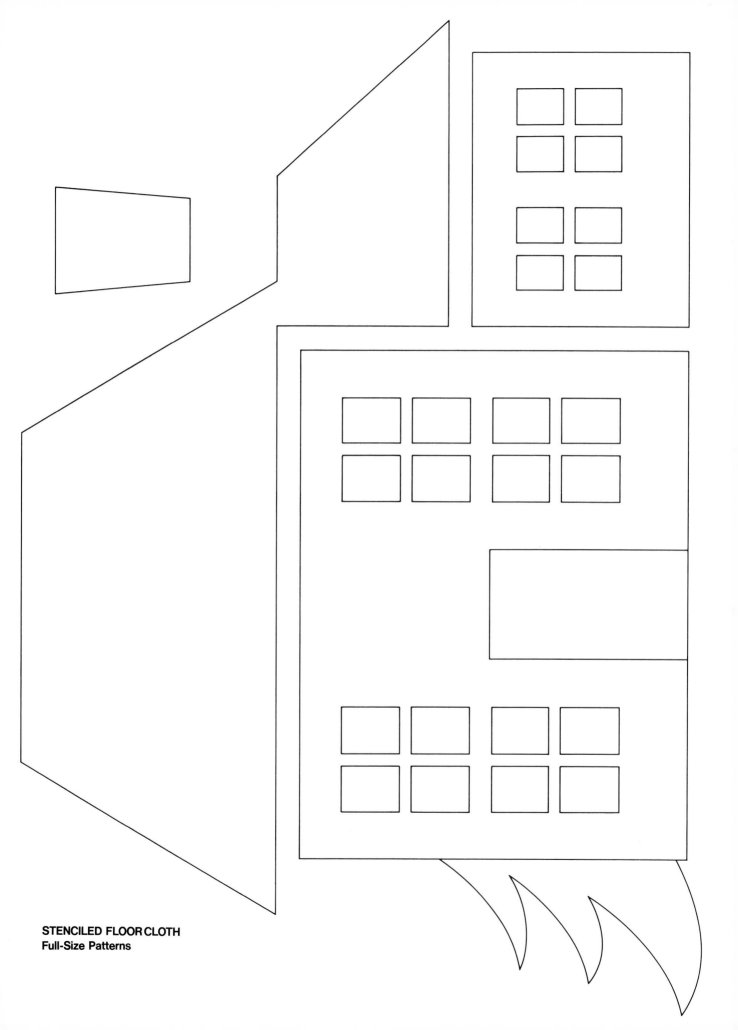

STENCILED FLOOR CLOTH
Full-Size Patterns

continued from page 86
Art Underfoot

Stenciled Place Mats

Shown on page 75.
Finished size: 12½x17½ inches

MATERIALS

8x13-inch rectangle of artist's
   canvas for each mat
Gesso
Acrylic paints in white, blue, red,
   and green
Acrylic varnish
Stencil paper
Mat knife
Stencil brushes

INSTRUCTIONS

Prepare canvas with gesso and base
coat of white acrylic as described,
page 86, for floorcloth.

Full-size patterns for the place
mats appear *opposite.* Cut stencils
for trees, heart, and leaves with mat
knife.

Stencil design on each mat. Position motifs as shown in the photo on
page 75. Protect stenciled mats with
several coats of acrylic varnish.

Braided Mats

Shown on page 76.

MATERIALS

Lightweight, silky fabrics in a
   variety of colors and prints
Pins, needles
Thread

INSTRUCTIONS

Note: Used clothing shops will pro-
vide you with a wonderful selection
of old dress fabrics suitable for this
project.

Cut fabrics into 1½- to 2-inch-
wide strips. Join strips of each color
into one long piece (stitch strips together, end-to-end, on bias, with ¼-
inch seams). Turn raw edges inward
to center; fold in half lengthwise
again. Roll strips into balls before
braiding.

Pin three different strips together
at one end. Stitch ends together to
keep from unwinding.

Taking care to keep raw edges
tucked in as you work, braid three
strands together until you have sufficient length to begin winding into a

STENCILED FLOORCLOTH
Full-Size Patterns

mat. Change colors from time to time and from strand to strand as design dictates. (Stitch new strands to original strand on the bias as previously described.)

TO MAKE THE ROUND MAT: Braid approximately 24 inches of length. Begin to coil the braid into a tight center circle. Work with the braid lying flat on a table or flat surface so that the finished mat will not buckle or curl. Pin and slip-stitch the edges of each round together.

Continue to braid, coil, and stitch until the mat measures the desired size.

To end, gradually trim the final strips down to ½ inch wide. Braid them into a tail and stitch to outer edge of mat.

TO MAKE THE OVAL MAT: Braid a 24-inch length of three fabric strips as described above. Fold braid back on itself after 3 inches, then coil the remainder of the braid around this center lozenge shape, gradually building up the oval.

Braid, coil, stitch, and finish the mat as described for the round mat, *above.*

Crocheted Rug

Shown on page 77.
Finished size: 36 inches in diameter

Skill Level
For the intermediate crocheter.
Gauge: 5 sc = 2 inches.

MATERIALS
Lightweight scrap fabric
Size K crochet hook or size to obtain gauge given above

INSTRUCTIONS
Cut fabric lengthwise or crosswise into strips ¾ to ⅞ inch wide.

Note: To change color, work last yo of last st in new color.

Note for small motif only: Each motif begins with black for Rnd 1.

STENCILED PLACE MATS
Full-Size Patterns

Arrange remaining colors to begin with lightest color on Rnd 2, changing to progressively deeper shades on successive rounds, working last rnd of each motif in black.

SMALL MOTIF (make 13): With black, ch 2.

Rnd 1: 7 sc in 2nd ch from hook, changing to next color on last st—7 sts. Continue to change color at end of each rnd, or as often as number of colors available permits. Note that on some small motifs, there are 1, 2, or 3 rnds worked in the same color, and on one pink and beige motif, beige rows separate 3 colors of pink and burgundy.

Rnd 2: Inc in each st around—14 sts.

Rnd 3: * 1 sc, inc in next st; rep from * around—21 sts.

Rnd 4: * 2 sc, inc in next st; rep from * around—28 sts.

Rnd 5: * 3 sc, inc in next st; rep from * around—35 sts.

Rnd 6: * 4 sc, inc in next st; rep from * around, changing to black on last st—42 sts.

Rnd 7: * 5 sc, inc in next st; rep from * around, end with sl st in next st—49 sts. End off.

continued

continued from page 89
Art Underfoot

CENTER MOTIF: *Note:* On large center section, Rnds 1 and 2 are black, with color changing at end of each rem rnd. Note that the colors are not kept together in color "families" as they are on small motifs.

Beg with black, ch 2.

Rnds 1 and 2: Work as for Rnds 1 and 2 of small motif, changing to next color on last st of Rnd 2.

Rnds 3–7: Work as for small motif, changing color at end of rnd, if number of colors available permits.

Work 17 rnds more, continuing to inc 7 sts in each rnd. Number of sts at end of each rnd is as follows: *Rnd 8:* 56; *Rnd 9:* 63; *Rnd 10:* 70; *Rnd 11:* 77; *Rnd 12:* 84; *Rnd 13:* 91; *Rnd 14:* 98; *Rnd 15:* 105; *Rnd 16:* 112; *Rnd 17:* 119; *Rnd 18:* 126; *Rnd 19:* 133; *Rnd 20:* 140; *Rnd 21:* 147; *Rnd 22:* 154; *Rnd 23:* 161; *Rnd 24:* 168 sts.

Place 13 small motifs in circle; sew 4 sts of each motif tog at points where motifs touch, forming ring. Place ring along outer edge of center motif. Fill in space between center

PENNY TABLE MAT
COLOR PLACEMENT DIAGRAM

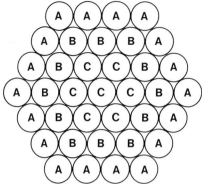

COLOR KEY
A-Black, Green, Beige
B-Black, White, Green
C-Black, Maroon, Red

motif and ring of smaller motifs by working Rnd 25 of center motif with black, placing dtrc opposite each point where smaller motifs are joined, working 3–4 sc opposite midpoint between smaller motif joinings, and modulating height of sts between dtrc and sc by using trc, dc, and hdc, and increasing as needed to keep rug flat.

Sew the outer ring to Rnd 25 of center motif. Sew the fabric ends to the wrong side.

Large Penny Rug
Shown on page 79.
Finished size: 34x52 inches

MATERIALS
1⅔ yards of red wool flannel
1¼ yards of 60-inch black felt

¼ yard of 60-inch felt in the following colors: yellow, red, orange, green, white, and lavender
Threads to match fabric colors
Fabric glue
Cardboard or plastic for templates

INSTRUCTIONS
Trace and cut out plastic or cardboard templates for each of the three circles and three teardrop patterns, *below.*

Trace and cut the following: large circle pieces—278 black; medium circle pieces—68 yellow, 74 orange, 112 white, 24 green; small circle pieces—60 red, 74 green, 60 lavender, 24 orange, 60 yellow; large teardrop pieces—62 black; medium teardrop pieces—62 orange; small teardrop pieces—62 yellow.

Using a good fabric glue and blanket stitches, assemble 62 teardrops for the border (layer small yellow on medium orange on large black teardrops). Assemble the following "pennies" on large black circle background: 60 in color combination A, 74 B, 52 C, 24 D, 8 E, and 60 F (see chart, *below*).

LARGE PENNY RUG
PLACEMENT DIAGRAM (¼ of pattern)

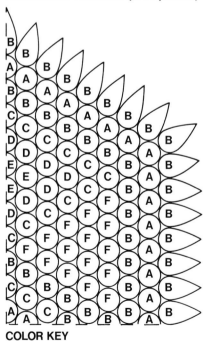

COLOR KEY
A-Yellow, Red   D-Green, Orange
B-Orange, Green   E-Yellow, Lavender
C-White, Lavender   F-White, Yellow

LARGE PENNY RUG
Full-Size Patterns

PENNIES

TEARDROP
BORDER

Spread out red flannel fabric and arrange pennies and teardrops in pattern (¼ of complete design shown, *opposite*). Glue and stitch pieces in place. Cut flannel ⅝ inch from outside edges of teardrop border. Turn under a narrow double hem, leaving ¼ inch of red showing; slip-stitch hem to back of rug.

Penny Table Mat

Shown on page 78.
Finished size: Approximately 16 inches in diameter

MATERIALS

¼ yard of 60-inch-wide black felt
⅛ yard of 60-inch-wide felt in the following colors: green, beige, white, maroon, and red
½ yard of red flannel fabric
Threads to match fabrics
Fabric glue
Cardboard or plastic for templates

INSTRUCTIONS

Trace and cut out templates for each of the three circle patterns, *opposite*. Trace and cut out the following pattern pieces: large circles—37 black; medium circles—18 green, 12 white, 7 maroon; small circles—18 beige, 12 green, 7 red.

Assemble "pennies" with glue and blanket stitches as follows: 18 in color combination A, 12 B, and 7 C (See diagram, *opposite, top*).

Spread out red flannel fabric and arrange pennies following piecing diagram, *opposite, top*. Stitch pennies in place. Trim flannel ½ inch from edges of outer row of pennies. Turn under a double hem and slip-stitch hem to back of table rug.

Floral Pattern Penny Runner

Shown on page 80.
Finished size: 20x60 inches

MATERIALS

22x57-inch rectangle of white background fabric
22x57-inch burlap for backing
1 yard of closely woven black wool fabric
Scraps of pink, green, yellow, orange, purple, and beige fabrics for flower appliqués
4⅓ yards of ¾-inch red flannel bias binding
Yellow, aqua, pink, white, and orange yarn or floss
Fabric glue

continued

COLOR KEY
A–Pink C–Yellow E–Purple
B–Green D–Orange F–Beige

FLORAL PATTERN PENNY RUNNER
PLACEMENT DIAGRAM
(¼ of pattern)

FLORAL PATTERN PENNY RUNNER
Full-Size Patterns

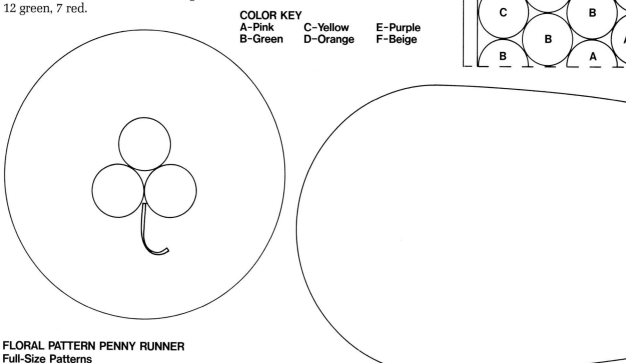

continued from page 91
Art Underfoot

INSTRUCTIONS

Using patterns, *page 91,* cut 114 four-inch circles and 18 tongue-shape border pieces from black wool (do *not* add seam allowances).

For flower appliqués, cut the following ½-inch circles: 36 pink, 36 green, 120 yellow, 42 orange, 72 purple, and 36 beige. For each flower, arrange three small circles in the center of a larger black circle and secure with dabs of fabric glue. Then outline each small circle with blanket stitches in a contrasting shade of single ply yarn or embroidery floss. Embroider a short aqua stem in chain stitch.

Complete the following appliquéd "pennies": 12 pink (A), 12 green (B), 40 yellow (C), 14 orange (D), 24 purple (E), and 12 beige (F).

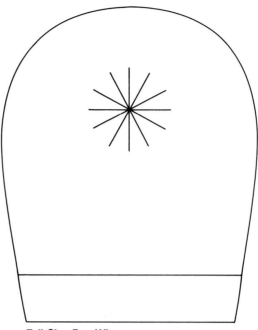

Full-Size Pen Wiper

EMBROIDERED HORSE RUG

1 Square = 1 Inch

Arrange appliquéd circles on rectangle of white fabric, following placement diagram, *top of page 91.* Secure each circle to background fabric with a dab of fabric glue.

Pin and baste burlap backing to wrong side of white fabric. Turn runner over to right side and stitch each circle in place with blanket stitches taken through all three layers of fabric. Use a contrasting shade of yarn or floss for blanket stitching on each set of pennies (refer to color photo on *page 80*).

Trim both layers of backing into lozenge shape, cutting approximately ¾ inch beyond appliquéd shapes. Use purchased binding, or cut and piece sufficient 2-inch-wide bias strips of red flannel to make 4⅓ yards of binding.

Fold raw edges of bias strip in toward center ¼ inch and press. Then fold strip in half and press down length of strip to create ¾-inch-wide bias binding. Pin and baste binding around edges of runner. Topstitch close to inside and outside edges of binding, then work a row of featherstitches in yellow yarn or floss along center of binding strip, all around runner.

Using yellow again, work a row of blanket stitches around the curved edge of each tongue-shape border piece. Position and pin nine border pieces on either end of runner (refer to photo on *page 80* for placement). Tongues should extend about ½ inch beneath bound edge of runner. Whipstitch bottom edge of each border piece to back of runner.

Embroidered Horse Rug

Shown on page 81.
Finished size: 30x42 inches

MATERIALS

14x22-inch oval of gray wool or felt (center)
Scraps of gray, brown, and black wool or felt (pen-wiper border)
24x36-inch oval of heavy cotton or hopsack fabric (backing)
Wool yarn in red, gold, white, yellow, and black

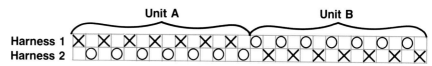

DIAGRAM FOR WARPING

INSTRUCTIONS

Enlarge pattern, *opposite,* and transfer to center of gray wool or felt oval.

Embroider mare and colt in outline and satin stitches. (Refer to the photograph on *page 81* for color and placement.)

Position and pin embroidered oval to center of backing fabric.

Cut enough pen-wiper shapes (full-size pattern, *opposite*) from gray, brown, and black wool or felt to make a border around the center oval. Outline each shape with buttonhole stitches in contrasting colors of yarn. Embroider a star on each pen wiper using a second color of contrasting yarn.

Stitch the first row of pen wipers, about ½ inch inward, completely around the outer edge of the backing fabric.

Working in toward the embroidered center, arrange two more rows of pen wipers around the edges. Pin and stitch them in place, making sure each row conceals the straight edges of the previous row. (Use the photograph on *page 81* as a placement reference.) The last row should tuck between the embroidered center and backing fabric. Use a buttonhole stitch through all three layers to finish.

Checkerboard Place Mats

Shown on page 8.
Finished size: 14½x18½ inches

MATERIALS

Lightweight cotton fabric torn in 1-inch-wide strips
Natural and colonial blue 8/4 carpet warp

Threads per inch: 14
Total threads: 196

INSTRUCTIONS

The instructions are for a table loom or two-harness floor loom.

WARPING THE LOOM: (Refer to the diagram, *above.*) To warp the loom for 2-inch blocks: Alternate light (O), then dark (X) threads for two inches (28 threads), then reverse dark, then light.

(A) unit: Harness 1 (X); harness 2 (O). Repeat two inches for 28 threads.

(B) unit: Harness 1 (O); harness 2 (X). Repeat two inches for 28 threads.

Repeat to seven total units.

WEAVING THE MATS: Weave blue carpet warp for the selvage. Weave in at least 1 inch to make a deep hem so that if fringe tatters in washing, the selvage can be turned under to form a hem.

Plain-weave one blue, then one natural, cotton filler, alternating light and dark to form a square block. End weave with four blue, two natural, and four blue to form a band. Repeat light, dark, and filler to make five blocks; repeat band, final block, and selvage, to complete mat.

Join filler with pieces that have been cut with a thin tapered end and twisted so that the joint cannot be noticed. The thin, twisted taper also should be used when joining light and dark fillers.

(*Note:* Tearing fabric is faster than cutting. Always tear with the length of cloth. Fold the cloth lengthwise in two folds; cut and tear strips, several at one time. When weaving, instead of putting filler on a shuttle, use a thin, flat ½-inch-wide stick with a grooved notch at one end to pass filler through the warp.)

ARTFUL EMBELLISHMENTS

♦

PAINTED FINISHES

*In Colonial times, wallpaper, rugs,
and fine wood furnishings were
luxuries that few could afford.
Undaunted, Americans relied on gaily
painted patterns and stenciled
designs to brighten their walls,
"carpet" their floors, and ornament
their plain pine furniture.*

ARTFUL EMBELLISHMENTS

S tenciling was a popular method of decorating walls and floors throughout Colonial America, and particularly in New England, where such work was usually done by itinerant artists. Often a craftsman would actually move in with the family whose house he was to stencil, bartering his artistic efforts in exchange for a week's or a whole winter's worth of room and board, depending on the complexity of the project.

Traditionally, the reusable stencils were cut from thin sheets of metal or stiff, oiled paper. A talented stenciler eventually developed a large repertoire of figurative and abstract patterns that could be mixed and matched to suit any surface and please almost any customer.

Today, with the resurgence of interest in this versatile craft, new developments in techniques and materials (such as transparent acrylic stencils and quick-drying paints) make it easy for even a novice to achieve excellent results.

Designs can be original or contemporary adaptations of traditional motifs.

Patterns and instructions begin on *page 106.*

ARTFUL EMBELLISHMENTS

Stenciling an entire room—or any large project—requires careful planning to ensure success.

First, decide how much and what kind of stenciling to use. Do you want an overall repeat pattern, just a few stenciled borders, or a combination of elements? Here, three different border patterns, and individual elements lifted from those patterns, are mixed with an occasional figurative accent (see close-up of willow tree, *below right*).

Select designs that work together and suit the scale of the room.

Choose a simple color scheme that complements other decorative elements. The border motifs shown here are stenciled in Colonial shades of red and blue, with the willow tree in gold and green—colors that repeat the dominant tones of the homespun coverlet and Oriental rug in the same room.

Take special care to position the pattern motifs to your best advantage. The finished design should both accent attractive architectural features of the room, and mask unsightly elements (such as the awkwardly situated door, *above right,* which has been stenciled over to minimize its impact).

ARTFUL EMBELLISHMENTS

Faux finishes—painted finishes designed to imitate the surface characteristics of more costly materials such as polished marble or fine-grained hardwoods— were frequently used to embellish floors and furniture in Colonial times. Traditional techniques range from the realistic to the fanciful, including wood graining, sponging, marbleizing, and vinegar painting, as well as spatter and comb painting.

In the hallway pictured here, three different techniques have been combined to imitate a traditional checkered marble floor.

As with stenciling, the introduction of new techniques and materials in recent years has brought the art of faux (French for "false") finishes within the grasp of any patient amateur. The availability of quick-drying paints, inexpensive tools, and sturdy polyurethane varnishes has made such projects easy to execute and extremely durable.

For complete instructions on how to re-create this floor, please turn to *page 107*. For a sampling of other faux-finish techniques, turn the page.

Artful Embellishments

Working on small projects—like the boxes, picture frames, miniature chest, and child's cradle pictured on these pages—offers an ideal way to experiment with traditional faux-finish techniques.

The delightful doll-size chest, *above left,* and several of the round wooden boxes, *opposite,* are examples of comb painting—one of the easiest and most versatile faux finishes. To comb-paint, you must first paint the object with a dark shade of acrylic, then brush on a second coat of lighter-colored paint. While the second coat is wet, comb in a pattern of arcs and wavy lines, using a notched piece of plastic or cardboard, or a regular hair comb.

The photo *below left* shows a winsome folk-art cradle decorated with vinegar painting. A mixture of dry tempera powder, water, and vinegar is brushed over a base coat of flat oil paint, then incised with strokes of a stick, finger, or pencil eraser, or wiped with wadded pieces of paper or cloth.

Also pictured, *opposite,* are treasure boxes and frames with tortoise-shell, marbleized, grained, and spatter-painted finishes.

For instructions on reproducing faux finishes, please turn to *page 113.*

ARTFUL
EMBELLISHMENTS

Chairs of every description were among the most common items of painted and stenciled furniture in 18th- and 19th-century America. The variety of decoration was limited only by the artist's skill and imagination, and by the decorative conventions of the period.

You, too, can turn nondescript secondhand chairs and simple pieces of unfinished furniture into one-of-a-kind hand-painted accents for the kitchen or dining room with the application of freehand or stenciled patterns. Experiment with adaptations of the gracefully drawn scrolls and borders, gilt highlighting, stenciled fruits and flowers, and abstract motifs found on the chairs pictured here.

Look for other authentic patterns in books and catalogs of Early American furniture, copy designs from chairs on display in local museums and historic houses, or adapt contemporary motifs that strike your fancy.

Use acrylic or oil paints to stencil or hand-paint the designs (see general how-to on *pages 112–115*). Protect finished chairs with a coat or two of clear polyurethane varnish.

Painted Chest

Shown on page 95.

MATERIALS
For painting design
Artist's oil or acrylic paints in a
  variety of colors
Artist's brushes
Tissue paper
Dressmaker's carbon
Clear acrylic spray paint

INSTRUCTIONS
The full-size patterns, *left* and *opposite,* were taken from the antique jewelry chest, *page 95.* You can use these patterns to embellish any piece you already own.

General directions for painting in this folk-art style appear on *page 115.*

Stenciled Walls

Shown on pages 96–99.

MATERIALS
Acrylic stencil paints
Stencil brushes in assorted sizes
Tracing paper
Stencil paper

INSTRUCTIONS
The room on *pages 96–99* has been stenciled in the traditional style. The patterns on *pages 108–109* and *page 110* may be used as full-size or may be adjusted in size according to your room. The larger the wall, the larger the stencil it will comfortably handle. The room featured on *pages 96–99* has 8-foot ceilings. Enlarging the patterns to the scale given will give you the same look you see in the photographs.

General directions for stenciling appear on *page 114.*

PAINTED CHEST
Full-Size Patterns

**PAINTED CHEST
Full-Size Pattern**

Marbled Floors

Shown on pages 100–101.

MATERIALS
Sandpaper
Masking tape
Waterproof marker or pencil
Striping brush or turkey feather
Paintbrushes
Oil-base primer
Oil-base paint in cream, white, gray, black, tan, dark green, and light green
Mat or semigloss varnish
Turpentine
Wood alcohol

INSTRUCTIONS
Sand the floor. Prime the floor with a good oil-base primer. Next, give it three or four coats of oil-base paint, allowing ample drying between each coat of paint. (A light color of base was used on the floor on *pages 100–101*.)

Lay out the pattern using a pencil or waterproof marker. Each square on the floor shown on *pages 100–101* is 10x10 inches. Placing squares on the diagonal will minimize the effects of walls that are out of square.

Leave an 8-inch-wide border around the perimeter of the room.

The white "tile" is done first. Paint all white squares with oil-base paint. Allow paint to dry. Apply a second coat of oil-base paint that is only slightly different from the white (off-white, light gray, cream, etc.). Before this coat is dry, work black, tan, and gray into it, blurring it so that the surface has the characteristic of marble. As this layer dries, go back over each square putting in more clear, sharp lines with a striping brush or turkey feather.

After all the paint on the lighter squares is *thoroughly* dry, you may proceed to the darker "tiles."

Use masking tape and squares of paper to completely cover the white squares so that you do not get dark paint on them. This procedure takes time, but it is one of the most important steps.

Work with only a few squares at a time. (Dark and light green oil-base paints were used for this floor.) Dab on a light green, then dab on dark green, leaving some of the light color showing through. Let the paint set for only a short time, then blur it with a brush to blend the edges of

the colors together. Allow the paints to dry thoroughly.

Spatter the dark "tiles" with turpentine. Let set, then spatter on alcohol thinner (wood alcohol). Because the two conflict, the turpentine and wood alcohol create pockmarks in the oil-base paint which give the appearance of fossil stone. This makes a nice contrast to the even-grained marbling that the white "tiles" represent.

When dark squares are dry, remove the masking tape and paper.

TO PAINT THE BORDER: Brush black paint over the light base coat. While the paint is still wet, wipe through the paint in places with a cloth dampened with turpentine. Add white veins with a brush after the paint is dry.

TO FINISH THE FLOOR: Use at least five coats of a high-quality polyurethane mat or semigloss varnish. Hand-rub each coat to remove the thick layer of varnish that is normally left from the brush. Allow the varnish to dry before going on to the next coat.

continued on page 110

STENCILED WALLS

1 Square = 1 Inch

108

STENCILED WALLS

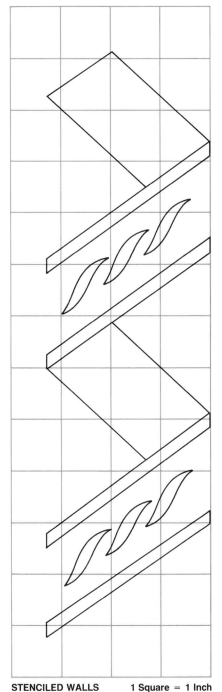

STENCILED WALLS   1 Square = 1 Inch

continued from page 107
Artful Embellishments

Painted Heart
Shown on page 14.

MATERIALS
½-inch-thick plywood
Liquitex 5000 Series No. 5 round
   brush
1-inch bristle brush
Sponge brushes for applying the
   base coat of paint and for
   varnishing
B.I.N. pigmented sealer
Vanilla-color base coat paint
Satin- or mat-finish varnish
Liquitex acrylic paints in the
   following colors: Chromium
   Green Oxide (CGO), Titanium
   White (W), Phthalo Blue (PHB),
   Burnt Umber (BU), Yellow
   Oxide (YO), Raw Sienna (RS),
   Naphthol Crimson (NC),
   Dioxazine Purple (DP), Hooker's
   Green (HG)
Cherry stain (for antiquing)
Natural sponge
Foil (for a paint palette)
Paper towels
Tracing paper
Pencil

INSTRUCTIONS
MIXING PAINT COLORS: Mauve
= 3 parts NC, 2 parts W, 1 part BU,
and 1 part DP.
   Blue = 3 parts PHB and 1 part BU.

TRANSFERRING THE PATTERN:
On the tracing paper, draw a heart
shape that measures 15 inches wide
and 17 inches tall. Cut the heart
shape from ½-inch plywood.
   Transfer the full-size patterns to
tracing paper. Then, transfer the
full-size motifs to the heart shape,
referring to the color photograph on
page 14 for arrangement.

PREPARING THE HEART: Base-
paint the entire heart with B.I.N. to
seal the wood and prevent knot-
holes from showing through the
paint. Sand with fine sandpaper.
   Base-paint the heart with two or
three coats of vanilla-color paint.
   Transfer the pattern to the heart.

SPONGING THE EDGE OF THE
HEART: Thin the mauve paint (mixture as earlier described) with water
using equal parts. Dab a natural
sponge into the watered-down
mauve mixture. Blot excess onto paper towel. Then, begin dabbing
along the edge of the heart, immediately outside the design.

PAINTING THE DESIGN: Paint the
edge of the heart with CGO.
   All decorative designs are done
with one brush—the Liquitex No. 5
round.

Scrolls: Fill in scrolls with RS, then
restroke with a double load of RS on
one side and W on the other side.
Hold the brush so you can see both
colors. With W to the inside, restroke halfway through the original
stroke.

Cross-hatching: Thin mauve paint
with an equal amount of water.
Paint crosshatch marks.

Dots and dot flowers: Paint with
blue mix and double-load with W
on top of the brush.

Leaves: Base-coat with a double
load of CGO and W. Use a long
stroke of HG along the side. Add a
shorter stroke of W.

Roses: Base-coat with mauve mix.
Shade bottom inside of rose with
BU. (Double-load brush side by side
with mauve and BU.) BU edge goes
to the bottom. BU oval goes to the
top inside of the rose. Restroke bottom petals with a double-load side-
by-side of W and mauve. (W goes to
the outside.) Petals and strokes going through the middle are also
painted in this manner. Add W dots
to the inside center.

Heart: Base-coat with mauve mix.
Stroke from top center to bottom
point with a double load of RS on
one side and W on the other side of
the brush. Hold the brush so you can
see both colors. W should be to the
inside.

continued

110

PAINTED HEART
Full-Size Patterns

Scrolls

Welcome

continued from page 110
Artful Embellishments

Border: Dip the end of a round brush in CGO and dot around the outside edge of the heart.

ANTIQUING THE HEART: Brush on cherry stain over the entire painted heart, completely covering the design. With a paper towel, wipe until the surface is as light or dark as you want it to be. If you wipe off too much stain, simply apply more. Smooth out the antiquing stain with a dry 1-inch bristle brush, pulling strokes in one direction only.

When the stain is dry, varnish the heart with three coats of satin- or mat-finish varnish.

Faux-Finished Boxes, Frames, and Furniture
Pictured on pages 102–103.

MATERIALS
For Tortoiseshell Frame (1)
Flat oil-base primer
Bright yellow ocher oil-base paint
Mat or semigloss polyurethane
    varnish
Artist's oil paints in the following
    colors: burnt umber, raw umber,
    red iron oxide, and black
Small artist's brushes
One 2-inch-wide paintbrush
Small sponge brush

For Fossil Marble Frame (2)
Flat oil-base primer
White gloss oil-base paint
Linseed oil
Paint thinner
Denatured alcohol
Artist's oils in the following colors:
    yellow ocher, white, and cobalt
    blue
Artist's brushes
Mat or semigloss polyurethane
    varnish

For Combed Box (3)
Flat oil-base primer
Acrylic paint in tan and blue
Cardboard
Sponge brush
Mat or semigloss polyurethane
    varnish

For Sponged Boxes (4, 6)
Flat oil-base primer
Acrylic paint in mustard yellow,
    tan, and red
Sponge brush
Small marine sponge
Mat or semigloss polyurethane
    varnish

For Grained Box (5)
Flat oil-base primer
Bright yellow ocher oil-base paint
    (mid-sheen)
Glazing liquid
Artist's oil paints in the following
    colors: burnt umber, vermilion,
    and green
Corncob
Paper towels or old rags
Three containers for mixing glazes
Mat or semigloss polyurethane
    varnish

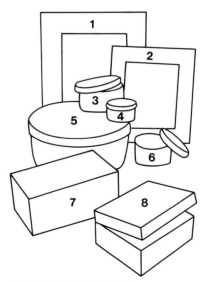

FAUX-FINISHED BOXES AND FRAMES

For Marbled Box (7)
Flat oil-base primer
Blue acrylic paint
Artist's oils in light blue and white
Medium-size foil roasting pan
    filled with water
Paint thinner
Waxed paper
Paper towels
Mat or semigloss polyurethane
    varnish

For Spattered Box (8)
Flat oil-base primer
Acrylic paint in red, mustard, tan,
    and blue
Sponge brush
Three toothbrushes
Mat or semigloss polyurethane
    varnish

INSTRUCTIONS
All of the pieces on *pages 102–103* are painted with faux (false) finishes. The four-drawer chest is comb-painted green over red; the cradle is combed in warm shades of brown.

Refer to the diagram, *below left,* to determine the finish on each box or frame. The materials lists will help you determine what you need. Then, use the general directions, *opposite* and on *pages 114–115,* for the various faux finishes.

Painted Chair Backs
Shown on pages 104–105.

MATERIALS
Oil-base paint
Acrylic paint
Stencil brush
Stencil paper or commercial stencil
Polyurethane varnish

INSTRUCTIONS
The chairs shown on *pages 104–105* are all antiques. The backs have been stenciled in traditional motifs. A variety of stencils for reproducing traditional decorations are available through mail-order and retail stores. A partial list of these outlets appears on *page 115.* General instructions for stenciling appear on *page 114.*

GENERAL INSTRUCTIONS FOR PAINTED FINISHES

Refer to the diagram, *opposite,* to identify the finishes on the projects on *page 103:* (1) Tortoiseshell, (2) Fossil Marble, (3) Comb, (4) Sponge, (5) Grain, (6) Sponge, (7) Marble, and (8) Spatter.

COMB PAINTING

Combing is a decorative paint technique that is limited only by your imagination. Depending on the tools, colors, and application technique you choose, you can create a finish to match any design mood.

To begin, prime the surface of the project with a good flat oil-base primer. Allow the paint to dry thoroughly. Sand the surface lightly.

Apply two coats of acrylic base paint, allowing ample drying time between coats. When the base paint is dry, apply one coat of a second color of acrylic. While that paint is wet, drag the comb through the paint to create the pattern. (*Note:* It is very important to paint on one small section at a time, then comb immediately, since acrylic paint dries quickly.)

Combs designed specifically for this purpose are available in most well-stocked paint and hardware stores. Or, make your own from a stiff piece of plastic or cardboard or a rubber dustpan; or use a hair comb.

There are a number of ways to produce a creative finish. The simplest method is to drag the comb straight down through the paint. Or, comb diagonally, starting at the upper left corner and working toward the lower right corner. Another popular version is cross-hatching—combing both vertically and horizontally to form a grid pattern. Wavy lines and arches are also quite interesting in a comb-painted finish.

After the paint has had ample drying time, varnish the entire surface of the project.

GRAINING

Prime the surface of the project with an oil-base primer. Lightly sand the project.

Paint over the primer with two coats of bright yellow ocher oil-base paint, allowing each coat to dry thoroughly before going to the next.

Mix artist's oil paint with glazing liquid until you reach the desired colors. You will want to end up with three different shades that work well together for graining. Apply each color to the project with a small rag. With one hand, hold one end of a corncob. Set it down on the wet paint. Use the other hand to pull the other end through the paint to create a half circle. Dab the area not covered with the cob graining with paper towels to create a mottled look. Use your fingertips to lightly touch the surface, creating small circular shapes.

You can get a very different look by moving the corncob in a wavy motion. You'll want to experiment to see what look you like best.

Allow all paints to dry thoroughly. Varnish your project with a good flat-finish varnish.

MARBLING

Marbling can be done on almost any surface. However, you must prepare the surface properly.

Before you begin to paint, lightly sand the surface of the area to be marbled. Wipe away any loose particles. Give the surface one coat of flat oil-base primer. When the primer is thoroughly dry, sand it again lightly.

Next, apply two coats of base paint; allow ample drying time between coats. (*Note:* The boxes shown were painted with acrylic base; the floor shown was painted with oil-base paint for a finish hard and durable enough to walk on.)

Mix artist's oils with enough paint thinner to obtain the consistency of light cream. Waxed paper works well as a mixing palette.

Easy Dipping Method
(for small projects)

Fill a container that has a surface larger than the project with water. Use a knife to drop a small amount of artist's oil (lighter than the base coat) onto the top of the water. The paint will disperse somewhat. Next, drop white artist's oil onto the water surface where there are empty spaces.

Use a knife to swirl the two colors of paint on the surface of the water.

Dip one side of the project at a time, just touching the top of the water. Blot the project on paper towels and repeat for the remaining sides. Allow the paint to dry thoroughly. Varnish the piece on all sides when the paint is dry.

Brushing Method
(for large projects including floors)

All three base coats must be dry before beginning.

Apply a coat of paint, very close in color to the base coat. Before the paint is dry, work black, tan, and gray artist's oils into it with a soft brush or crumpled cotton rag to give the character of marble. As this paint dries, you can intensify the effect by going back over it with a striping brush, or turkey or goose feather, and small amounts of the artist's oil. Use both light and heavy strokes, as well as a combination of jagged and smooth strokes, to create realistic, uneven colors.

After all paint is dry, varnish with several coats of polyurethane mat or semigloss varnish.

FOSSIL MARBLING

Prime project with one coat of oil-base paint. Allow the paint to dry, then sand lightly. Apply a second coat of oil-base paint. Sand again so that the surface is very smooth.

continued

113

continued from page 113
General Instructions

With a cotton rag, apply a thin coat of linseed oil over all surfaces.

Mix yellow ocher with white; add enough paint thinner to get the consistency of milk. Repeat this step with a second color of artist's oil paint. Apply these two colors to the surface of the project in a checkerboard fashion. Dab the paint lightly with a rag to remove any excess paint.

Dip a small paintbrush into paint thinner and spatter the thinner over the painted surface. Small shapes will appear.

Use the same procedure with denatured alcohol. Different shapes will appear.

Allow the project to dry thoroughly. Varnish all sides.

TORTOISESHELL
Prime the project with a flat oil-base primer. When the paint is dry, lightly sand the surface. Paint the project with two coats of yellow ocher oil-base paint, allowing ample drying time between coats.

Mix varnish with burnt umber, raw umber, and red iron oxide to obtain a pleasing wood-stain color. Apply the colored varnish to the surface using a sponge brush. Apply enough of the varnish mixture to give it a transparent quality. The base coat of yellow should always be visible to some degree, beneath the sponge-brush strokes.

Quickly make squiggles in the varnish with an artist's brush. With another brush, draw short broken lines diagonally using burnt umber oil paint.

Use black artist's oil paint and dab the paint on the surface of the project in a diagonal pattern, similar to the burnt umber, but touch the surface less frequently. With the 2-inch-wide brush, dry-brush the surface diagonally in one direction, then diagonally the other way. Finish by repeating the first diagonal brushing.

Allow the paints to dry thoroughly. Varnish the entire surface; dry.

SPONGE PAINTING
Depending on the type of sponge you choose to work with, you can create a host of different effects with this technique. Before beginning, experiment with different sponge shapes and pore sizes.

Color selection also affects the final look of a sponged finish. For a subtle, more formal look, select colors that are fairly close together. Two colors with great contrast will give you a more playful look for children's projects, bathroom accessories, etc. Sponging several colors over the base coat will create an even greater decorating impact.

Begin with a clean, smooth surface. Fill cracks and holes with spackling compound or patching plaster, then sand smooth.

Paint your project with a flat oil-base primer. Allow the primer to dry. Lightly sand the surface.

Paint the surface with two coats of acrylic paint, drying between each coat.

Select a second color of paint to contrast with the base coat. Dip a marine sponge into the second color of acrylic. Use small amounts of paint; blot the sponge on paper to remove the excess. Dab the sponge on newspaper to get most of the paint off the sponge. Then, lightly dab the surface of the project to create the pattern. When all the paint has thoroughly dried, varnish all surfaces.

RAG ROLLING
Rag rolling is a painting technique closely related to sponging.

Almost any type of cloth is suitable for rag rolling—sheets, cheesecloth, chamois, lace netting, terry, or burlap. Each will produce a different look.

There are essentially two techniques used in rag rolling. One involves simply dabbing a freshly painted surface with a wadded piece of cloth. The other entails wrapping crinkled fabric around a roller and rolling it across fresh

paint. Gloss or semigloss paint should be used for the rag rolling, since it will not be absorbed by the rag, as would flat paint. Once the rag-rolled surface is dry, you may choose to sponge on a second color.

SPATTER PAINTING
Paint the project with an oil-base primer; dry and lightly sand.

Apply two coats of the acrylic paint base coat, allowing each coat to dry before going to the next.

Dip the bristles of a toothbrush into a contrasting color of acrylic paint. Draw a finger over the bristles to spatter the paint onto the surface of the project. Repeat the procedure with two additional colors of paint for a more interesting look. Allow all paint to dry. Varnish all surfaces.

STENCILING
The ability to create a beautifully stenciled wall, floor, or piece of furniture is not limited to formally trained artists. Because you can do it yourself, stenciling is an inexpensive decorating technique.

Stencil work is suitable to a number of decorating styles, depending on the pattern you select. A wide variety of predesigned and precut stencils is available at decorating centers, paint stores, and crafts stores. A number of museums and historical villages have copied stencil patterns from their own historic walls and have made the patterns available in kits for do-it-yourselfers.

You can also create your own designs, or you may choose to use our patterns on *pages 108–110*.

To stencil walls and furniture
Applying stencils to walls or furniture takes planning. Measure the motif as well as the length of the area you will apply it to. Divide the length of the area by the size of the stencil to compute the number of times the design will be repeated. Plan for a neat arrangement at the corners. Lightly mark the spots where the stencil will appear.

Position the stencil and anchor it with masking tape at the corners.

Put a small amount of paint into a can lid or paint tray. Dip the tip of the stencil brush into the paint and remove the excess by dabbing the brush onto a piece of paper. The secret to successful stenciling is to use a nearly dry brush; this produces the best print. When you apply the paint, it should be almost powdery.

Hold the brush perpendicular to the stencil and use an up-and-down motion to apply the paint. Do not stroke or drag the paint across the stencil, or it will smear under the edges. To achieve the best results, work from the edges of the stencil toward the center. When done, carefully remove the stencil.

As you go along, you might want to alternate the design by flipping the stencil over each time it is painted. Wipe the stencil each time it is moved to prevent paint smears.

To stencil floors

Sand off all of the old varnish, wax, or paint before stenciling a floor. If you need only to remove wax, you can scrub with a heavy-duty floor cleaner intended for this purpose and avoid full-scale sanding.

Measure the area you wish to stencil and apply the design in the same way you would wall or furniture stencils. After painting any floor design, wait 24 hours and then seal the floor with two or more coats of polyurethane. Finish with a good coat of wax.

TOLE AND DECORATIVE PAINTING

The word "tole" is French for tin. Beginning as early as the middle of the 18th century, tole painting was a popular means of decorating tin trays, cups, teapots, and other household goods.

While the French were painting on tin, others were creating their own style of folk art. Beautiful designs of flowers, birds, and fruit were being painted on chairs, trunks, wooden bowls and boxes, cupboards, and other furnishings.

You, too, can embellish almost any item in your home with folk-art designs. An unlimited selection of decorative-painting books is available in crafts, and bookstores. Following are a few tips that may help you achieve the painted finish you desire.

One simple brushstroke, resembling a large comma, is all you need to know. With practice, you can create truly professional results.

Always purchase good-quality artist's oils. Inexpensive paints may crack with age.

Waxed paper is great for mixing colors. There's no messy cleanup; just throw the "palette" away when you finish.

Use a good-quality sable watercolor brush for painting. Select several sizes depending on the detail you plan to create. Keep an extra brush on hand for mistakes, dipping the brush in turpentine and using it as you would an eraser if a bit of paint goes outside of the pattern line.

Lay a sheet of tracing paper over the design you wish to copy. Trace the design. Do not use carbon paper to transfer the design onto your project. Carbon will smear. Use dark graphite on light backgrounds and light graphite for dark backgrounds. Sandwich the graphite between the tracing paper and your project to transfer the design.

Protect your clothing and table surface; artist's oils will stain. Keep paper towels or rags close by for cleanup.

Use turpentine to clean your brushes and to keep them soft and easy to use.

Prepare the item you are to decorate so that it has a smooth surface. For wood, fill in any cracks or holes, and sand the surface. Seal the surface with a wood sealer. For tin, clean any rust spots with a wire brush. Wash tin, new or old, with soap and hot water, rinsing thoroughly. Rinse with vinegar to neutralize metal acids. Prime the tin with a rust-retardant metal paint.

Apply a base coat in the color of your choice to both tin and wooden objects. If you plan to use an antiquing finish on the piece, start out with a bright background color. Antiquing will tone the paint color down considerably.

A satin-finish base coat is recommended to make the decorative painting adhere easily.

For the decorative painting, mix equal parts of varnish and artist's oil to get a whipping-cream consistency. Dip the dry brush into turpentine, dab it lightly on a tissue, then dip it into the paint mixture. Now, you are ready to paint.

When you have completed the entire design, and the paint is thoroughly dry, you may wish to use an antiquing glaze over the entire surface to give the piece some "age." Finish your project by adding a coat of high-quality polyurethane varnish for protection.

Mail-order sources for stencils

There are many mail-order sources from which you can obtain stencil designs. Here is a small sampling of addresses to write for catalogs or more information:

Adele Bishop, Inc., a division of Wall Link, P.O. Box 3349, Dept. WWI, Kinston, NC 28501. A catalog is available for $3.00.

Stencil House, P.O. Box 109, Hooksett, NH 03106. A catalog is available for $2.50.

Gail Grisi Stenciling, Inc., P.O. Box 1263, Haddonfield, NJ 08033. A catalog is available for $2.00 (refundable with first order).

Plaid Enterprises, Inc., P.O. Drawer E, Norcross, GA 30091.

StenArt, Inc., P.O. Box 114, Pitman, NJ 08071. A catalog is available for $2 (refundable with first order).

A CHILD'S WORLD

◆

HANDMADE PLAYTHINGS

Not so very long ago, it seems, imagination was all it took to turn the most humble toys into exciting treasures. Any doll would do as a fairy princess, and picture puzzle blocks could set a child to dreaming of castles, kings, and high adventure.

A Child's World

Long before the age of television cartoons and commercials, familiar images of childhood prevailed in the nursery. Then, as now, favorite storybook characters were the most frequent inspiration for children's toys and decor.

Elves, fairies, and other woodland creatures were stock figures in children's books of the Victorian era, and the delightful redwork design on the curtain, *top left,* was no doubt inspired by a nursery-tale illustration of that period.

During the last quarter of the 19th century, Kate Greenaway's winsome depictions of childhood won the hearts of parents and children alike. Stitcheries inspired by her drawings soon appeared on everything from tea towels to quilt tops. The scene of dancing children, *left,* is a particularly charming design.

The Little Red School House was another beloved icon of childhood—one that found special favor among quilters from about 1850 through the early decades of this century. More than a dozen variations of this quilt block exist—the simplest being the pieced pattern shown here.

Instructions for all projects shown begin on *page 128.*

A CHILD'S WORLD

Rag dolls have always been popular playthings for children. Their homely features, handmade costumes, and huggable bodies have an enduring appeal that fancier, store-bought models can't quite match. In pioneer days, a simple doll like the homespun miss, *left,* was often a child's only toy and dearest companion.

As the 19th century progressed, printed cloth dolls modeled after characters from fairy tales and favorite children's books began to appear on the market. Most of these were designed to be cut, stitched, and stuffed at home. The seamstress could then add a few embellishments of her own—like the touches of embroidery and bead buttons on the rabbit, *far left*.

In contrast, the swashbuckling Puss in Boots character, *near left,* is entirely homemade— the outline traced from a picture book, perhaps, and then embroidered.

Picture block puzzles, *left, center,* were another popular pastime for children. (You can make a similar set of blocks using six different prints or wrapping paper pictures cut into squares and glued to blocks of scrap pine.)

121

A Child's World

Children's playthings of the past were often simply scaled-down versions of grown-up furnishings.

In the 19th century, exquisite doll furniture was fashioned from the finest woods and crafted with the same attention to detail and finishing that one would expect to find on the finest pieces of "real" furniture.

To make your own version of the heirloom doll bed, *below,* scout the lumberyard or hardware store for well-turned spindles, finials, and balusters that can be cut to size and pieced together to make a four-poster design. Join the posts with wood strips, and, using a jigsaw, cut a shapely headboard from plywood. Nail plywood to the bottom, and stain or paint as desired. Add a mattress, a canopy of lace, and a coverlet stitched in your favorite quilt pattern (this one is a simple nine-patch design).

The Shaker-style cabinet, *opposite,* is a handsome way to display antique doll dishes or other treasured miniatures. Create your own cupboard by following the easy instructions included in this chapter.

A CHILD'S WORLD

The sturdy little table-and-chairs set pictured here is just the right size for serious tête-à-têtes between small children and large dolls—a common occurrence in almost any nursery, in any era.

The fanciful chaise longue, *below,* would surely have thrilled a Victorian child with its elegant shape and floral upholstery—a perfect replica of the fainting couch in Mama's room, most likely. You might want to reproduce this intriguing piece for your favorite antique doll.

If you're interested in adding an old-fashioned note to the nursery (or to any other room in the house), antique dolls like these make delightful accessories. A variety of reproduction kits (including ceramic heads, hands, and feet, along with instructions for making muslin bodies and elaborate period costumes) are available at reasonable prices from mail-order firms and in some doll specialty shops. (Consult doll and hobby magazines for sources.)

Child's Picture Blocks

Shown on pages 120–121.
Finished size of each block: 1½x1½ inches

MATERIALS
Scraps of 2x2- or 2x4-inch lumber
Six pictures from antique-
    reproduction children's
    storybooks, all with images of
    about equal size
Rubber cement (for paper crafts)
Sharp crafts knife
Ruler
Polyurethane spray finish

INSTRUCTIONS
Note: Reproduction prints or story-books can be obtained from many sources. We used pictures from books printed by The Evergreen Press, Walnut Creek, California. We also purchased old prints from a lo-cal antiques store.

Each finished block measures 1½ inches square. Determine how many 1½-inch-square pieces you will be able to cut from each of the pictures you have chosen. From lumber, cut that number of 1½-inch-square blocks. Sand all sides.

Measure and mark 1½-inch squares on each picture. Use a ruler and sharp crafts knife to cut each picture apart as marked.

Lightly coat back of each picture square and one side of each block with rubber cement designed for pa-per crafts. (Work with only a few blocks at a time so that cement does not dry before you finish.) Press pa-per to blocks, wiping away any ex-cess glue. Repeat for all 1½-inch squares cut from one picture. Allow first side of each block to dry thor-oughly; continue procedure for all six sides.

When all sides are covered, you should be able to turn blocks and see six different pictures.

When rubber cement is thorough-ly dry, coat blocks with polyure-thane spray finish.

Corn-Husk Doll

Shown on page 117.
Finished size: 9½ inches tall

MATERIALS
Dried corn husks (packages of
    bleached husks are available in
    crafts stores)
Dried corn silk for hair
Small plastic-foam ball for head
Beige thread
Straight pins
Medium-weight florist's wire
Cotton balls
White glue

INSTRUCTIONS
Soften husks by soaking them in warm water; work with husks while they are still damp.

While husks are soaking, cut two 7-inch lengths of florist's wire. Insert end of one piece of wire into plastic-foam ball; secure with white glue. Cover ball with a corn husk; tightly tie husk with thread at bottom of ball. Cover thread with a narrow strip of husk to form neck.

For arms: Wrap second piece of wire with a length of husk. Secure ends by tying small strips of husk ½ inch from each end, wrapping each strip in a tight roll to form a hand. Tie hands in place with thread.

Center husk-covered wire hori-zontally, just below neck of doll, and tie in place with thread.

To make puffed sleeves: Arrange three or four husks so that they ex-tend from shoulders to 1 inch below hands. Wrap husks tightly with thread at shoulders and hands, then pull husks from beyond hands back up over arms; trim at shoulders and wrap ends tightly with thread.

For bust and waist: Place two cotton balls in center of a corn husk and fold long sides toward center. Fold husk in half across width and slip it onto lower part of body wire, sliding it up to meet arms. Wrap a piece of thread around bottom of husk to form waist. Wrap thread back and forth over shoulders and around waist to join pieces.

For bodice: Center a 3-inch-wide piece of husk on each shoulder for dress bodice. Cross husks over bust and over back, gathering at waist. Secure with several twists of thread.

For skirt: Raise doll's arms. Arrange five or six corn husks with ends ex-tending from over head to 1 inch be-low waist. Wrap thread around waist to secure ends, then pull husks down over waist to form skirt.

For hair: Gather a bunch of dried corn silk for hair, making a strip at least ½ inch wide and about 8 inch-es long. Lay strands of silk across doll's forehead; stitch in place with one long running stitch through foam ball. Braid hair at sides, wrap ends with thread, and trim.

For hat: Fold and pin a corn husk over top of head to form a cap. Trim edges as necessary.

Braid narrow strips of husk to form trim; pin in place to cover front and back edges of cap, letting ends fan out over shoulders (see photo, *page 117*). Trim ends evenly; add small husk bows at each side of cap.

CHILDREN DANCING REDWORK EMBROIDERY

1 Square = 1 Inch

TO FINISH DOLL: Fashion an apron from one husk and tie around doll's waist with a narrow length of corn husk.

Let doll dry overnight, then glue any loose corn husks in place with dabs of white glue.

Children Dancing Redwork Embroidery

Shown on page 118.
Design size: 12x18 inches

MATERIALS
Cotton or linen fabric in size
   needed for desired project
Red embroidery floss
Embroidery hoop
Embroidery needle
Dressmaker's carbon

INSTRUCTIONS
Enlarge pattern, *above,* to size, and transfer to fabric for project of your choice. (Design is suitable for doilies, curtains, pillow tops, wall hangings, and other crafts projects.)

Embroider design using two strands of red floss in a simple outline stitch (see stitch diagrams, *page 252*).

Fringe, hem, or finish embroidered fabric as appropriate.

Woodland Redwork Embroidery

Shown on page 118.
Design size: 12½x18 inches including repeat

MATERIALS
Linen or cotton fabric in size
   needed for desired project
Red embroidery floss
Embroidery hoop and needles
Dressmaker's carbon

INSTRUCTIONS
Enlarge pattern, *page 128,* to size, and transfer to fabric for project of your choice (doily, curtain, pillow top, etc.). As pictured, pattern is 18 inches wide, including repeat of one figure from each end of design.

Embroider design using two strands of red floss in outline stitch (see stitch diagrams, *page 252*).

Fringe, hem, tuck, or otherwise finish fabric as desired.

127

WOODLAND REDWORK

1 Square = 1 Inch

continued from page 127
A Child's World

Schoolhouse Quilt

Shown on page 119.
Finished size is 68x90 inches. (Each finished block is 10 inches square.)

MATERIALS
5½ yards of backing fabric
4½ yards of white fabric
1 yard of red fabric
¾ yard of navy fabric
Quilt batting
Plastic or cardboard for templates
Graph paper

INSTRUCTIONS
CUTTING INSTRUCTIONS: Enlarge pattern, *right*. Make plastic or cardboard templates for patterns A–K. Draw a 10½-inch square on graph paper. Make a template of

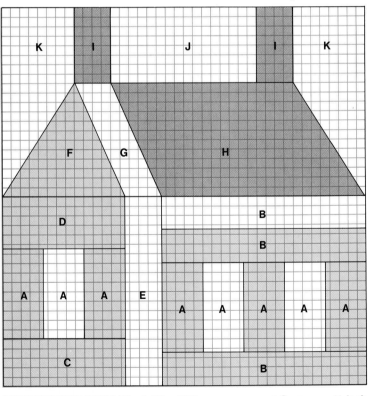

SCHOOLHOUSE QUILT (Block Size 10")

1 Square = ¼ Inch

this square (dimensions include ¼-inch seam allowances).

From white fabric, cut borders as follows (dimensions include ¼-inch seam allowances): two 9½x70½-inch side borders, one 6½x68½-inch top border, and one 14½x68½-inch bottom border.

Use 10½-inch-square template to cut 17 squares from white fabric.

From remaining white fabric, cut pieces as follows (numbers to cut for one block are in parentheses): 54 (three) of A, 36 (two) of K, and 18 (one) *each* of B, E, G, and J.

From red fabric, cut pieces as follows: 90 (five) of A, 36 (two) of B, and 18 (one) *each* of C, D, and F.

From navy fabric, cut 36 (two) of I and 18 (one) of H.

TO PIECE THE QUILT: Referring to photograph on *page 119,* piece 18 Schoolhouse blocks.

The pieced blocks alternate with white blocks in seven horizontal rows of five blocks each. Alternate three house blocks with two plain blocks for odd rows. Alternate three plain blocks with two house blocks for even rows. Join seven rows, alternating odd and even rows.

Sew a 9½x70½-inch border to opposite sides of quilt top. Sew 6½x68½-inch border to quilt top. Sew 14½x68½-inch border to quilt bottom.

TO FINISH THE QUILT: Cut backing fabric into two 2¾-yard pieces. Split one piece in half *lengthwise.* Sew split pieces to opposite long sides of full-width piece.

Layer and baste together quilt top, batting, and quilt back.

Quilt "in the ditch" immediately next to seams around all of house pieces. Quilt white areas in a diagonal grid of 1½-inch diamonds.

When quilting is completed, trim batting and backing even with quilt top. Trim batting ¼ inch smaller than top and backing. Turn edges of top and backing in ¼ inch toward batting. Whipstitch edges together.

RABBIT DOLL　　　　　　　　　　　　**1 Square = 1 Inch**

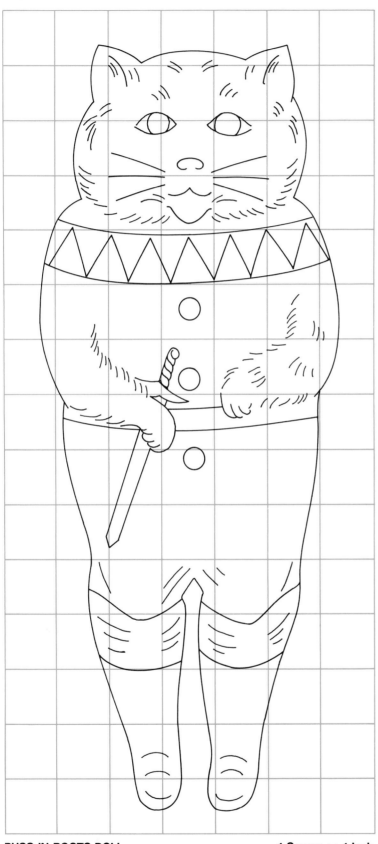

PUSS IN BOOTS DOLL   1 Square = 1 Inch

continued from page 129
A Child's World

Rabbit Doll

Shown on page 120.
Finished size: 15 inches tall

MATERIALS
1 yard of linen or cotton fabric
Red and green acrylic paints
Small artist's brushes
Pearl embroidery cotton in red, beige, and pink (or colors of your choice)
Black and gold metallic floss
Five small beads for buttons on vest and shirt
Fine-point black permanent marker
Polyester fiberfill

INSTRUCTIONS
Enlarge pattern, *page 129,* and trace outline and all details onto half of fabric with permanent marker. Flop pattern and trace outline only for back of doll. Leave at least 1½ inches of fabric between front and back traced images; do not cut out pieces until embroidery is completed.

Spread fabric faceup on newspapers; paint portions of design as follows: Paint coat with a light wash of green; paint pants and bow tie with a light wash of red. Allow paint to dry completely before beginning embroidery.

Embroider design as follows: Using red floss and the outline stitch (see stitch diagrams, *page 252*), outline cuffs, lapels, creases in pants, bow tie, and red buttons on cuffs and jacket.

Accent features and ears with outline stitches in beige; add pink accents to eyes and ears.

Embroider watch and chain with black and gold metallic thread. Add small beads for buttons on vest and shirt front.

Cut out front and back of doll ⅝ inch beyond stitching. With right sides facing, stitch back to front, leaving a 5-inch opening along one side for turning and stuffing. Clip seams, turn, press, stuff doll, and slip-stitch opening closed.

Puss in Boots Doll

Shown on page 121.
Finished size: 14 inches high

MATERIALS

½ yard linen or cotton fabric
Embroidery floss in black, brown, and blue
Polyester fiberfill
Dressmaker's carbon

INSTRUCTIONS

Enlarge pattern, *opposite,* and trace outline and details onto half of linen or cotton fabric.

Flop pattern and trace outline only (for back) onto fabric; leave at least 1½ inches between traced outlines. Do not cut out pieces until embroidery is completed.

Embroider cat in outline (stem) stitch (see stitch diagrams, *page 252*) in the following colors: outline, arms, and fur in brown; collar, cuffs of boots, sword handle, outlines of eyes, nose, mouth, and whiskers in black.

Embroider the pupils and three buttons in blue satin stitch.

Embroider outline of back in brown outline stitch. Cut out front and back of doll ⅝ inch beyond stitching. With right sides facing, stitch back to front, leaving a 5-inch opening along one side for turning and stuffing. Clip seams, turn, press, stuff doll, and slip-stitch opening closed.

Rag Doll

Shown on page 120.
Finished size: 18 inches high

MATERIALS

1½ yards of muslin for doll, slip, and pantaloons
Brown yarn for hair
Polyester fiberfill
¾ yard of calico for dress and cap
Two 8x2½-inch strips of black ribbing for stockings
Scraps of elastic and bias binding
Small snaps
Brown embroidery floss (or color of your choice)

INSTRUCTIONS

The doll pictured on *page 120* is of the simplest design: back and front are identical silhouettes, stitched together and stuffed. Legs are hinged at the hip so doll can sit, and hair is only a fringe of bangs beneath the doll's cap.

The face on the original doll was sketched and embroidered on a separate circle of muslin, which was then appliquéd in place on the front of the doll—most likely because the maker had difficulty drawing a face and wanted to experiment before stitching on the doll. (In these instructions, the face is embroidered on the doll before front and back pieces are cut out and assembled.)

TO MAKE DOLL: Enlarge pattern, *page 132,* and trace front and back on muslin, adding ½-inch seam allowances all around.

Trace face on front of doll and embroider with three strands of brown cotton floss. Work mouth and eyes in outline stitch, and pupils in satin stitch; use two small straight stitches or French knots to mark nostrils, if desired. (See stitch diagrams, *page 252.*)

Cut out doll front and back. With right sides facing, stitch back and front together, leaving a 5-inch opening along one side for turning. Trim seams, clip curves, turn, and press. Stuff doll firmly with fiberfill, stitching across legs at hips as indicated by dotted lines on pattern.

To make fingers, machine- or hand-stitch along lines indicated on pattern, stitching through stuffing. Tie threads off carefully so stitching will not pull loose.

For hair: Cut a 2x6-inch strip of cardboard. Wrap about 5 inches of the strip with loops of brown yarn. Slip loops off cardboard and stitch down center of loops to make doll's bangs. Pin and stitch this fringe of hair just in front of the seam along crown of doll's head.

TO MAKE DOLL'S CLOTHES: Enlarge patterns for bodice, sleeves, and pantaloons, *page 132,* and make paper patterns. (All patterns include seam allowances, as indicated.)

For dress bodice: For front, cut one bodice piece on center fold of calico. Then cut a left and a right bodice back by adding a ½-inch seam allowance to center fold of front. Also cut two sleeves from calico.

Stitch bodice front and backs together at shoulders and side seams. Hem left and right backs so that pieces will overlap slightly at center opening of back. Seam sleeves along bottoms and insert into armholes. Bind neckline and sleeve edges with bias strips of calico.

For dress skirt: Cut a 10x36-inch rectangle of calico. Seam short ends and gather along one long edge to fit bottom of bodice. Pin and stitch skirt to bodice. Hem skirt, adding snaps at center of dress back, as necessary.

For slip: Cut slip bodice front and backs, cutting neckline lower as indicated by dotted line on pattern. Assemble as described for dress bodice. Turn under narrow hems at neck and armholes.

Cut a 10x24-inch piece of fabric for slip skirt. Seam and assemble to slip bodice as for dress bodice and skirt. Hem slip skirt.

For pantaloons: Cut two of pantaloons pattern piece. Stitch seam AB on each leg. Then, pin and stitch the two legs together along crotch seam (CAC). Turn down top of pantaloons to make narrow casing for elastic. Slip in elastic, fit to doll's waist, and tie off. Stitch casing closed. Hem legs.

For stockings: Seam each 2½x8-inch length of ribbing lengthwise to make a tube. Roll seam to center of tube; seam across bottom of each tube to make stocking. Turn stockings right side out.

continued

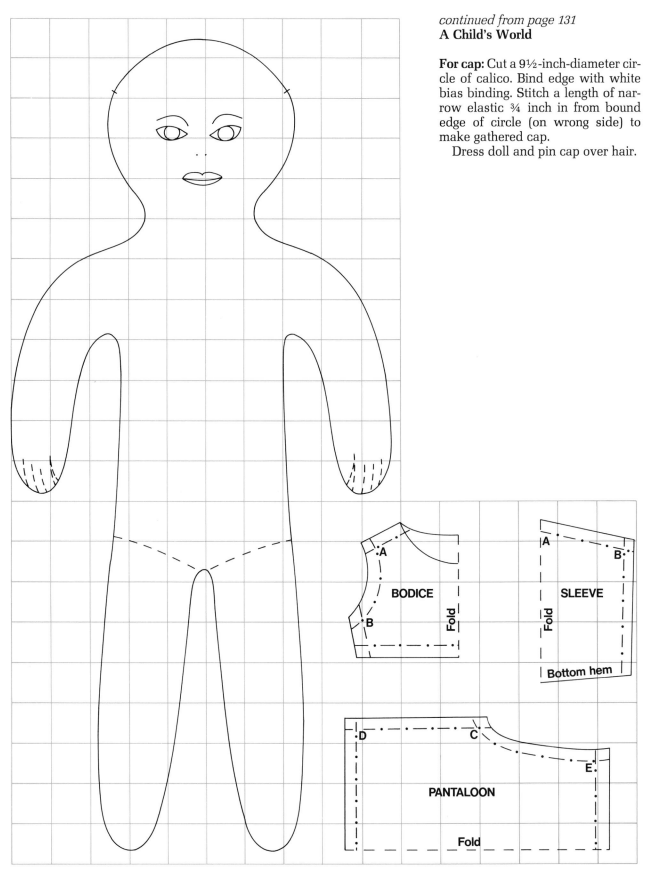

continued from page 131

A Child's World

For cap: Cut a 9½-inch-diameter circle of calico. Bind edge with white bias binding. Stitch a length of narrow elastic ¾ inch in from bound edge of circle (on wrong side) to make gathered cap.

Dress doll and pin cap over hair.

BODICE

A

B

Fold

SLEEVE

A

B

Fold

Bottom hem

PANTALOON

D

C

E

Fold

Reversible Doll Quilt

Shown on page 122.
Finished size: 17¼x17¼ inches

MATERIALS
About ¾ yard each of light and
dark calico
Thread

INSTRUCTIONS
One side of the quilt (Side A, pictured on *page 25*) consists of 169
squares arranged in 13 rows of 13
squares each. The reverse side (Side
B, shown on *page 122*) is pieced per
the assembly diagram, *below*.

TO PIECE SIDE A: Cut and piece
169 1¾-inch squares of light and
dark calico. Arrange the squares in
13 rows of 13 squares each, alternating dark and light squares; use ¼-
inch seams throughout. Press seams
toward darker squares in each row;
press seams between each row
open. Set piece for Side A aside.

REVERSIBLE DOLL QUILT

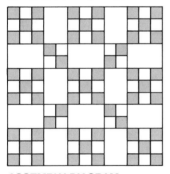

ASSEMBLY DIAGRAM

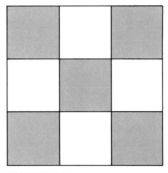

DIAGRAM A

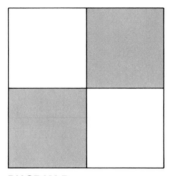

DIAGRAM B

TO PIECE SIDE B: Cut 53 dark and
44 light 1¾-inch squares of calico.
    Piece the squares into nine Nine-
Patch and four Four-Patch squares,
per diagrams A and B, *above*. Use
¼-inch seams throughout.
    Next, cut twelve 3x4¼-inch rect-
angles from calico. Arrange pieced
squares and cut rectangles per assembly diagram, *left*. Press all
seams open.

TO ASSEMBLE QUILT: With wrong
sides facing, place Side A on top of
Side B. Pin and baste the two sides.
    Piece random lengths of 1-inch-
wide strips of calico to form a 70-
inch length of binding. Bind edges of
doll quilt with this strip. Using regular sewing thread, tack the two layers of quilt together at corners of
each large Nine-Patch block.

Doll's Cupboard

Shown on page 123.
Finished size: 11x19x42¾ inches

MATERIALS
½-inch pine lumber
¾-inch pine lumber
¾x¾-inch pine cove molding
Two 1½x1½-inch hinges with
    screws
1 magnetic catch and strike plate
1 brass door pull
Saber saw
Wood glue
Wood putty
No. 17x1¼-inch finish nails

INSTRUCTIONS
When cutting and piecing doll's chi-
na cupboard, refer to the assembly
drawings on *page 134*.
    Cut two 4½x42¼-inch pieces of
¾-inch stock. Cut two 5¾x19-inch
pieces of ¾-inch stock. These
boards will be used to form sides.
    Edge-join one of the longer boards
to a shorter one, placing the ends of
the boards even at one end. Repeat
process for second set of side
pieces.
    Lay out the radius center points
on the bottom of one set of side
pieces. Using a compass, mark the
radii. Using a straightedge, connect
the tops of the radii. Repeat this on
the other set of A pieces.
    Using a saber saw, cut out the
bottom of each side set. Sand
smooth.
    Cut four 4⅜x39¾-inch pieces of
½-inch stock. Edge-join the four
pieces to form back. The back
should measure 17½x39¾ inches.
    Cut two 4⅞x17½-inch pieces of
¾-inch stock. Edge-join the two
boards to form bottom shelf.
    Glue, finish-nail, and clamp side
pieces to bottom, then to bottom
shelf.

continued

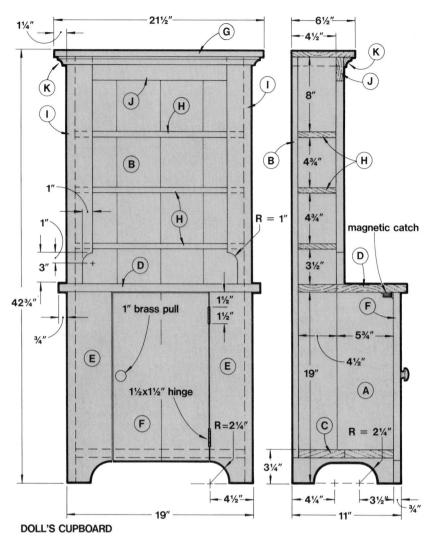

DOLL'S CUPBOARD

Bill of Materials					
Part	T	W	L	Material	Qty.
A	¾"	10¼"	42¼"	Pine	2
B	½"	17½"	39¾"	Pine	1
C	¾"	9¾"	17½"	Pine	1
D	¾"	11¼"	20½"	Pine	1
E	¾"	4½"	19"	Pine	2
F	¾"	10"	16¾"	Pine	1
G	½"	6½"	21½"	Pine	1
H	½"	4"	17½"	Pine	3

Part	T	W	L	Material	Qty.
I	¾"	2½"	22½"	Pine	2
J	¾"	2½"	14"	Pine	1
K	¾"	¾"	—	Moulding	3

Supply List
(2) 1½x1½" hinges with screws (1) magnetic door catch No. 17x1¼" finish nails (1) 1" brass pull Wood putty

continued from page 133
A Child's World

Cut one 4x17½-inch piece of ¾-inch stock. Cut one 7¼x20½-inch piece of ¾-inch stock. Center and edge-join the shorter board to the longer board to form D (countertop).

Cut two 4½x19-inch pieces of ¾-inch stock for E (lower front stiles). Using a compass, with the lower inside corner as center point, mark the radius on each E piece.

Using a saber saw, cut out the radius on each E piece. Sand smooth.

Locate and crosscut two ¹⁄₁₆-inch-deep mortises 1½ inches long into F (door).

Cut two pieces of ¾-inch stock to 5 inches wide x 16¾ inches long. These boards will be used to form F (door).

Edge-join the two boards together for F (door).

Place the hinges on all the mortises on E and F and mark the screw-hole locations. Drill all screw holes.

Drill a ¹⁄₁₆-inch hole into F for the brass pull. Install pull.

Glue and finish-nail E pieces to A pieces and C. Glue and finish-nail D to A pieces, B, and F.

Screw hinges onto E, then screw to F.

Attach magnetic catch to bottom of D and attach strike plate to back of F.

Cut one 6½x21½-inch piece of ½-inch stock for G (top). Center, glue, and finish-nail G to A pieces and B.

Cut three 4x17½-inch pieces of ½-inch stock for H (shelves). Locate, glue, and finish-nail H pieces to A pieces and B.

Cut two 2½x22½-inch pieces of ¾-inch stock for I (upper front stiles).

Lay out the radius center points on I pieces. Using a compass, mark the radii. Using a square, finish marking the I pieces.

With a saber saw, cut out the curved shape on the bottom of each I piece. Sand smooth.

Cut a 2½x14-inch piece of ¾-inch stock for J (upper rail). Test-fit I

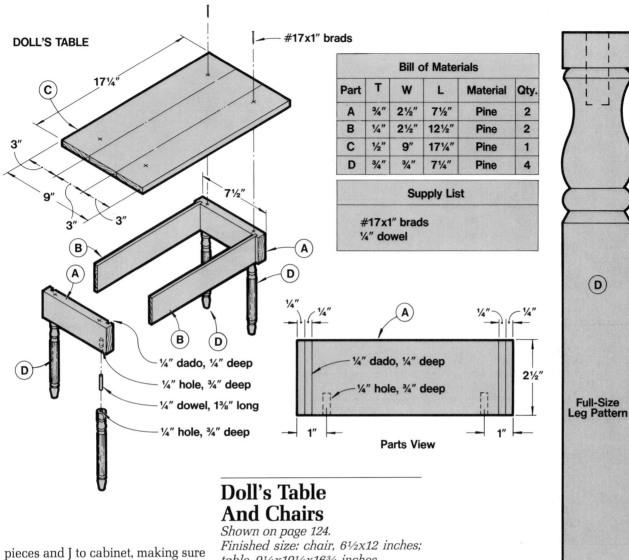

DOLL'S TABLE

17¼"

3"

9"

3"   3"

C

B

A

A

B   D

D

#17x1" brads

7½"

A

D

D

¼" dado, ¼" deep

¼" hole, ¾" deep

¼" dowel, 1⅜" long

¼" hole, ¾" deep

Bill of Materials					
Part	T	W	L	Material	Qty.
A	¾"	2½"	7½"	Pine	2
B	¼"	2½"	12½"	Pine	2
C	½"	9"	17¼"	Pine	1
D	¾"	¾"	7¼"	Pine	4

Supply List
#17x1" brads
¼" dowel

¼"   ¼"   ¼"   ¼"

A

¼" dado, ¼" deep

¼" hole, ¾" deep

2½"

1"   1"

Parts View

D

**Full-Size
Leg Pattern**

pieces and J to cabinet, making sure J is not too short or too long for I pieces to be flush with A pieces.

Glue and clamp I pieces to J.

Glue and finish-nail I pieces and J to A pieces, H pieces, and G.

Cut two 6-inch pieces of cove molding for K (cove molding). Crosscut one end of each piece to a 45-degree bevel.

Cut one 20½-inch piece of cove molding for front of cabinet. Crosscut both ends to a 45-degree bevel.

Glue and finish-nail K pieces to sides and top front of cabinet.

Using a hammer and a nail set, tap all finish nails below the surface of the wood. Fill all nail holes with pine-colored wood putty. Finish-sand all surfaces of cupboard. Stain, paint, or varnish as desired.

Doll's Table
And Chairs

Shown on page 124.
Finished size: chair, 6½x12 inches;
table, 9¼x10¼x16¾ inches

MATERIALS

1½-inch, ¼-inch, ½-inch, and ¾-inch birch lumber
½x36-inch birch dowel
¼x36-inch birch dowel
Stationary belt sander
Table saw
Lathe to turn legs (or use purchased legs)

INSTRUCTIONS

TO MAKE THE TABLETOP: Cut two 2½x7½-inch pieces of ¾-inch birch for A (short sides).

Crosscut a ¼-inch-wide dado ¼ inch deep into both ends of each A piece. (See detail drawing, *above.*)
continued

135

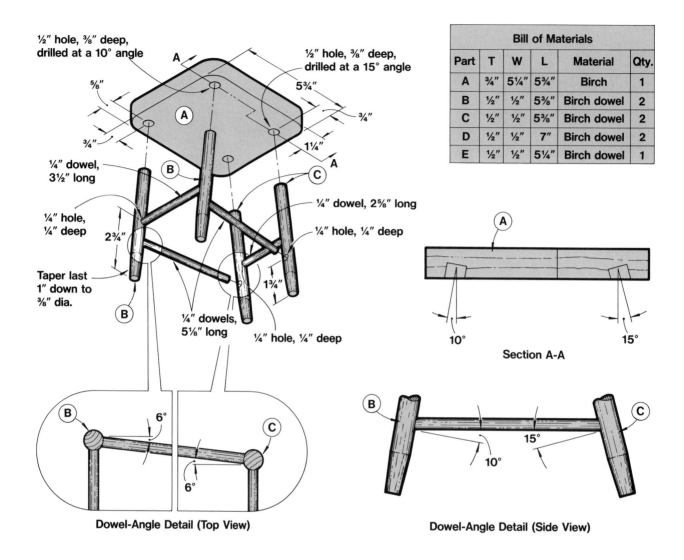

½" hole, ⅜" deep, drilled at a 10° angle

½" hole, ⅜" deep, drilled at a 15° angle

5¾"

⅝"

A

¾"

¾"

1¼"

A

¼" dowel, 3½" long

B

C

¼" dowel, 2⅝" long

¼" hole, ¼" deep

2¾"

¼" hole, ¼" deep

Taper last 1" down to ⅜" dia.

1¾"

B

¼" dowels, 5⅛" long

¼" hole, ¼" deep

Bill of Materials					
Part	T	W	L	Material	Qty.
A	¾"	5¼"	5¾"	Birch	1
B	½"	½"	5⅝"	Birch dowel	2
C	½"	½"	5⅝"	Birch dowel	2
D	½"	½"	7"	Birch dowel	2
E	½"	½"	5¼"	Birch dowel	1

A

10°

15°

Section A-A

B

C

15°

10°

Dowel-Angle Detail (Side View)

B

6°

C

6°

Dowel-Angle Detail (Top View)

continued from page 135
A Child's World

Drill two ¼-inch holes ¾ inch deep on the bottom of each A piece. (*Note:* Use a drill press if you have one available.)

Cut two 2½x12½-inch pieces of ¼-inch birch for B (long sides).

Glue and clamp A pieces and B pieces together.

Edge-join three 3x18-inch pieces of ½-inch birch for C (tabletop).

Crosscut one end of C square, then crosscut C to 17¼ inches on the other end.

Center, glue, and nail C to A and B pieces.

TO MAKE THE TABLE LEGS: Starting with a 1x1-inch turning square 8 inches long, use a lathe to

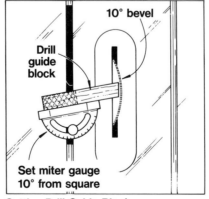

10° bevel

Drill guide block

Set miter gauge 10° from square

Cutting Drill Guide Block

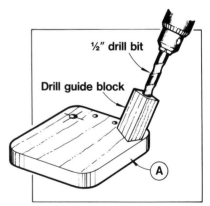

½" drill bit

Drill guide block

A

Drilling Holes for D Pieces

136

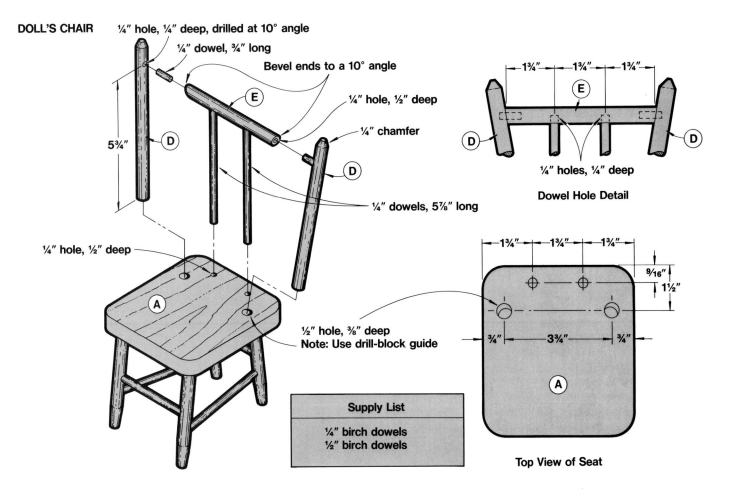

DOLL'S CHAIR

¼" hole, ¼" deep, drilled at 10° angle

¼" dowel, ¾" long

Bevel ends to a 10° angle

E

¼" hole, ½" deep

¼" chamfer

5¾"

D

D

D

¼" dowels, 5⅞" long

¼" hole, ½" deep

A

½" hole, ⅜" deep
Note: Use drill-block guide

Supply List

¼" birch dowels
½" birch dowels

1¾" — 1¾" — 1¾"

E

D — D

¼" holes, ¼" deep

Dowel Hole Detail

1¾" — 1¾" — 1¾"

9/16"

1½"

¾" — 3¾" — ¾"

A

Top View of Seat

turn the square down to a ¾-inch diameter for D (leg).

Measure a 7¼-inch length on the leg piece and mark the ends with a parting tool. (This will show you where to start shaping the leg, and also will give you the overall length of the leg.)

Using the full-size leg pattern, *page 135*, as a guide, start turning the leg to the approximate shape. Once you have roughed out the shape, sand the leg smooth while it is still turning on the lathe.

Drill a ¼-inch hole ¾ inch deep into the top of the leg.

Repeat steps to make three more legs.

ALTERNATIVES TO MAKING LEGS: If you do not have a lathe, you can use a purchased baluster or turned leg from the lumberyard. Choose one that is similar in size and shape to the one shown. Cut it to correct length.

ASSEMBLING THE TABLE: Crosscut four 1⅜-inch pieces from ¼-inch dowel. Glue the dowels into A pieces. Glue and clamp the D pieces onto the dowels in A pieces.

Allow ample drying time.

TO MAKE THE CHAIR SEAT AND LEGS: Cut a 5¼x5¾-inch piece of ¾-inch birch for A (seat).

Drill two ½-inch holes ⅜ deep at a 10-degree angle into the front bottom of A for B (legs). (See Section View A-A, *opposite.*)

Drill two ½-inch holes ⅜ deep at a 15-degree angle into the back bottom of A for C (legs). (See Section A-A and the exploded view, *opposite.*)

Crosscut four 5⅜-inch pieces from ½-inch dowel for B and C pieces.

Using a stationary belt sander, sand and taper the last inch of each B and C piece to a ⅜-inch diameter.

Drill ¼-inch holes ¼ inch deep into B and C pieces for the dowels that run side to side. (*Note:* These holes are not angled.)

Drill ¼-inch holes ¼ inch deep into B and C pieces for the dowels that run front to back. (*Note:* These are compound angle holes and need to be drilled as accurately as possible. See drawing of dowel angle details, *opposite.*)

Crosscut the ¼-inch dowel to lengths shown on the dowel angle details.

Dry-fit all dowels with A, B, and C pieces to assure proper fit.

Glue and clamp dowels to A, B, and C pieces.

TO MAKE BACKREST: Crosscut a 4-inch piece of 1½x1½-inch birch for drill guide block. Drill a ½-inch hole in the middle of the block.

Set the miter gauge on a table saw to a 10-degree angle. Then, set the
continued

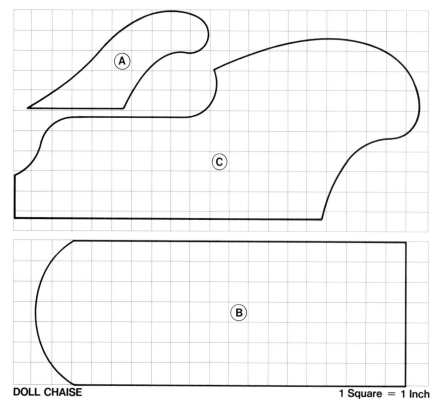

DOLL CHAISE   1 Square = 1 Inch

Doll Chaise
Shown on page 125.
Finished size: about 14x24 inches

MATERIALS
½-inch pine for couch
Four 3½-inch spindles for legs
One 6¼x2-inch dowel and five
    6¼x⅜-inch dowels
Scrap of lightweight cardboard
Firm quilt batting
1 yard of light- to medium-weight
    upholstery fabric
1 yard of lightweight muslin
2 yards of narrow cording
Jigsaw and router
Finishing nails
Small upholstery brads
Wood glue

INSTRUCTIONS
Enlarge patterns, *upper left,* and cut pieces from ½-inch pine with jigsaw. Cut two pieces of A and one each of B and C. Referring to assembly diagram, *lower left,* nail and glue A pieces to top of B.

Nail and glue a length of 2-inch dowel between curved tops of A pieces. Nail and glue the smaller dowel pieces evenly spaced between A pieces, as shown.

Cut a piece of lightweight cardboard to size; fit over dowels between A pieces as support for padding; glue cardboard in place.

Pad frame with layers of batting, cutting and shaping as necessary. Stretch muslin over padded frame and tack to secure. Cover couch with fabric, cutting and piecing to follow curves of couch. Cover upper portion of couch first, taking small tucks around curve of headrest; stitch and tack in place. Cover lower part of couch next, trimming seam with fabric-covered cording. Tack fabric to underside of couch.

For chaise back, sculpt a decorative edge along C with router. Paint or stain piece as desired.

Pad front of chaise, below sculpted edge, with batting; glue in place. Cover with upholstery fabric. Trim with fabric-covered cording. Nail and glue back and four legs in place. Paint or stain legs as desired.

continued from page 137
A Child's World

saw blade to a 10-degree bevel. (See cutting drill guide block drawing, *page 136.*) Crosscut one end of block. This will give you a 10-degree angle back and a 10-degree angle outward. Using this block, drill two holes into the top of A. (See drawing, *page 137,* for drilling holes for D.)

Drill two ¼-inch holes ½ inch deep into the top of A for ¼-inch dowels. (*Note:* These holes are not angled.)

Crosscut two pieces of ½-inch dowel to lengths shown on *page 137* for D (chair backrest dowels). Drill a ¼-inch hole ¼ inch deep at a 10-degree angle into D pieces for dowel pins.

Using a stationary belt sander, sand an approximate 45-degree chamfer on the tops of D pieces.

Crosscut a ½-inch dowel to length shown on *page 137* for E (horizontal chair backrest dowel). Drill a

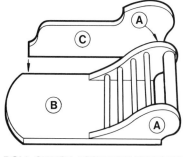

DOLL CHAISE ASSEMBLY DIAGRAM

¼-inch hole ½ inch deep into both ends of E.

Crosscut a 10-degree bevel on both ends of E.

Crosscut two 5⅞-inch pieces of ¼-inch dowel for the backrest. Crosscut two ¾-inch pieces of ¼-inch dowel for dowel pins. Test-fit D pieces, E, and the dowels. Glue and clamp assembly together.

FINISHING THE TABLE AND CHAIRS: Once all pieces are thoroughly dry, lightly sand any rough areas. You are then ready to paint or stain the table and chairs as desired.

Muslin Doll

Shown on page 17.
Finished size: small doll, 11 inches
tall; large doll, 14 inches tall

MATERIALS

¾ yard of muslin for each doll
Polyester fiberfill
Acrylic paints
Antiquing oil
Varnish
Tea (for staining fabric)
Ribbons and lace trim
Tissue paper

INSTRUCTIONS

Enlarge the pattern, *right,* onto tissue paper. (*Note:* Two scales are given, one for the small doll and one for the large doll. Assembly instructions are the same for both dolls.)

TO MAKE THE DOLL: From muslin, cut out all pieces. With right sides facing, stitch arm back and front sets together; clip curves and turn right side out. Stuff firmly with polyester fiberfill.

With right sides facing, stitch body back and body front together, leaving a 1-inch opening along the left side and a 3½-inch opening along the right side of the doll (between Xs on pattern). Trim seams and clip curves. Turn right side out through the larger opening.

Insert the left arm into the left-side opening. Slip-stitch closed through all layers.

Stuff both legs. Stitch across legs at hiplines indicated by dotted-and-dashed lines on pattern.

Stuff body and head firmly through the larger opening. Insert right arm; slip-stitch right-side opening closed.

TO PAINT THE DOLL: Varnish doll's head, arms, and legs. Paint all features and hair. Coat head, arms, and legs with antiquing oil.

TO AGE FABRIC FOR CLOTHING: Blot muslin randomly with a sponge dipped in strong tea. Rinse stained fabric thoroughly and allow to dry.

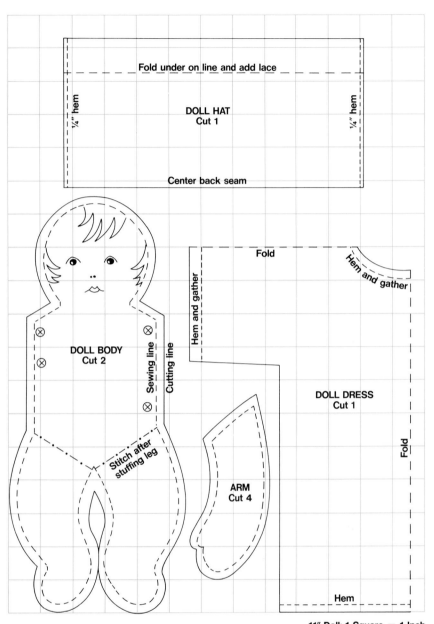

MUSLIN DOLL

11″ Doll: 1 Square = 1 Inch
14″ Doll: 1 Square = 1¼ Inch

TO MAKE THE DRESS: Fold fabric in fourths so that there are two folds. Place the shoulder and center front and back on folds as indicated on pattern, *above*. Cut out.

Open up the dress fabric. Refold so that right sides are facing with side seams aligned. Machine-stitch under the arms and down the sides. Hem the sleeves and bottom of the dress. Machine-stitch cotton lace to the dress bottom.

Hand-baste around the sleeve edge and neckline. Place the dress over the doll body; tighten and tack sleeve and neckline.

TO MAKE THE HAT: Cut hat from fabric. Fold one edge under as indicated on pattern and machine-stitch. Sew lace over seam line.

With right sides facing, machine-stitch along center back. Hem lower edge of hat. Shape the hat to the doll's head by making a large pleat on each side of the back center seam at the base of the doll's neck. Tack pleat in place. Hand-stitch ribbon ties in place.

PRACTICE MAKES PERFECT

◆

A SELECTION OF SAMPLERS

In the days before printed patterns, how-to books, and store-bought kits were readily available, needle-arts enthusiasts honed and displayed their skills by creating marvelous design "scrapbooks" in the form of stitchery samplers.

PRACTICE MAKES PERFECT

Needlework was one of the important components of a fashionable young lady's education in early America. Fancy stitchery was a major part of the curriculum—strictly taught and diligently practiced—at every one of the boarding schools, academies, and exclusive seminaries for young ladies that flourished in the New World following the Revolution.

However, the more tedious disciplines of so-called "plain sewing"—including dressmaking, darning, and the mastery of simple cross-stitch letters, numbers, and motifs for marking family garments and household linens—were learned by girls of every social class at a very early age. For these were practical skills, necessary to the running of a household (whether as mistress or servant), and thus a not-to-be-neglected part of every girl's education.

Pictured in the foreground here is a contemporary adaptation of cross-stitch motifs found on the antique sampler in the background. The original was stitched by Anna Maria Werner of Montgomery County, Pennsylvania, nearly two hundred years ago.

PRACTICE MAKES PERFECT

Earnest young ladies continued to stitch samplers in big cities and tiny towns across the country throughout the 19th century.

Since close adherence to prescribed patterns was encouraged (and original touches in design and execution frowned upon), experts can often identify the school or teacher under whose tutelage a given sampler was stitched.

Pictured *below* is a colorful sampler worked with wool yarns on linen canvas—materials favored by many immigrants of German descent in the middle decades of the 19th century. This particular example was stitched by Henrietta Goepp, who settled in the Amana Colonies in Iowa in the early 1850s.

Opposite is a more sophisticated pictorial sampler dating from 1872. Stitched by Miss Mary S. Salgleish, it is typical in style and composition of the more carefully planned, beautifully bordered sampler designs that became popular during the last half of the 19th century.

PRACTICE MAKES PERFECT

Cross-stitch and embroidery were not the only needlework techniques to yield pretty practice pieces, although these are the samplers most highly prized by today's collectors of American folk art.

But textile chapbooks of patterns and stitches in *every* technique were routinely—if not always systematically——assembled by needle-art enthusiasts. This was particularly true during the 19th century when American women began at last to have both the time and the opportunity to explore new needlework techniques.

Knitting samplers—like the runner of openwork stitches, *right*—were often rolled up and tucked into Victorian workbaskets, and rarely appeared on display.

Similarly, the framed collection of crochet pattern scraps, *above,* is an assemblage of edging and medallion designs originally worked up as reference—or sampler— copies of favorite or unfamiliar patterns. Arranging these pieces in a frame is a charming 20th-century fancy. Collect or crochet pattern scraps of your own, and frame to make a similar collage.

146

Practice Makes Perfect

Since commercially printed quilt patterns were not widely available until well into the 19th century, sampler quilts like this one offered an early and ingenious way to keep track of new or best-loved pattern blocks. An expert stitcher might piece all the blocks herself over a period of years, but, more often, pattern-block samplers were assembled as friendship quilts. In such cases, each block was designed and stitched by a different friend or relative, and the blocks were pieced together in celebration of a special family occasion.

This particular quilt boasts 64 different squares arranged in eight rows of eight blocks each. The pieced squares alternate with red blocks to create a sense of rhythm and coherence in the overall design.

Interestingly, each square is carefully embroidered with the name of the quilt-block pattern, all drawn in the same hand. This suggests that the sampler may have been the work of a single quilter.

To create your own sampler quilt, choose pattern blocks that fit neatly on same-size squares and restrict fabric selections to a single basic palette.

148

ALPHABET SAMPLER

Alphabet Sampler

Shown on page 141.
Finished size: 7¼x17¾ inches or 79x194 stitches

MATERIALS
12x21 inches of 11-count Aida cloth or hardanger cloth
Red embroidery floss

INSTRUCTIONS
PREPARING THE PATTERN: Chart the complete pattern, *above* and *opposite,* onto graph paper using felt-tip marking pens. Or, you may work directly from our pattern. The shaded stitches on the portion of the pattern on *page 151* indicate where the pattern on *page 150* overlaps. *Do not repeat these stitches.*

TO STITCH THE DESIGN: Separate the red embroidery floss and use three strands for working the cross-stitches.

Begin working the alphabet at the upper left-hand corner. Leave 2 inches of plain fabric on all sides for mounting the finished needlework.

Stitch each counted cross-stitch over one thread of Aida fabric or two threads of hardanger.

TO FINISH THE SAMPLER: If necessary, lightly press the stitchery on the back side of the fabric. Frame as desired.

Pennsylvania Sampler

Shown on pages 142–143.
Finished size: 9x10½ inches, excluding the border of plain fabric, or 115x135 stitches

MATERIALS
15x16 inches of 26-count even-weave fabric
Embroidery floss in the colors listed in the color key

INSTRUCTIONS
PREPARING THE PATTERN: Using felt-tip marking pens, transfer the diagram on *page 153* to graph paper. Make a mirror image of the border to complete the pattern. (Color key is on *page 152.*)

TO STITCH THE DESIGN: Separate the embroidery floss and use two strands for working the cross-stitches.

Locate the center of the pattern and the center of the fabric; begin stitching the design here. Work the cross-stitches over two fabric threads.

Stitch the design from the center and work to the outer edges.

TO FINISH THE SAMPLER: Block the finished embroidery by pressing it carefully on the back side with a damp press cloth and a warm iron. Frame the sampler as desired.

House Sampler
Shown on page 144.
Finished size: 13x19½ inches or 143x215 stitches

MATERIALS
17x24 inches of hardanger cloth· or any even-weave fabric with 22 threads per inch
Embroidery floss in the colors listed on the color key

INSTRUCTIONS
Note: The charts for the samplers featured on *pages 144–145* are given in both colors and symbols. Example: The pink squares will have different symbols inside. The combinations will designate which color in the pink/red family is used for that particular stitch. The same rule applies to all colors.

PREPARING THE PATTERN: Chart the complete pattern, *pages 154–155,* onto graph paper, or work directly from our chart.

TO STITCH THE DESIGN: Locate the center of the pattern and the center of the fabric. Begin working outward from this point.

Separate the embroidery floss and use three strands over two threads of fabric.

TO FINISH THE SAMPLER: Press the fabric on the back side, if necessary. Frame as desired.

continued from page 151
Practice Makes Perfect

Child's Yarn Sampler

Shown on page 145.
Finished size: 97x112 stitches (size will vary depending upon which fabric you choose)

MATERIALS

18x20 inches of 7-mesh needlepoint canvas, 14x16 inches of 10-mesh needlepoint canvas or 13x15 inches of 11-count Aida cloth or hardanger cloth

Embroidery floss in the colors listed in the color key or similar colors of 3-ply Persian yarn

INSTRUCTIONS

PREPARING THE PATTERN: Chart the complete pattern, *page 156,* onto graph paper, or work directly from our chart.

TO STITCH THE DESIGN: The antique sampler on *page 145* was stitched on an old style of needlepoint canvas that had a horizontal blue line every inch. Because the background is open in cross-stitch, you can see the blue line in the photograph of the old sampler, *page 145.* You may use either a needlepoint canvas with yarn or floss, or a cross-stitch fabric with floss to stitch this sampler. A handy guide to fabric and floss appears on *page 159.* The sampler on *page 145* used 4-ply yarn on 7-mesh canvas.

Begin working the alphabet in the upper left-hand corner. Leave at least 3 inches of border fabric for mounting the finished needlework. Work all cross-stitches.

TO FINISH THE SAMPLER: Lightly press the sampler on the back side of the fabric. Frame as desired.

Knitted Sampler

Shown on pages 146–147.
Finished size: 13¼x70 inches, including fringe

Skill Level

For the expert knitter.

MATERIALS

5 balls of DMC Cébélia #20 crochet cotton (50-g ball) in natural

Size 2 knitting needles or size to obtain gauge given below

Gauge: Over garter st, 9 sts = 1 inch.

INSTRUCTIONS

The authentic character of the antique sampler photographed on *pages 146–147* has been retained as much as possible while eliminating the irregularities. Motifs have been centered (with one exception as noted), all letters and numerals of a single pattern have been made the same height, and the same number of stitches has been maintained throughout the sampler.

All even-numbered rows of pattern stitches are wrong-side rows; they are knit. This is not specified in each pattern instruction, but be sure each pattern ends with this wrong-side knit row before beginning to count number of rows worked in garter stitch between patterns. The number of garter stitch rows so specified includes both right- and wrong-side rows.

There are two kinds of eyelets. Small eyelets are created by one yo; large eyelets are created by two consecutive yo's. In working the row following the two yo's, knit into first loop and purl into the second loop.

Cast on 120 sts. Work 4 rows garter st.

EYELET BORDER PATTERN:
Row 1: K 1, * yo, k 2 tog; rep from * across, end k 1.
Row 3: K 2, * yo, k 2 tog; rep from * across.

Rep Rows 1 and 2.
Work 8 rows garter st.

HOURGLASS PATTERN:
Note: Pat is worked 4 times across each row.

Row 1: K 1, (k 2 tog, yo twice) twice, k 3 tog, k 14, k 3 tog, (yo twice, k 2 tog) twice, k 1.

Row 3: K 2, (k 2 tog, yo twice) twice, k 3 tog, k 12, k 3 tog, (yo twice, k 2 tog) twice, k 2.

Row 5: K 3, (k 2 tog, yo twice) twice, k 3 tog, k 3, k 2 tog, yo twice, k 2 tog, k 3, k 3 tog, (yo twice, k 2 tog) twice, k 3.

Row 7: K 4, (k 2 tog, yo twice) twice, k 3 tog, (k 2 tog, yo twice, k 2 tog) twice, k 3 tog, (yo twice, k 2 tog) twice, k 4.

Row 9: K 5, (k 2 tog, yo twice) twice, k 3 tog, k 1, k 2 tog, yo twice, k 2 tog, k 1, k 3 tog, (yo twice, k 2 tog) twice, k 5.

Row 11: K 6, (k 2 tog, yo twice) twice, k 3 tog, k 4, k 3 tog, (yo twice, k 2 tog) twice, k 6.

Row 13: K 7, (k 2 tog, yo twice) twice, k 3 tog, k 2, k 3 tog, (yo twice, k 2 tog) twice, k 7.

Row 15: K 8, (k 2 tog, yo twice) twice, k 3 tog twice, (yo twice, k 2 tog) twice, k 8.

Row 17: K 8, k 3 tog, (yo twice, k 2 tog) twice, (k 2 tog, yo twice) twice, k 3 tog, k 8.

Row 19: K 7, k 3 tog, (yo twice, k 2 tog) twice, k 2, (k 2 tog, yo twice) twice, k 3 tog, k 7.

Row 21: K 6, k 3 tog, (yo twice, k 2 tog) twice, k 4, (k 2 tog, yo twice) twice, k 3 tog, k 6.

Row 23: K 5, k 3 tog, (yo twice, k 2 tog) twice, k 6, (k 2 tog, yo twice) twice, k 3 tog, k 5.

Row 25: K 4, k 3 tog, (yo twice, k 2 tog) twice, k 2, k 2 tog, yo twice, k 2 tog, k 2, (k 2 tog, yo twice) twice, k 3 tog, k 4.

Row 27: K 3, k 3 tog, (yo twice, k 2 tog) twice, k 1, (k 2 tog, yo twice, k 2 tog) twice, k 1, (k 2 tog, yo twice) twice, k 3 tog, k 3.

continued

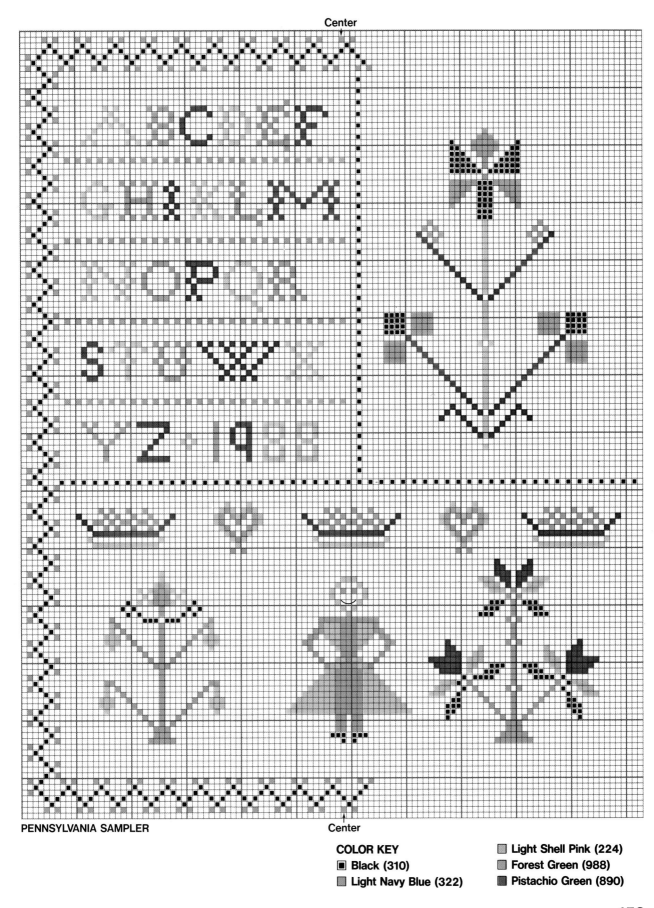

PENNSYLVANIA SAMPLER

Center

Center

COLOR KEY

◼ Black (310)

◼ Light Navy Blue (322)

◻ Light Shell Pink (224)

◼ Forest Green (988)

◼ Pistachio Green (890)

153

HOUSE SAMPLER

154

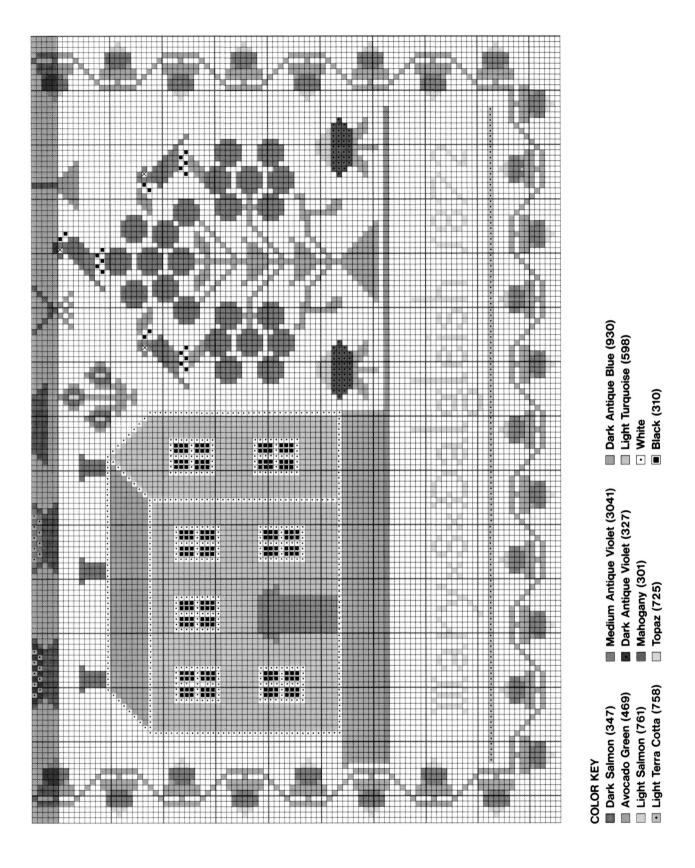

COLOR KEY

▨ Dark Salmon (347)	▩ Medium Antique Violet (3041)	▨ Dark Antique Blue (930)
▨ Avocado Green (469)	▪ Dark Antique Violet (327)	▨ Light Turquoise (598)
▨ Light Salmon (761)	▨ Mahogany (301)	⊡ White
⊡ Light Terra Cotta (758)	▨ Topaz (725)	▪ Black (310)

CHILD'S YARN SAMPLER   Start on star

COLOR KEY

- ⊞ Topaz (725)
- ▢ Medium Tangerine (741)
- ▨ Dark Golden Wheat (832)
- ⊞ Light Terra Cotta (758)
- ⦂ Dark Bittersweet (720)
- ⊞ Dark Burnt Orange (900)

- ▨ Medium Salmon (3328)
- ◩ Dark Coral (349)
- ◉ Dark Salmon (347)
- ▣ Garnet (816)
- ■ Dark Garnet (814)

- ⦂ Medium Mauve (316)
- ■ Dark Mauve (315)
- ▨ Dark Antique Blue (930)
- ■ Navy Blue (823)
- ◎ Light Avocado Green (471)

- ▨ Avocado Green (469)
- ■ Dark Green (561)
- ◪ Light Pecan (372)
- ▨ Mahogany (301)
- ■ Dark Beige Gray (640)

continued from page 152
Practice Makes Perfect

Row 29: K 2, k 3 tog, (yo twice, k 2 tog) twice, k 4, k 2 tog, yo twice, k 2 tog, k 4, (k 2 tog, yo twice) twice, k 3 tog, k 2.

Row 31: K 1, k 3 tog, (yo twice, k 2 tog) twice, k 14, (k 2 tog, yo twice) twice, k 3 tog, k 1.

Rep Rows 1–32 three times more. Work 6 rows garter st.

EYELET BORDER PATTERN:

Work Rows 1–4 of Eyelet Border Pat, then rep Rows 1 and 2.

Work 6 rows garter st.

SMALL DIAMOND PATTERN:

Pat is repeated 4 times across each row.

Row 1: K 13, k 2 tog, yo twice, k 2 tog, k 13.

Row 3: K 11, (k 2 tog, yo twice, k 2 tog) twice, k 11.

Row 5: K 9, (k 2 tog, yo twice, k 2 tog) 3 times, k 9.

Row 7: K 7, (k 2 tog, yo twice, k 2 tog) 4 times, k 7.

Row 9: K 5, (k 2 tog, yo twice, k 2 tog) 5 times, k 5.

Row 11: Rep Row 7.

Row 13: Rep Row 5.

Row 15: Rep Row 3.

Row 17: Rep Row 1.

Work 4 rows garter st.

"X'S" PATTERN:

Note: Pattern is repeated 4 times across each row.

Row 1: K 1, (k 2 tog, yo) 3 times, k 16, (yo, k 2 tog) 3 times, k 1.

Row 3: K 2, (k 2 tog, yo) 3 times, k 14, (yo, k 2 tog) 3 times, k 2.

Row 5: K 3, (k 2 tog, yo) 3 times, k 12, (yo, k 2 tog) 3 times, k 3.

Row 7: K 4, (k 2 tog, yo) 3 times, k 10, (yo, k 2 tog) 3 times, k 4.

Row 9: K 5, (k 2 tog, yo) 3 times, k 8, (yo, k 2 tog) 3 times, k 5.

Row 11: K 6, (k 2 tog, yo) 3 times, k 6, (yo, k 2 tog) 3 times, k 6.

Row 13: K 7, (k 2 tog, yo) 3 times, k 4, (yo, k 2 tog) 3 times, k 7.

Row 15: K 8, (k 2 tog, yo) 3 times, k 2, (yo, k 2 tog) 3 times, k 8.

Row 17: K 7, (yo, k 2 tog) 3 times, k 4, (k 2 tog, yo) 3 times, k 7.

Row 19: K 6, (yo, k 2 tog) 3 times, k 6, (k 2 tog, yo) 3 times, k 6.

Row 21: K 5, (yo, k 2 tog) 3 times, k 8, (k 2 tog, yo) 3 times, k 5.

Row 23: K 4, (yo, k 2 tog) 3 times, k 10, (k 2 tog, yo) 3 times, k 4.

Row 25: K 3, (yo, k 2 tog) 3 times, k 12, (k 2 tog, yo) 3 times, k 3.

Row 27: K 2, (yo, k 2 tog) 3 times, k 14, (k 2 tog, yo) 3 times, k 2.

Row 29: K 1, (yo, k 2 tog) 3 times, k 16, (k 2 tog, yo) 3 times, k 1.

Work 4 rows garter st.

SQUARES AND RECTANGLES PATTERN:

Note: Pattern is repeated 4 times across each row.

Row 1: K 2, (k 2 tog, yo) 4 times, k 10, (k 2 tog, yo) 4 times, k 2.

Rows 3, 5, and 7: Rep Row 1.

Row 9: K 10, (k 2 tog, yo) 5 times, k 10.

Rows 11, 13, 15, 17, 19, 21, and 23: Rep Row 9.

Rep Rows 1-24 once, then rep Rows 1-8.

Work 10 rows garter st, placing markers on last wrong-side row as follows: K 44, place marker, k 38, place marker, k last 38 sts.

LARGE INITIALS PATTERN:

Note: Each section of pattern is divided by markers as follows:

With right side facing, section on right is 38 sts for the letter "P," the center is 38 sts for the divider pattern, and section on left is 44 sts for the letter "C."

Row 1: K 20, (yo, k 2 tog) 3 times, k 6, (yo, k 2 tog) 3 times, sl marker, k 38, sl marker, k 6, (yo, k 2 tog) 9 times, k 20.

Rows 3 and 5: Rep Row 1.

Rows 7, 9, and 11: K 26, (yo, k 2 tog) 3 times, k 6, sl marker, k 17, k 2 tog, yo twice, k 2 tog, k 17, sl marker, (yo, k 2 tog) 3 times, k 18, (yo, k 2 tog) 3 times, k 14.

On rem odd-numbered rows of Large Initials Pattern, center section bet markers is worked as for Rows 7, 9, and 11, and will not be given in remaining instructions. Division between "P" and "C" on following rows is indicated as "sl marker."

Rows 13, 15, and 17: K 26, (yo, k 2 tog) 3 times, k 6, sl marker, k 30, (yo, k 2 tog) 3 times, k 8.

Rows 19, 21, and 23: K 14, (yo, k 2 tog) 6 times, k 6, (yo, k 2 tog) 3 times, sl marker, k 30, (yo, k 2 tog) 3 times, k 8.

Rows 25, 27, and 29: K 8, (yo, k 2 tog) 3 times, k 12, (yo, k 2 tog) 3 times, k 6, sl marker, k 30, (yo, k 2 tog) 3 times, k 8.

Rows 31, 33, and 35: K 8, (yo, k 2 tog) 3 times, k 12, (yo, k 2 tog) 3 times, k 6, sl marker, (yo, k 2 tog) 3 times, k 18, (yo, k 2 tog) 3 times, k 14.

Rows 37, 39, and 41: K 14, (yo, k 2 tog) 6 times, k 12, sl marker, k 6, (yo, k 2 tog) 9 times, k 20.

Work 8 rows garter st, removing markers on last row.

SMALL INITIALS AND DATE:

Row 1: K 13, (yo, k 2 tog) twice, k 4, (yo, k 2 tog) twice, k 6, k 2 tog, yo twice, k 2 tog, k 12, k 2 tog, yo twice, k 2 tog, k 14, k 2 tog, yo twice, k 2 tog, k 8, k 2 tog, yo twice, k 2 tog, k 12, (yo, k 2 tog) 6 times, k 15.

Row 3: K 13, (yo, k 2 tog) twice, k 4, (yo, k 2 tog) twice, k 7, k 2 tog, yo twice, k 2 tog, k 12, k 2 tog, yo twice, k 2 tog, k 11, (k 2 tog, yo twice, k 2 tog) twice, k 6, k 2 tog, yo twice, k 2 tog, k 12, (yo, k 2 tog) 6 times, k 15.

Row 5: K 17, (yo, k 2 tog) twice, k 11, k 2 tog, yo twice, k 2 tog, k 12, k 2 tog, yo twice, k 2 tog, k 9, (k 2 tog, yo twice, k 2 tog, k 4) twice, k 2 tog, yo twice, k 2 tog, k 8, (yo, k 2 tog) twice, k 12, (yo, k 2 tog) twice, k 11.

Row 7: K 17, (yo, k 2 tog) twice, k 12, k 2 tog, yo twice, k 2 tog, k 12, k 2 tog, yo twice, k 2 tog, k 8, (k 2 tog, yo twice, k 2 tog, k 4) twice, k 2 tog, yo twice, k 2 tog, k 8, (yo, k 2 tog) twice, k 12, (yo, k 2 tog) twice, k 11.

Row 9: K 17, (yo, k 2 tog) twice, k 12, k 2 tog, yo twice, k 2 tog, k 12, k 2 tog, yo twice, k 2 tog, k 8, (k 2 tog, yo twice, k 2 tog, k 4) twice, k 2 tog, yo twice, k 2 tog, k 28, (yo, k 2 tog) twice, k 7.

Row 11: Rep Row 9.

continued

continued from page 157
Practice Makes Perfect

Row 13: K 11, (yo, k 2 tog) 3 times, k 4, (yo, k 2 tog) twice, k 7, k 2 tog, yo twice, k 2 tog, k 12, k 2 tog, yo twice, k 2 tog, k 11, (k 2 tog, yo twice, k 2 tog) twice, k 6, k 2 tog, yo twice, k 2 tog, k 28, (yo, k 2 tog) twice, k 7.

Row 15: Rep Row 13.

Row 17: K 7, (yo, k 2 tog) twice, k 6, (yo, k 2 tog) twice, k 10, k 2 tog, yo twice, k 2 tog, k 12, k 2 tog, yo twice, k 2 tog, k 11, k 2 tog, yo twice, k 2 tog, k 2, k 2 tog, yo twice, k 2 tog, k 5, k 2 tog, yo twice, k 2 tog, k 28, (yo, k 2 tog) twice, k 7.

Row 19: K 7, (yo, k 2 tog) twice, k 6, (yo, k 2 tog) twice, k 9, k 2 tog, yo twice, k 2 tog, k 12, k 2 tog, yo twice, k 2 tog, k 11, (k 2 tog, yo twice, k 2 tog, k 4) twice, k 2 tog, yo twice, k 2 tog, k 28, (yo, k 2 tog) twice, k 7.

Row 21: K 7, (yo, k 2 tog) twice, k 6, (yo, k 2 tog) twice, k 8, (k 2 tog, yo twice, k 2 tog, k 4) 6 times, k 2 tog, yo twice, k 2 tog, k 8, (yo, k 2 tog) twice, k 12, (yo, k 2 tog) twice, k 11.

Row 23: K 7, (yo, k 2 tog) twice, k 6, (yo, k 2 tog) twice, k 9, k 2 tog, yo twice, k 2 tog, k 2, k 2 tog, yo twice, k 2 tog, k 6, k 2 tog, yo twice, k 2 tog, k 2, k 2 tog, yo twice, k 2 tog, k 5, (k 2 tog, yo twice, k 2 tog, k 4) twice, k 2 tog, yo twice, k 2 tog, k 8, (yo, k 2 tog) twice, k 12, (yo, k 2 tog) twice, k 11.

Row 25: K 11, (yo, k 2 tog) 3 times, k 4, (yo, k 2 tog) twice, k 6, (k 2 tog, yo twice, k 2 tog) twice, k 8, (k 2 tog, yo twice, k 2 tog) twice, k 8, (k 2 tog, yo twice, k 2 tog) twice, k 6, k 2 tog, yo twice, k 2 tog, k 12, (yo, k 2 tog) 6 times, k 15.

Row 27: K 11, (yo, k 2 tog) 3 times, k 4, (yo, k 2 tog) twice, k 8, (k 2 tog, yo twice, k 2 tog, k 12) twice, k 2 tog, yo twice, k 2 tog, k 8, k 2 tog, yo twice, k 2 tog, k 12, (yo, k 2 tog) 6 times, k 15.

Work 8 rows garter st.

DATE WITH CROSS MOTIF:
Note: For design continuity, the date of this pattern is worked directly above the date of the previous pattern, with block motifs replacing the initials, even though the pattern is not centered.

Row 1: K 31, k 2 tog, yo twice, k 2 tog, k 12, k 2 tog, yo twice, k 2 tog, k 14, k 2 tog, yo twice, k 2 tog, k 8, k 2 tog, yo twice, k 2 tog, k 39.

Row 3: K 13, (k 2 tog, yo) 3 times, k 13, k 2 tog, yo twice, k 2 tog, k 12, k 2 tog, yo twice, k 2 tog, k 11, (k 2 tog, yo twice, k 2 tog) twice, k 6, k 2 tog, yo twice, k 2 tog, k 17, (k 2 tog, yo) 3 times, k 16.

Row 5: K 13, (k 2 tog, yo) 3 times, k 13, k 2 tog, yo twice, k 2 tog, k 12, k 2 tog, yo twice, k 2 tog, k 9, (k 2 tog, yo twice, k 2 tog, k 4) twice, k 2 tog, yo twice, k 2 tog, k 17, (k 2 tog, yo) 3 times, k 16.

Row 7: K 13, (k 2 tog, yo) 3 times, k 14, k 2 tog, yo twice, k 2 tog, k 12, k 2 tog, yo twice, k 2 tog, k 8, (k 2 tog, yo twice, k 2 tog, k 4) twice, k 2 tog, yo twice, k 2 tog, k 17, (k 2 tog, yo) 3 times, k 16.

Row 9: K 13, (k 2 tog, yo) 3 times, k 14, k 2 tog, yo twice, k 2 tog, k 12, k 2 tog, yo twice, k 2 tog, k 8, (k 2 tog, yo twice, k 2 tog, k 4) twice, k 2 tog, yo twice, k 2 tog, k 17, (k 2 tog, yo) 3 times, k 16.

Row 11: K 7, (k 2 tog, yo) 3 times, k 6, (k 2 tog, yo) 3 times, k 8, k 2 tog, yo twice, k 2 tog, k 12, k 2 tog, yo twice, k 2 tog, k 8, (k 2 tog, yo twice, k 2 tog, k 4) twice, k 2 tog, yo twice, k 2 tog, k 11, (k 2 tog, yo) 3 times, k 6, (k 2 tog, yo) 3 times, k 10.

Row 13: K 7, (k 2 tog, yo) 3 times, k 6, (k 2 tog, yo) 3 times, k 7, k 2 tog, yo twice, k 2 tog, k 12, k 2 tog, yo twice, k 2 tog, k 11, (k 2 tog, yo twice, k 2 tog) twice, k 6, k 2 tog, yo twice, k 2 tog, k 11, (k 2 tog, yo) 3 times, k 6, (k 2 tog, yo) 3 times, k 10.

Row 15: Rep Row 13.

Row 17: K 7, [[k 2 tog, yo) 3 times, k 6] twice, k 2 tog, yo twice, k 2 tog, k 12, k 2 tog, yo twice, k 2 tog, k 11, k 2 tog, yo twice, k 2 tog, k 2, k 2 tog, yo twice, k 2 tog, k 5, k 2 tog, yo twice, k 2 tog, k 11, (k 2 tog, yo) 3 times, k 6, (k 2 tog, yo) 3 times, k 10.

Row 19: K 13, (k 2 tog, yo) 3 times, k 11, k 2 tog, yo twice, k 2 tog, k 12, k 2 tog, yo twice, k 2 tog, k 11, (k 2 tog, yo twice, k 2 tog, k 4) twice, k 2 tog, yo twice, k 2 tog, k 17, (k 2 tog, yo) 3 times, k 16.

Row 21: K 13, (k 2 tog, yo) 3 times, k 10, (k 2 tog, yo twice, k 2 tog, k 4) 6 times, k 2 tog, yo twice, k 2 tog, k 17, (k 2 tog, yo) 3 times, k 16.

Row 23: K 13, (k 2 tog, yo) 3 times, k 11, k 2 tog, yo twice, k 2 tog, k 2, k 2 tog, yo twice, k 2 tog, k 6, k 2 tog, yo twice, k 2 tog, k 2, k 2 tog, yo twice, k 2 tog, k 5, (k 2 tog, yo twice, k 2 tog, k 4) twice, k 2 tog, yo twice, k 2 tog, k 17, (k 2 tog, yo) 3 times, k 16.

Row 25: K 13, (k 2 tog, yo) 3 times, k 12, [(k 2 tog, yo twice, k 2 tog) twice, k 8] twice, (k 2 tog, yo twice, k 2 tog) twice, k 6, k 2 tog, yo twice, k 2 tog, k 17, (k 2 tog, yo) 3 times, k 16.

Row 27: K 33, (k 2 tog, yo twice, k 2 tog, k 12) twice, k 2 tog, yo twice, k 2 tog, k 8, k 2 tog, yo twice, k 2 tog, k 39.

Work 6 rows of garter st.

EYELET BORDER PATTERN
Work Rows 1–4 of Eyelet Border Pat twice.

Work 6 rows garter st.

LARGE DIAMOND PATTERN:
Row 1: K 20, * k 2 tog, yo twice, k 2 tog, k 34; rep from *, k 2 tog, yo twice, k 2 tog, k 20.

Row 3: K 18, * (k 2 tog, yo twice, k 2 tog) twice, k 30; rep from *, (k 2 tog, yo twice, k 2 tog) twice, k 18.

Row 5: K 16, * (k 2 tog, yo twice, k 2 tog) 3 times, k 26; rep from *, (k 2 tog, yo twice, k 2 tog) 3 times, k 16.

Row 7: K 14, * (k 2 tog, yo twice, k 2 tog) 4 times, k 22; rep from *, (k 2 tog, yo twice, k 2 tog) 4 times, k 14.

Row 9: K 12, * (k 2 tog, yo twice, k 2 tog) 5 times, k 18; rep from *, (k 2 tog, yo twice, k 2 tog) 5 times, k 12.

Row 11: K 10, * (k 2 tog, yo twice, k 2 tog) 6 times, k 14; rep from *, (k 2 tog, yo twice, k 2 tog) 6 times, k 10.

Row 13: K 8, * (k 2 tog, yo twice, k 2 tog) 7 times, k 10; rep from *, (k 2 tog, yo twice, k 2 tog) 7 times, k 8.

Row 15: Rep Row 11.
Row 17: Rep Row 9.
Row 19: Rep Row 7.
Row 21: Rep Row 5.
Row 23: Rep Row 3.
Row 25: Rep Row 1.
Row 27: Knit.
Row 29: K 1, * k 2 tog, yo twice, k 2 tog, k 34; rep from * twice more, k 2 tog, yo twice, k 2 tog, k 1.

Row 31: K 3, (k 2 tog, yo twice, k 2 tog), k 30, * (k 2 tog, yo twice, k 2 tog) twice, k 30; rep from *, k 2 tog, yo twice, k 2 tog, k 3.

Row 33: K 1, (k 2 tog, yo twice, k 2 tog) twice, k 26, * (k 2 tog, yo twice, k 2 tog) 3 times, k 26; rep from *, (k 2 tog, yo twice, k 2 tog) twice, k 1.

Row 35: K 3, (k 2 tog, yo twice, k 2 tog) twice, k 22, * (k 2 tog, yo twice, k 2 tog) 4 times, k 22; rep from *, (k 2 tog, yo twice, k 2 tog) twice, k 3.

Row 37: K 1, (k 2 tog, yo twice, k 2 tog) 3 times, k 18, * (k 2 tog, yo twice, k 2 tog) 5 times, k 18; rep from *, (k 2 tog, yo twice, k 2 tog) 3 times, k 1.

Row 39: K 3, (k 2 tog, yo twice, k 2 tog) 3 times, k 14, * (k 2 tog, yo twice, k 2 tog) 6 times, k 14; rep from *, (k 2 tog, yo twice, k 2 tog) 3 times, k 3.

Row 41: K 1, (k 2 tog, yo twice, k 2 tog) 4 times, k 10, * (k 2 tog, yo twice, k 2 tog) 7 times, k 10; rep from *, (k 2 tog, yo twice, k 2 tog) 4 times, k 1.

Row 43: Rep Row 39.
Row 45: Rep Row 37.
Row 47: Rep Row 35.
Row 49: Rep Row 33.
Row 51: Rep Row 31.
Row 53: Rep Row 29.
Row 55: Knit.
Rep Rows 1–26.
Work 8 rows garter st.

TRIPLE EYELET BORDER PATTERN:
Work Rows 1–4 of eyelet border pat; work Rows 1 and 2. Work 4 rows garter st. Rep these 10 rows twice more.

ARROW PATTERN:
Row 1: K 16, * (k 2 tog, yo twice, k 2 tog) 3 times, k 26; rep from *, (k 2 tog, yo twice, k 2 tog) 3 times, k 16.

Row 3: K 18, * (k 2 tog, yo twice, k 2 tog) twice, k 30; rep from *, (k 2 tog, yo twice, k 2 tog) twice, k 18.

Rows 5, 7, and 9: K 20, * (k 2 tog, yo twice, k 2 tog), k 34; rep from *, (k 2 tog, yo twice, k 2 tog), k 20.

Row 11: Rep Row 1.
Row 13: Rep Row 3.
Row 15: Rep Row 5.
Work 2 rows garter st.

INVERTED "V" PATTERN:
Note: Pattern is repeated 3 times across each row.

Row 1: K 3, (k 2 tog, yo twice) twice, k 3 tog, k 20, k 3 tog, (yo twice, k 2 tog) twice, k 3.

Row 3: K 4, (k 2 tog, yo twice) twice, k 3 tog, k 18, k 3 tog, (yo twice, k 2 tog) twice, k 4.

Row 5: K 5, (k 2 tog, yo twice) twice, k 3 tog, k 16, k 3 tog, (yo twice, k 2 tog) twice, k 5.

Row 7: K 6, (k 2 tog, yo twice) twice, k 3 tog, k 14, k 3 tog, (yo twice, k 2 tog) twice, k 6.

Row 9: K 7, (k 2 tog, yo twice) twice, k 3 tog, k 12, k 3 tog, (yo twice, k 2 tog) twice, k 7.

Row 11: K 8, (k 2 tog, yo twice) twice, k 3 tog, k 10, k 3 tog, (yo twice, k 2 tog) twice, k 8.

Row 13: K 9, (k 2 tog, yo twice) twice, k 3 tog, k 8, k 3 tog, (yo twice, k 2 tog) twice, k 9.

Row 15: K 10, (k 2 tog, yo twice) twice, k 3 tog, k 6, k 3 tog, (yo twice, k 2 tog) twice, k 10.

Row 17: K 11, (k 2 tog, yo twice) twice, k 3 tog, k 4, k 3 tog, (yo twice, k 2 tog) twice, k 11.

Row 19: K 12, (k 2 tog, yo twice) twice, k 3 tog, k 2, k 3 tog, (yo twice, k 2 tog) twice, k 12.
Work 8 rows garter st.

EYELET BORDER PATTERN:
Work Rows 1–4 of Eyelet Border Pat, then work Rows 1 and 2.

Work 4 rows garter st.
Bind off loosely.
Make fringe 1¼-inch finished length, attaching with Turk's-head knots.

Cross-Stitch Materials

Counted cross-stitch may be worked on many types of fabrics. Even-weave fabrics are the best choice because they have the same number of horizontal and vertical threads per inch. The result is embroidery stitches that are uniform in size.

Hardanger cloth is one of the more common fabrics used for counted thread work. The thread count is always 22 threads per inch.

Aida cloth is another commonly used fabric. It appears to be made of tiny squares, each defining the area for one stitch. It comes in many thread counts.

Mono needlepoint canvas was used a great deal in colonial times. The background is left unstitched. Both yarn and floss can be used for cross-stitch.

Many other specialty fabrics are available to choose from. Measure fabric threads carefully. A fabric that varies by as little as one thread in one direction can throw off the stitch shape and the finished size.

Following is a handy guide to fabric, needle, and thread combinations:

For 10-mesh needlepoint canvas, use a size 22 tapestry needle and 6 strands of floss.

For 11-count Aida, use a size 24 tapestry needle and 3 strands of floss.

For 14-count Aida, use a size 24 tapestry needle and 2 strands of floss.

For 18-count Aida, use a size 24 tapestry needle and 1 or 2 strands of floss.

For hardanger, use a size 26 tapestry needle and 1 strand of floss.

A Place for Everything

◆

Storage and Display

Closets were few and cupboards costly in early American homes. Everyday items were often stored in ornamental containers designed for display—beautifully crafted boxes and baskets, carved shelves, and embroidered catchalls that were both pretty and practical.

A PLACE FOR EVERYTHING

Gaily patterned bandboxes were popular across America from 1800 until about 1850. Usually round or oval in shape, such boxes were regularly used by both men and women to keep and carry all sorts of personal paraphernalia—hats, gloves, collars, muffs, wraps, and various trinkets.

The earliest boxes were made of painted wood. As they became more popular, wooden ones were replaced by lighter cardboard versions. These were covered with fancy printed papers and often lined with newspaper.

Contemporary craftsmen are turning out beautiful new examples of this useful old item. Most of the new boxes, like those pictured here, are fashioned from sturdy cardboard and covered with fancy wallpaper or fabric. To make your own bandboxes, start from scratch, or scour garage sales and thrift shops for cardboard hatboxes of recent vintage that can be covered and lined with paper or fabric to replicate the older boxes.

Whether antique or reproduction, bandboxes are a marvelous way to store all sorts of odds and ends.

Instructions for projects in this chapter begin on page 170.

163

A PLACE FOR EVERYTHING

Soon after the tools became commercially available, woodburning evolved as one of the favorite non-needlework crafts of late 19th-century America. It seems that everyone from kids at Scout camp to artistic ladies with a bit of leisure time took to creating a great variety of intricately patterned woodburned projects—storage boxes, towel racks, whatnot shelves, picture frames, and numerous other objects, both useful and ornamental.

The woodburning tool itself is quite simple to use. Successful control of the hot tip and careful execution of the delicate patterns require a bit of patience and a sure hand.

Pictured here are patterned boxes and a charming small towel rack, complete with an oval cutout frame to hold a favorite picture.

Purchased boxes and various unfinished shapes of pine and other softwood are easiest to embellish with woodburned designs. Project patterns and woodburning instructions begin on page 170.

A PLACE FOR EVERYTHING

As needlework magazines, transfer patterns, and mail-order kits proliferated around the turn of this century, American housewives began stitching decorative covers and fancy cases for every item in sight. Pretty pillow slips covered with bouquets of flowers and moralizing maxims were all the rage.

Equally popular were tidy little linen bags and fabric envelopes designed for stashing everything from milady's collars and kerchiefs to the week's allotment of laundry and sewing.

Charming stitchery projects like those pictured here often began as line drawings and appropriate phrases preprinted on linen or cotton cloth, all ready for the embroiderer's needle. Such designs were usually stitched with red cotton floss, using simple stem or outline stitches, and hence were referred to as "redwork."

Flowers, birds, butterflies, and fanciful scrollwork were among the most popular patterns, along with sweet-faced children and old-fashioned adages. "A stitch in time saves nine" blazoned across a sewing pocket, for example, might gently remind a young housewife to attend to the mending tucked inside.

167

A PLACE FOR EVERYTHING

Over the years, inventive wood-smiths have used the simplest of tools to shape native materials (pine, oak, and handsome hardwoods) to meet specific storage and display needs.

The wall-hung bin *right* keeps onions easily accessible. The openings between the slats allow air to freely circulate, forestalling rot and mildew.

Below left, a Shaker-style cheesebox is embellished with painted folk-art motifs.

Opposite is a classic silverware caddy—just the thing to keep kitchen utensils (or office supplies) in order.

Cut from walnut, the graceful display shelf *above* boasts a small mirrored panel.

The woodburned storage bin, *above right*, offers a handsome way to keep cooking staples ever ready.

Right, the six drawers of this spice cabinet are designed to hold everything from culinary flavorings to stamps and rubber bands. Hang the cabinet on the wall or stand it on a countertop, as space allows.

Patterns and instructions begin on page 170.

Bandboxes

Shown on pages 162–163.

MATERIALS

Artist's mat board or illustration
 board
Printed paper, wallpaper, or fabric
 for covering box
Paper or fabric for lining
Crafts glue
Utility knife with sharp blade
Metal straightedge
Emery board or medium
 sandpaper
Paintbrush (for spreading glue)
Artist's brush
2 spring-type clothespins

INSTRUCTIONS

TO MAKE THE BASE: Make a pattern using any size round or oval. Trace the circle or oval onto the right side of the mat board. Cut out the shape with a utility knife and smooth the edges with emery board or sandpaper.

TO MAKE THE BOX SIDE BAND: Cut a strip of mat board 4 inches to 9 inches wide (depending on how deep you want the box to be) and ¾ inch to 1 inch longer than the circumference of the base. Cut out the strip using a utility knife and metal straightedge. Sand the edges.

 Cut a strip of printed paper or fabric 2 inches wider and 2 inches longer than the side band. Using crafts glue that has been lightly thinned with water, center the paper or fabric strip over the band and glue in place. Smooth out all wrinkles or air bubbles as you go. Turn the band over; paint the edges of the paper or fabric with the crafts glue and press in place on the back of the band. Let the paper- or fabric-covered band dry thoroughly.

ATTACHING THE BASE AND SIDES: Place the base wrong side up on the table. Hold the side band at each end and gently bend it around the base. Be careful not to let the band crease. Overlap the ends and

be sure the band fits snugly all the way around the base. Mark the overlap with a pencil mark.

 Remove the band; glue overlapping ends together, holding the overlap in place with a clothespin until the glue is completely dry.

 Cut a piece of paper or fabric 1 inch larger than the base. Cover the bottom of the base with glue, then center the paper or fabric over the base and smooth it in place. Place a weight (a book will do) on top of the base to keep it flat; allow the base materials to dry thoroughly.

 Snip the paper or fabric outside of the cardboard base at ½-inch intervals all around the base. Crease the tabs toward the base.

 Place the band on the table, top edge up; slip the bottom, covered side down, inside the band, pushing it down against the table. Place glue on the back of each tab, then press it to the side band of the box to firmly attach the side to the base. Use an artist's brush to press the tabs smooth, adding more glue over the top to keep them in place. Allow the glue to dry thoroughly.

TO MAKE THE LID: Set the box base down on the right side of a piece of mat board. Trace around the box with a pencil. (*Note:* Leave at least a hairline gap between the edge of the box and the pencil mark.) Remove the box and even out the line, if necessary.

 Cut out the top with a utility knife; smooth edges. Measure around the lid and cut out a rim band following the directions for the side band. (The depth of the box will determine the depth of the rim.)

 Cover the top and rim band with paper or fabric, and assemble as for base and side band.

 Line the box with paper or fabric, if desired.

Woodburned Boxes And Towel Rack

Shown on pages 164–165.

MATERIALS

Unfinished wooden boxes
Woodburning tool
Sandpaper
Soft cloth
Graphite paper
Tracing paper
Stain
Clear matte varnish
Brushes
Fine-tip pen

For towel rack:

⅜-inch birch-veneered plywood
11⅝-inch length of ⅜-inch dowel
Saber saw

INSTRUCTIONS

The designs, *opposite* and *page 172,* can be woodburned on any unfinished wooden boxes or other wooden accessories. Following are instructions for making a towel rack.

CUTTING OUT THE PIECES: Transfer the outline for Backboard A, *page 172,* onto tracing paper. Use graphite paper to trace the shape onto plywood. Cut out the shape with a saber saw; using a fine-grade sandpaper, sand all surfaces in one direction.

 Transfer Bracket B pattern, *page 172,* and cut out two brackets; sand the brackets smooth. Drill one ⅜-inch hole in each bracket as marked on the pattern.

WOODBURNING THE DESIGN: Transfer the design onto tracing paper. Position pattern on the wood. Slip the graphite underneath the design and tape it in position. Use a fine-tip pen to trace all elements of the pattern onto the wood. Remove tracing and graphite papers.

 Following the manufacturer's instructions for your woodburning tool, woodburn all design lines.

 Always move the pen toward you. To keep your hand steady, rest your hand on the wood and use your

continued

WOODBURNED BOX

1 Square = 1 Inch

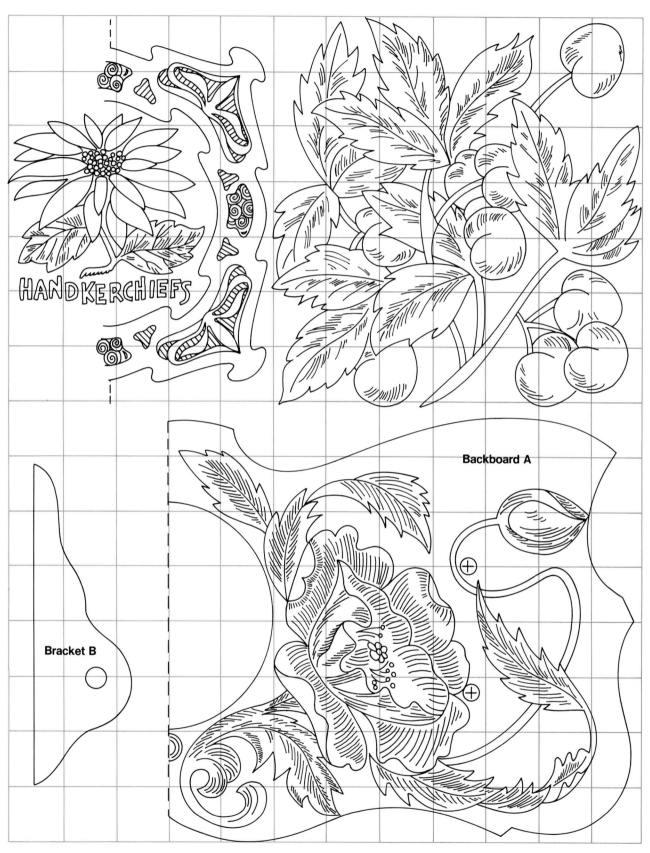

WOODBURNED BOXES AND TOWEL RACK

1 Square = 1 Inch

172

continued from page 170
A Place for Everything

fingers to guide the pen. Remember that the slower you go, the darker the line will appear. Erase all of the carbon transfer lines after you finish burning and before you seal or stain the wood.

Once the entire design is etched, wipe a light color of stain into all recesses and over surface of wood; quickly wipe stain off with a soft cloth. This will make the design lines contrast more sharply with the surface of the rack.

Apply one coat of matte varnish to all surfaces; allow varnish to dry thoroughly.

ASSEMBLING THE RACK: Stain and seal B pieces and dowel to match A.

Glue and nail one of the brackets in position on A. (See circled Xs on back pattern, and refer to color photograph, *page 165.*) Insert dowel into brackets, and glue and nail second bracket to A. Dowel should be tight enough to stay in place between the brackets.

When all glue is dry, apply a second coat of matte varnish.

Attach a wire hanger to A.

Redwork Embroidery
Shown on pages 166–167.

MATERIALS
White or off-white muslin or
  cotton fabric
Red embroidery floss
Embroidery hoop (optional)
Embroidery needle
Dressmaker's carbon or water-
  erasable marking pen
Tissue paper

INSTRUCTIONS
All projects on *pages 166–167* were embroidered using a single, simple stitch: the outline or stem stitch (see diagram, *page 252*). This stitch is flexible enough to follow any line or curve.

REDWORK EMBROIDERY 1 Square = 1 Inch

REDWORK EMBROIDERY 1 Square = 1 Inch

continued

173

continued from page 173
A Place for Everything

The loop of the stitch may lie above or below the needle, whichever is comfortable for you. But to create neat, smooth lines of stitches, work all loops in the same way. For graceful curves, you may wish to decrease slightly the length of the stitches on curved lines.

TO TRANSFER THE DESIGN: Enlarge any of the designs on *pages 173–175*. Using dressmaker's carbon paper or a water-erasable marking pen, transfer the design to the center of the fabric. (Leave plenty of fabric around the design; you can trim away excess after the embroidery is completed.)

TO WORK THE DESIGN: Place the fabric in an embroidery hoop (optional). Using two strands of red embroidery floss, work the design in outline stitches. When all embroidery is completed, press the wrong side of the fabric.

Stitch the finished needlework onto a pocket, bag, pillow, or any project of your choice.

Onion Box

Shown on page 168.
Finished size: 12x13½ inches

MATERIALS
¼-inch pine lumber
½-inch pine lumber
No. 17x¾-inch finish nails
No. 17x1¼-inch finish nails
Band saw

INSTRUCTIONS
Cut two 6x13½-inch pieces of ½-inch stock. Glue and clamp (edge-join) the two pieces to form A (back). Crosscut A to measure 13¼ inches long.

1 Square = 1 Inch

Enlarge pattern, *near right, below,* for the top portion of A. (Flop the pattern to complete A.) Cut out the pattern. Trace the pattern onto the ½-inch pine. Use a band saw to cut out A. Sand edges smooth.

Drill a ⅛-inch hole about ⅜ inch deep at a 15-degree angle into the back of A for hanging. (See assembly diagram, *page 176.*)

Enlarge and transfer pattern for B (ends), *far right, below,* onto paper; cut out the pattern. Cut two 4x5½-inch pieces of ½-inch stock for B. Trace pattern for B onto both pieces of stock. Using a band saw, cut the two B pieces to shape. Sand edges smooth.

Glue and nail B pieces to A, making sure the faces of B pieces are flush with the edges of A and the bottoms of B pieces are flush with the bottom of A.

Cut six 1³⁄₁₆x12-inch pieces of ¼-inch stock for C (slats).

Starting at the top of B pieces, glue and nail the C pieces to B pieces. (Refer to exploded view, *page 176,* for spacing.) Leave about ⅛ inch space between each C piece.

Sand and stain or varnish all surfaces of the box.

Painted Cheesebox
Shown on page 168.

The cheesebox shown on *page 168* is an antique. The pattern for the design appears on *page 176.* Use this design and the General Instructions for Painted Finishes, *page 115,* to embellish any boxes or furniture you wish to decorate.

REDWORK EMBROIDERY　　　　　　　　1 Square = 1 Inch

ONION BOX

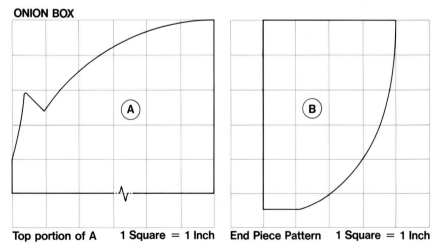

Top portion of A　　1 Square = 1 Inch　　End Piece Pattern　　1 Square = 1 Inch

Bill of Materials					
Part	T	W	L	Mat.	Qty.
A	½"	12"	13¼"	Pine	1
B	½"	4"	5½"	Pine	2
C	¼"	1³⁄₁₆"	12"	Pine	6

Supply List
#17x¾" finish nails
#17x1¼" finish nails

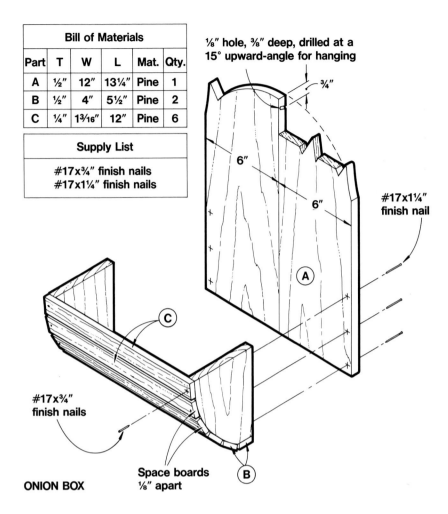

⅛" hole, ⅜" deep, drilled at a 15° upward-angle for hanging

¾"

6"

6"

#17x1¼" finish nail

Ⓐ

#17x¾" finish nails

Space boards ⅛" apart

Ⓒ

Ⓑ

ONION BOX

PAINTED CHEESEBOX

continued from page 175
A Place for Everything

Silverware Tray
Shown on page 168.
Finished size: 7¾x12¼ inches

MATERIALS
⅜-inch pine lumber
¼-inch pine lumber
No. 17x¾-inch brads
No. 17x1-inch brads
Wood glue
Scroll saw
Table saw

INSTRUCTIONS
Cut two 2x11¾-inch pieces of ⅜-inch stock for A (sides).

Cut two 2x7¼-inch pieces of ⅜-inch stock for B (ends).

Using a table saw, bevel the ends of A and B pieces to 45-degree angles. Glue, nail, and clamp A and B pieces together, referring to drawing, *opposite, top right,* and the color photograph, *page 168, bottom right.*

Cut three 2¾x12½-inch pieces of ¼-inch stock. Edge-join the stock; glue and clamp.

Recut stock to 7¾x12¼ inches for C (bottom). Center, glue, and nail C to A and B pieces.

Enlarge pattern for D (handle), *opposite, top left.* Flop pattern to complete shape.

Cut a 3x11-inch piece of ⅜-inch stock for D. Trace pattern for D onto stock. Drill a ⅛-inch hole into the inner cut in D for a place to start cutting with the scroll saw.

1 Square = 1 Inch

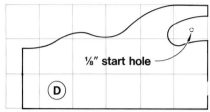

Handle Pattern (Half Pattern)

⅛" start hole

D

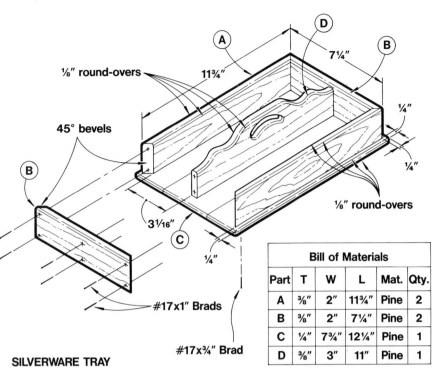

SILVERWARE TRAY

⅛" round-overs

45° bevels

A

11¾"

D

7¼"

B

¼"

¼"

B

⅛" round-overs

3¹⁄₁₆"

C

¼"

#17x1" Brads

#17x¾" Brad

Bill of Materials					
Part	T	W	L	Mat.	Qty.
A	⅜"	2"	11¾"	Pine	2
B	⅜"	2"	7¼"	Pine	2
C	¼"	7¾"	12¼"	Pine	1
D	⅜"	3"	11"	Pine	1

Release the upper arm clamp from the blade on the scroll saw. Slip hole in D over the blade.

Clamp the upper arm back onto the blade and cut out the handle opening.

Using the scroll saw, cut the remainder of D to shape. Sand.

Sand an approximate ⅛-inch round over on all designated parts as shown in drawing, *top right.*

Center, glue, and nail D to B and C pieces.

Whatnot Shelf

Shown on page 169.
Finished size: 10½x20½ inches

MATERIALS
½-inch mahogany lumber
⅛-inch mirror cut to shape
Silicone seal
No. 6x1-inch flathead wood screws
Crafts knife
Scroll saw
Drill press with ⁹⁄₆₄-inch bit
Router with rabbet and cove bits
Stain or varnish

INSTRUCTIONS
PREPARING THE PATTERN: Enlarge patterns for A (back), *below,* and B (shelf) and C (bracket), *page 178.* Flop patterns for A and B at centerlines to complete the patterns. Mark screw-hole locations, mirror-cutout outline, and mirror-rabbet outline.

Using a sharp crafts knife, cut out all pattern pieces, including the mirror opening. (Do not cut out mirror-rabbet outline.)

CUTTING OUT THE BACK: Edge-join two pieces of ½x6x21-inch ma-

---

hogany stock to form a 1x12x21-inch piece. Trace pattern A onto this piece of wood. (Save your pattern to use when cutting the mirror.) Cut along the outside edge of A.

CUTTING OUT THE DESIGN: Use a scroll saw to drill ⅛-inch holes as marked on the mirror-back pattern, *below.* On the scroll saw, undo the top arm clamp for the blade. Slip one of the holes in A over the saw blade. Clamp and tension the *continued*

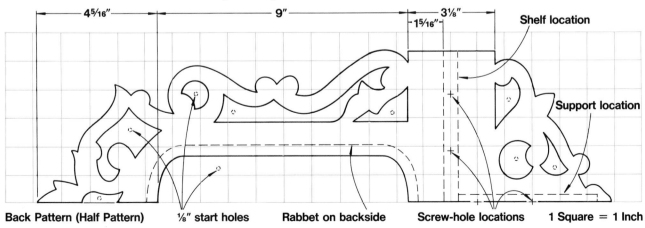

4⁵⁄₁₆"   9"   3⅛"

1⁵⁄₁₆"

Shelf location

Support location

Back Pattern (Half Pattern)   ⅛" start holes   **Rabbet on backside**   **Screw-hole locations**   1 Square = 1 Inch

---

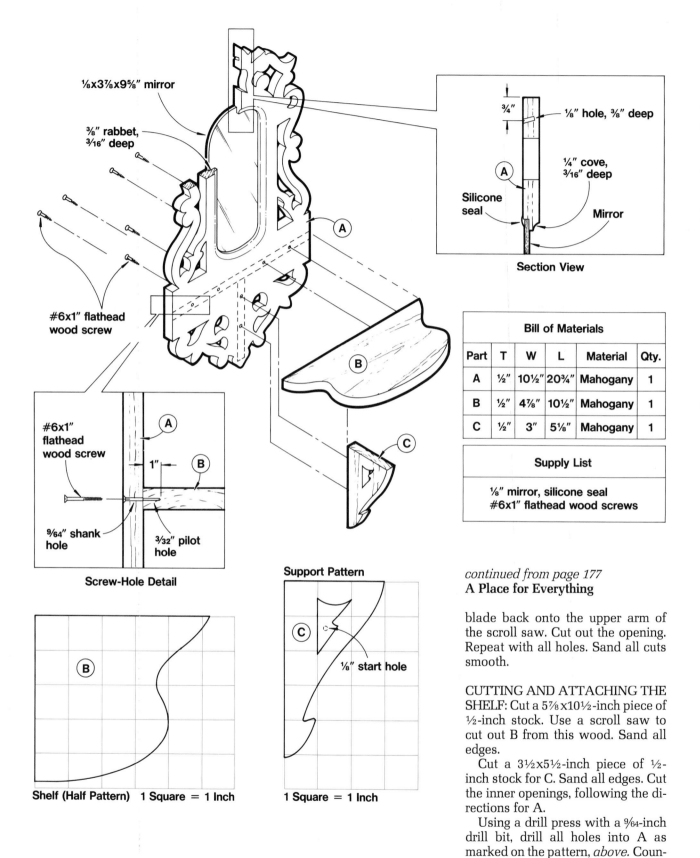

⅛x3⅞x9⅝″ mirror

⅜″ rabbet, 3/16″ deep

#6x1″ flathead wood screw

¾″

⅛″ hole, ⅜″ deep

A

¼″ cove, 3/16″ deep

Silicone seal

Mirror

Section View

A

B

C

Screw-Hole Detail

#6x1″ flathead wood screw

A

B

1″

9/64″ shank hole

3/32″ pilot hole

Support Pattern

C

⅛″ start hole

1 Square = 1 Inch

B

Shelf (Half Pattern)   1 Square = 1 Inch

Bill of Materials					
Part	T	W	L	Material	Qty.
A	½″	10½″	20¾″	Mahogany	1
B	½″	4⅞″	10½″	Mahogany	1
C	½″	3″	5⅛″	Mahogany	1

Supply List
⅛″ mirror, silicone seal #6x1″ flathead wood screws

continued from page 177
A Place for Everything

blade back onto the upper arm of the scroll saw. Cut out the opening. Repeat with all holes. Sand all cuts smooth.

CUTTING AND ATTACHING THE SHELF: Cut a 5⅞x10½-inch piece of ½-inch stock. Use a scroll saw to cut out B from this wood. Sand all edges.

Cut a 3½x5½-inch piece of ½-inch stock for C. Sand all edges. Cut the inner openings, following the directions for A.

Using a drill press with a 9/64-inch drill bit, drill all holes into A as marked on the pattern, *above*. Countersink all holes into the back of A to fit a No. 6 flathead wood screw.

178

Using a router with a ⅜-inch rab-beting bit, rout a ⅜-inch rabbet ³⁄₁₆ inch deep into the back of A around the mirror cutout.

Using a router and a ¼-inch cove bit, rout a ¼-inch cove ³⁄₁₆ inch deep into the front of A around the mirror cutout.

Drill a ⅛-inch hole ⅜ inch deep at a 15-degree upward angle into the back of A. (See section-view detail, *opposite.*)

Clamp B onto A and drill through the holes in A into B, using a drill and a ³⁄₃₂-inch drill bit. (See screw hole detail, *opposite.*)

Glue and screw B to A.

Repeat to fasten C to A.

Finish-sand and stain or varnish all surfaces.

Ask a clerk at a store that sells mirrors and glass to cut a ⅛-inch mirror from the pattern of the mir-ror-rabbet outline. Fit the mirror into the rabbet in A and put a silicone seal fillet onto the back of A and the back of the mirror. (See section-view detail, *opposite.*)

Sugar Canister

Shown on page 169.
Finished size: 11x8½x8 inches

MATERIALS
½-inch pine lumber
Two 1x1-inch full brass hinges with screws
No. 17x1-inch finish nails
Table saw
½-inch dado blade
Router with chamfer bit
Wood glue
Sandpaper
Stain or varnish
Woodburning tool

INSTRUCTIONS
TO CUT THE PIECES: Cut four 7½x10-inch pieces of ½-inch stock for A (sides).

Using a table saw, bevel the edge of each A piece to a 45-degree angle as shown on the exploded-view drawing, *above.*

Cut one 8½x8½-inch piece of ½-inch stock for B and C (top). Using a router with a chamfer bit, rout a ½-

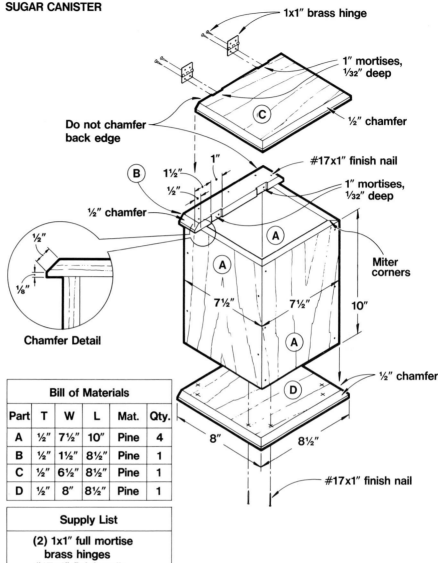

SUGAR CANISTER

1x1" brass hinge

1" mortises, 1/32" deep

½" chamfer

Do not chamfer back edge

#17x1" finish nail

1" mortises, 1/32" deep

Miter corners

½" chamfer

#17x1" finish nail

1½"

1"

½"

½" chamfer

7½"   7½"   10"

8"   8½"

½"
⅛"

Chamfer Detail

Bill of Materials					
Part	T	W	L	Mat.	Qty.
A	½"	7½"	10"	Pine	4
B	½"	1½"	8½"	Pine	1
C	½"	6½"	8½"	Pine	1
D	½"	8"	8½"	Pine	1

Supply List
(2) 1x1" full mortise brass hinges
#17x1" finish nails

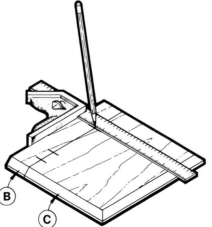

Marking the Mortises

inch chamfer on the sides and front edge of the BC piece. (*Note:* Do not chamfer back edge.)

Using a table saw, rip a 1½-inch-wide strip from the back of the stock for B. Then, rip C to 6½ inches wide.

Lay B and C pieces flat and flush just as they will lie when closed on the top of the sugar box. Mark the mortise locations with a square on both pieces of the wood. (See drawing for marking mortises, *left.*) This will ensure that mortises line up.

continued

continued from page 179
A Place for Everything

Set up the table saw with a ½-inch dado blade about 1/32 inch above the tabletop. Using a miter gauge, crosscut the mortises into B and C for the hinges. Place hinges into the mortises in C and drill the screw holes. Repeat for B.

Cut an 8x8½-inch piece of ½-inch stock for D (bottom). Using a router with a chamfer bit, rout a ½-inch chamfer around the sides and front of D.

TO ASSEMBLE THE CANISTER: Glue and nail A pieces together for canister sides. Center, glue, and nail D to canister sides, making sure the back of D is flush with the back of canister, and the remaining three sides of D extend evenly beyond the other three canister sides.

Glue and nail B to canister back, making sure the back of B is flush with the canister back and with D. Piece B should hang over canister sides evenly.

Screw hinges to B, then to C. Finish-sand the canister; woodburn a desired pattern on the front or sides, and stain or varnish as desired.

Oak Spice Box
Shown on page 169.
Finished size: 5¾x6x20 inches

MATERIALS
½-inch oak lumber
⅛-inch hardboard
Jigsaw
Table saw
Wood glue
Sandpaper
Stain (optional)
Clear matte varnish
6 drawer handles or knobs

INSTRUCTIONS
CUTTING THE PIECES: From ½-inch oak, cut the following pieces: one back, 5x21½ inches; two sides, 6x18½ inches; six shelves, 5½x5½ inches; one bottom, 5x5½ inches; six drawer fronts, 1 15/16 x4 15/16 inches; six drawer backs, 1 13/16 x4 15/16 inches; 12 drawer sides, 1 13/16 x4⅜ inches.

From ⅛-inch hardboard, cut a total of six drawer bottoms measuring 4 15/16 x5½ inches.

Referring to the diagrams, *below,* draw the arches and circle cutouts on the back and sides.

Using a jigsaw, cut out the arches and circles. Sand all surfaces.

Using a table saw, dado a ½-inch groove on both sides for each shelf.

ASSEMBLING THE SPICE BOX: Glue and clamp the back to both sides. Glue and clamp the shelves and bottom in place.

Glue and clamp drawer fronts, sides, backs, and bottoms together.

Finish-sand all surfaces. Seal with clear matte varnish. Stain, if desired.

Add handles or knobs, as desired.

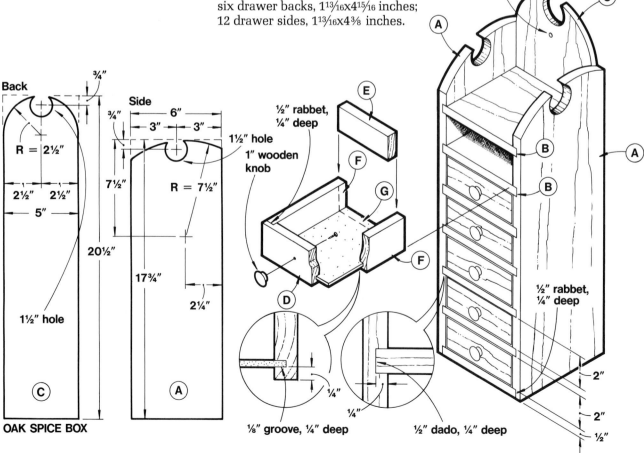

Back

R = 2½"

2½" 2½"

5"

20½"

1½" hole

C

Side

6"
3" 3"

¾"

7½"

R = 7½"

17¾"

2¼"

A

¼" hole

C

A

B

B

A

½" rabbet, ¼" deep

E

F

G

F

D

⅛" groove, ¼" deep

½" dado, ¼" deep

1½" hole
1" wooden knob

½" rabbet, ¼" deep

2"

2"

½"

OAK SPICE BOX

Hearts-and-Hands Mirror Frame

Shown on page 12.
Finished size: 14¼x17⅜ inches

MATERIALS
¾-inch pine
½-inch x 18-gauge brass
  escutcheon pins
⅜-inch corrugated nails
Sandpaper
Wood glue
Router with rabbet bit
Tin
Acrylic paints in blue, red,
  magenta, aqua, and white
Artist's brush
Heavy-duty scissors

INSTRUCTIONS
Cut two 2x15-inch pieces of pine.
Cut two 2x18-inch pieces of pine.

BUILDING THE FRAME: Rabbet
⅜x⅜ inch along one side of each
pine strip. Recut two of the pieces to
14⅜ inches and two of the pieces to
17½ inches. Miter all corners.

Glue and clamp sides together.
Fasten with two corrugated nails at
the back of each corner.

Cut a ¾-inch radius on each corner. Sand all surfaces. Paint frame
with blue acrylic paint.

ADDING THE TIN CUTOUTS: Us-
ing full-size patterns, *right,* cut four
hand, four heart, 10 star, and two
bird shapes from tin. Paint shapes in
bright colors using color photograph
on *page 12* as a guide. Using brass
escutcheon pins, secure shapes to
frame. (*Note:* Use two pins on corner hearts; use one pin for each of
the other tin cutouts.)

Dip end of artist's brush in magenta paint and dab random dots on
frame between tin cutouts.

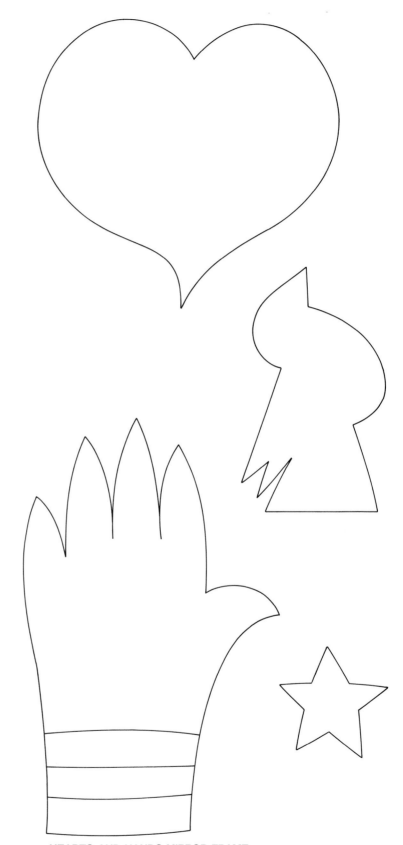

HEARTS-AND-HANDS MIRROR FRAME
Full-Size Patterns

NATURE'S BOUNTY

♦

CRAFTING WITH NATURAL MATERIALS

America's first settlers brought little with them in the way of familiar luxuries, but the new land provided its own delights. Here they discovered an abundance of plants, trees, and flowers to beguile the eye, sweeten the home, and ease the harshness of daily life.

NATURE'S BOUNTY

The fragile beauty and delicious fragrance of flowers and herbs—not to mention their culinary and medicinal properties—have been a source of pleasure and inspiration to peoples of every culture.

The early colonists and, later, immigrants from every corner of the globe brought with them to these shores their treasured family recipes for potpourris and pomanders, perfumes and scented potions, plus arcane herbal remedies for ills of the body and aches of the soul. With them, too, came age-old techniques for harvesting, drying, and preserving useful and ornamental plants of every description.

New recipes and techniques soon evolved, blending English and European traditions with native American Indian lore, modified by the results of on-site experimentation. Through trial and error, the colonists learned to deal with local climate and soil conditions, as they avidly explored new uses for the unfamiliar flowers, herbs, and other versatile plants that grew in their new homeland.

Whether planted in elegant colonial Williamsburg or a Spartan prairie community, every household garden boasted a well-tended patch of herbs and flowers destined for cooking and curing purposes. Where time and climate permitted, there were almost always a few flowers "just for show" as well.

Today, even urban dwellers who haven't so much as a clump of geraniums or a sprig of rosemary growing in a window box can still create glorious dried flower arrangements and sweet-smelling potpourris simply by relying on the large selection of dried materials (flowers, herbs, spices, and fixatives) available from retail and mail-order sources across the country.

A few of the pretty possibilities are pictured here: dainty country wreaths of dried flowers, a "bird's nest" wreath and one of twined rose hips, a miniature pressed flower picture, and an extravagant Victorian wreath and companion trinket box fashioned from tiny dried rosebuds.

Instructions for these projects, as well as recipes for potpourri and directions for making the dried Apple-Slice Wreath shown on page 183, begin on page 194.

NATURE'S BOUNTY

For texture and variety, toss a few wildflowers and roadside finds in amongst the more delicate cultivated blossoms in your dried arrangements.

The beribboned wreath shown here is a mix of roses, hydrangea, and common clover, with yarrow, statice, and a scattering of wild herbs and grasses.

NATURE'S BOUNTY

Corn was the most basic food crop of Colonial America, particularly in the region now known as the Southern Highlands (the mountainous areas of Maryland, the Virginias, the Carolinas, Georgia, Kentucky, Tennessee, and Alabama).

While the grain provided basic sustenance for both man and beast, the corn husks also had their uses. Strong, pliable, and resilient, they could be stuffed into mattresses, woven into chair seats, plaited into ropes and baskets, or shaped into dolls to amuse children.

The versatile "shucks" (as they are called in the Highlands) had decorative uses as well. When dampened, they could be tinted with natural dyes and coaxed into graceful flower shapes, like those in the bouquet *above*. Or, dried husks might be combined with dried gourds and seedpods to make a handsome harvest wreath, *right*.

Today, prepackaged corn husks are available in many crafts shops throughout the country, for those crafters—both rural and urban—who want to try their hand at re-creating these designs.

NATURE'S BOUNTY

Christmas was the most festive season of the year for the early colonists—a time when family gatherings, feasts, and festivities were the order of the day.

Lavish though the hospitality was, seasonal decorations of the period were far simpler than those of today. Rich or poor, the colonial housewife invariably turned to the materials at hand to embellish her home for the holidays.

The centerpiece for a Christmas table in pre-Revolutionary Williamsburg, for example, might have been this elegantly simple sweep of fruit, greens, cones, and nuts, arranged in graceful curves, *right*.

Elsewhere in the room, the mistress of the house might place small arrangements of holly, and magnolia pods and leaves in honor of the season, *above*.

NATURE'S BOUNTY

Gracing the sideboard, *opposite,* is a handsome pyramid of apples and boxwood, a traditional 18th-century design with English antecedents.

The pineapple crowning the cone was a popular symbol of hospitality in colonial days, and often appeared—carved, painted, stenciled, or stitched—in decorative motifs of the period.

A tiny wreath, *below,* of dried apple slices laced on wire and tied with a red ribbon encircles a brass candlestick. Freshly clipped holly and sprigs of greenery complete the arrangement.

Preserving Flowers And Grasses for Wreaths And Bouquets

There are several different ways of drying flowers, weeds, and grasses for use in the projects pictured in this chapter. Read through the following suggestions in order to determine the most appropriate method for preserving the plant material you plan to work with.

Air Drying
Most traditional everlastings—flowers, weeds, and grasses—as well as most herbs, can be dried naturally, without the use of chemical desiccants or other materials. Air drying is the simplest and often the most effective way of drying these plants—all you need is a warm, dark, dry, clean, well-ventilated space. An attic is ideal, but a large closet works equally well.

For air drying, flowers should be cut before they are in full bloom. Most foliage does not dry well and should be removed immediately after flowers are harvested. Separate flowers by kind and gather 10 or 12 stems of one kind of flower into a bunch. Secure stems tightly together with a piece of string or rubber band, but avoid crushing flower heads together. Flowers need to spread loosely, thus allowing air to circulate and preventing distortion of the flower shapes.

Suspend flowers from nails or pegs in a warm, dry place for three to five weeks until completely dry. Keep in mind that sunlight will fade the flowers, and that dampness or dirt will impair the appearance of the dried blossoms.

After flowers and grasses are dry, they can continue to hang, blossoms down, until needed.

Materials that are particularly suitable for air drying include the following:

Statice (several pastel shades)
Cornflower (blues, pink, white)
Yarrow (rose, white, yellow, gold)
Dusty miller (gray)
Baby's-breath (white, pink)
Strawflower (reds, yellows, corals, bronzes)
Bells-of-Ireland (green)
Ammobium (white)
Lunaria (also known as money plant, silver-gray in color)
Celosia (reds, pinks, creams)
Nigella (brown seedpods)
Chinese lantern (red, orange, brown)
Thistle
Most other wild grasses and seedpods

Drying fresh garden flowers requires somewhat different methods from those described above for preserving everlastings and other wild materials.

Fresh flowers can be successfully dried all year-round, whenever they are available and not just during their "natural" blooming season.

Start by picking or buying a bouquet of your favorite blossoms—zinnias, carnations, black-eyed susans, roses, daffodils, yarrow, pansies, or daisies. A mixed bouquet is usually more interesting than one made of a single variety of flower.

Keep in mind that the drying process tends to darken and intensify natural colors, so it's best to start with whites, brights, and pastels.

Drying with Sand or Borax
Flowers have been successfully dried with sand for centuries. All this method requires is lots of fine, clean sand and ample containers.

The flowers are placed in the container and then covered with sand. The container is left open to allow for evaporation. The flowers will dry in good color and with wonderfully lifelike shapes in three to five weeks.

An alternative to sand is a mixture of one part borax to three parts finely ground cornmeal. The borax and cornmeal should be mixed together and all lumps eliminated.

TO DRY FLOWERS: Pour about an inch or two of sand or borax mixture into the bottom of the container (a shoe box will do). Cut flowers to within 1 inch of the head and mount each flower head on a 6- to 8-inch length of florist's wire. Bend the wires to the side and position flowers with heads facing up on the sand or borax mixture in the box. Now gently pour more sand or borax over the flower until it is completely covered, filling all the spaces *between* the petals with the mixture as well.

Try to keep only one kind of flower in each container, as different types of flowers dry at different rates. Leave containers open and check flowers periodically to see if they are "done." Most flowers should be completely dried in three to five weeks, depending on the warmth and dryness of the room in which they are kept.

Flowers may be left in sand or borax until you're ready to work with them, or they may be removed and stored upright until needed.

Drying with Silica Gel
A sandlike material available in crafts and hobby shops, silica gel is a desiccant that actually draws moisture from the flowers, drying them much more quickly than they can be dried in sand or borax.

If you're using silica gel, the flowers must be placed in airtight containers; otherwise the gel absorbs moisture from the air and the flowers are spoiled.

Prepare flowers as described above (clip stems, insert and bend wires) and place each flower faceup on a ½-inch layer of gel at the bottom of the container. Sprinkle or sift gel over the flowers, poking it in and around the petals until flowers are completely covered. Be careful not to distort the natural shapes of the blossoms.

Cover the containers and tape the edges closed to make sure that no air gets in. Leave the containers in a dry, dark place for about 10 days, perhaps longer, depending on the size of the flower and the thickness of the petals.

After 10 days, check the flowers—the petals should be dry but not brittle. If the petals still feel fresh and supple, leave the flowers in the containers and continue to check them every two or three days. (*Note:* Flowers that are left too long in the gel will fade and eventually fall apart.)

When the flowers are dry, carefully remove them from the silica gel; then gently shake the crystals from the flower petals.

Although silica gel is more expensive than either sand or the borax/cornmeal mixture, it should be noted that flowers dried in gel retain more vivid colors and a more lifelike appearance than those dried in the more traditional manner.

Drying in a Microwave

A microwave oven can dry flowers and leaves more quickly and easily than the regular silica gel method. It also preserves the color and shape of the blooms much better than conventional drying methods do.

You will need the following materials and supplies:
Several choice buds or flowers at the peak of their bloom, and a selection of nicely shaped leaves
Silica gel *or* a mixture of two parts cornmeal to one part borax
Plastic, glass, paper, or ceramic bowl or cup to contain the gel and a bloom
A fine-mesh sieve or strainer
A heat-resistant glass or ceramic container for water
Toothpicks, artist's brush, florist's wire, and floral tape

Microwave drying differs slightly from the other drying methods described above, so follow these directions carefully.

Select flowers that are firm in shape, and cut stems to within 1 inch of the blossoms. Bright, light-colored blooms can be preserved better than darker flowers, and thick-petaled blossoms are better than more delicate varieties. Pour about 1½ inches of silica gel or the cornmeal and borax mixture into a bowl. The container should be large enough to allow 2 inches between the top layer of the gel and the top of the bowl. This allows for expansion of the gel during heating.

Place a single flower in the bowl, blossom up. Don't let the bloom touch the sides of the bowl. Using a sieve, gently sift the gel granules over the top of the flower. Use a toothpick to spread the gel under the petals, and around and inside the center of the flower; the bloom should be *completely* covered.

Pour 8 ounces of water into a glass or ceramic container (a measuring cup works fine). Place the water in one corner of the microwave oven. It remains there for the entire drying process.

Put the gel-covered flower in the oven. *Do not cover the container.* Dry one flower at a time to find proper timing. Drying times will vary depending on the number of flowers in the oven.

Set your oven timer. The color of the gel will change from blue to pink as moisture is absorbed and the flower dries. Drying times range from several seconds to three minutes, depending on the bloom's size and texture, on whether you use gel or cornmeal and borax, and on your oven's heating capacity.

Keep a record of drying time and size and type of each flower. Use the listings below as a guide for each bloom:

Zinnia—2 minutes
Carnation—2 minutes
Black-eyed susan—2 minutes
Rose—2 minutes
Daffodil—1½ minutes
Daisy—1 minute
Pansy—45 seconds
Leaves—2 minutes

When the timer stops, remove the flower container from the oven and set the bowl on newspaper. **Don't touch the gel;** allow it to cool for 20 minutes.

Pour off the top layer of the gel. Gently lift out the flower, which will be limp, and place it on top of the remaining gel in the bowl. Let the flower rest until it is firm enough to handle (5 to 20 minutes). Save the remaining gel. Once cold, it can be reused to dry other materials.

When the flower is firm, *gently* remove the remaining gel granules from the blossom with an artist's brush. Avoid tearing the petals.

Place the dried bloom atop a container of cool gel. Allow it to rest overnight uncovered until it feels firm to your touch.

continued

continued from page 195
Nature's Bounty

Insert a length of florist's wire through the flower stem and into the head; or simply attach the stem to a length of wire with a twist of floral tape. Add leaves, if desired.

Note: Do not add wire to the flowers until they are dried and ready for assembly. Using metal in a microwave oven can void the oven's warranty and can eventually cause the oven to malfunction.

Preparing Dried Flowers for Use
To arrange the dried flowers in a bouquet or incorporate them in a wreath, attach florist's wire to the short stems of those that have been dried in sand, borax, or silica gel. Secure the wire to the stems with a twist of florist's tape, then wrap the tape down the length of the wire. (Florist's wire and tape are both available at crafts and hobby shops or through your local florist.)

Flowers that have been air dried can be used just as they are, though you may occasionally want to mist these plants to make them more pliable as you work.

Caring for Dried Flowers
To help your creations withstand changes in the atmosphere, spray the flowers with a light coat of vinyl sealant. This spray helps the flowers resist moisture, and protects them from dust. To freshen and restore colors, spray the flowers periodically with another light coating of sealant.

Although dried flowers are often referred to as "everlastings," they are not imperishable. Dried flower arrangements and wreaths of dried materials should be refreshed with new materials from time to time.

Apple-Slice Wreath
Shown on page 183.

MATERIALS
For one 12-inch wreath
Small Jonathan apples
Straw heart- or circle-shape wreath
Wire hanger or drying screen
Hot-glue gun
Wheat stalks
Ribbon
Clear varnish

INSTRUCTIONS
Slice apples crosswise into pieces ¼ inch thick. Leave the skin on the apples for color.

TO DRY THE SLICES: If you have a wire drying rack, place the slices in a single layer on the rack to dry. Be sure the rack rests in a dry area. Turn the slices twice daily.

If you do not have a rack, here's an easy substitute. Clip one end of a clothes hanger and hook the slices over the bottom to dry. Hang up the slices in a dry area. (The apples probably will take two weeks to dry. Humidity will cause the process to take a bit longer.)

Once the apple slices are completely dry, use a strong crafts glue or a hot-glue gun to secure them in place on a straw heart- or circle-shape wreath.

Spray the slices with clear varnish. Embellish with wheat stalks and a country bow.

Potpourri
Shown on pages 182-183.

INSTRUCTIONS
There are dozens of different recipes for potpourris—some for scenting the room, others for freshening the linens, and still others for keeping the moths at bay. You may concoct your own special blend of flowers, herbs, and spices by following these suggestions.

FLOWERS: Some flowers are used in the mixture for their scent (rose and jasmine, for example), and others are included just to add color and texture to the mix (bachelor's-button and daisy). All of the following flowers dry well and retain a lovely color: rose, marigold, calendula, clematis, bachelor's-button, pansy, peony, aster, nasturtium, zinnia, larkspur, delphinium, sweet alyssum, dianthus, and cornflower.

Pick the flowers on a dry, sunny day, just before they've reached the height of their bloom. To ensure good ventilation, dry the flower petals on wire screens. Set the screens in a cool, dry, shady place for about two weeks, or until the flower petals are crackly. Also dry a few whole buds and flower heads to add textural interest to your potpourri mix.

For every quart of dried petals, you'll need to add a heaping spoonful of mixed herbs and spices. Favorite herbs include rosemary, mint, lavender, thyme, lemon balm, lemon verbena, and sage. Oft-used spices are cloves, cinnamon, cardamom, coriander, nutmeg, mace, allspice, and anise. Most of these herbs and spices are available at natural food stores or herbalist shops.

To preserve the scent of your heavenly mixture, you will also need to mix in a large spoonful of fixative. Orrisroot is one that is readily available at pharmacies.

If the scent of the mixture is not quite strong enough, or if you need to "refresh" an aging mixture, add a few drops (no more) of essential oils in one of the following fragrances: rose, lavender, rosemary, rose geranium, honeysuckle, lilac, or bergamot. These oils, too, are available at herbal shops and through a variety of mail-order sources.

Pour the mixture of petals, herbs, spices, and essential oils into an airtight container and set it aside to cure for three to four weeks. Stir the mixture every few days to blend the fragrances and prevent mildew.

Distribute the finished potpourri in lovely bowls to scent your rooms, or tuck it into small sachet bags to scent drawers and closets.

TRADITIONAL POTPOURRI: This is a catchall recipe for flowers and herbs collected from a summer garden. Vary ingredients and proportions depending on available materials.

Mix together the following:
3 ounces of rose petals
2 ounces of lavender flowers
1 ounce each of peony, jasmine, camomile, carnation, and marigold flowers for scent
1 ounce each of lemon balm, marjoram, hyssop, southernwood, rosemary, and meadowsweet, plus ½ ounce each of thyme, peppermint, and crushed bay leaves
Sprinkle in 1 ounce of strawflowers and bachelor's-buttons for color.

Next, add the following:
4 tablespoons each of cinnamon, allspice, and cloves, plus one tablespoon of grated nutmeg
2 ounces each of crushed orange peel and orrisroot
2 drops each of rose, honeysuckle, carnation, lilac, and lavender oils
Cure mixture as described above and distribute in pretty containers about the house.

LAVENDER SACHET RECIPE: This recipe is made entirely from herbs and spices.

Mix together the following:
3 ounces of thyme
½ ounce each of rosemary, wormwood, and melilot
1 ounce of lavender
¼ ounce each of tansy and mint
1 teaspoon each of cloves and orrisroot.
Crush all the ingredients together into a fine powder and spoon the powder into small fabric bags to make sachets for your linen closet.

Rosebud Box and Wreath

Shown on pages 184–185.

MATERIALS
Dried rosebuds (150–200 to cover a 4x6-inch oval box top)
White glue
Round or oval wooden box in desired size
Wood stain and varnish
Gold braid or lace trim to edge box top
Straw or moss-covered wreath
Satin ribbon for bow

INSTRUCTIONS
(*Note:* A selection of dried rosebuds may be purchased through mail-order sources listed at the end of this chapter, or you may dry your own.)

To dry your own rosebuds, pick the buds at midday during summer months. Look for tight buds that show color. Dry buds in one of the following ways:

AIR DRYING: Place buds on a rack made of wire screening for one week, or until they have visibly dried. Then "cure" them for about four hours by placing them in a slow (100 degree) oven.

SILICA GEL: Pour 1 to 2 inches of silica gel (available in crafts stores) into a container and insert buds, tips up, into granules. Sprinkle flowers with gel until they are completely covered. Cover container tightly and store in a dark, dry place for two to six days, checking periodically until flowers are dry.

BORAX: Using ordinary household borax, follow drying instructions for silica gel, *above,* except place the buds, tips down, in the borax, and do not cover container while drying.

When flowers are dry, store in an airtight container until needed.

TO DECORATE THE BOX: Stain and varnish the box as desired. Glue rosebuds on the lid by starting in the center and working out toward the edges. Glue buds as closely together as possible.

When glue is completely dry, add a row of lace trim or gold braid around the top edge of the box.

TO MAKE THE WREATH: Starting in center of straw or moss-covered wreath form, glue rosebuds, tips up, over entire surface (including sides) of wreath. Place buds as closely together as possible. When glue is completely dry, trim wreath with a satin bow.

Bird's Nest Wreath/Ornaments

Shown on page 185.

MATERIALS
Dried vetiver root or mosses for bird's nest
Dried flowers
Narrow satin ribbons
Florist's wire or twine
White glue

INSTRUCTIONS
(*Note:* If vetiver root or mosses are not available, project can be made with excelsior nests from crafts or hobby shops.)

With vetiver root or mosses, form a 4- to 5-inch-diameter circle to make the bottom of the nest. Secure with twine or wire.

Next, build strands of root or moss upward on outer edges of base circle to form sides of nest; secure with twine or wire.

With glue, add small bunches of dried flowers, ribbon bows, and ribbon streamers around the edge of the nest.

continued from page 197
Nature's Bounty

Dried Herb Wreath

Shown on pages 184–185.

MATERIALS

Selection of dried herbs and
   foliage plants (thyme, artemisia,
   marjoram, etc.)
Dried flowers (pearly everlasting,
   statice, rosebuds, strawflower,
   etc.)
Florist's wire, white glue
Narrow satin ribbons

INSTRUCTIONS

To dry materials, hang plants in
small bunches in a cool, dry place
until dried (or refer to general drying
instructions, pages 194–195).

To make wreath, begin with
greens gathered into small bundles.
Lay bundles flat on a table. Wind
thin wire around the stems of one
bundle, keeping material flat against
table. Add small bundles of dried
greens to what has already been
wired. Continue adding material until length of greens can be formed
into a 4- to 6-inch-diameter circle.
Wire ends of wreath together.

Add dried herbs or flowers to
wreath for accent. Use wire to attach larger blossoms and glue to secure tiny flowers and buds.

To finish, embellish with ribbons.
Weave ribbon through wreath or tie
in a bow with streamers, if desired.

Small Rose-Hip Wreath

Shown on page 185.

MATERIALS

Wild rose hips on vine, with or
   without leaves
Pruning shears, heavy gloves
Florist's wire

INSTRUCTIONS

Clip vines in the fall from rosebush
(wear heavy gloves to protect
hands). Remove leaves from vines,
if desired. Twist one vine to form a
3- to 4-inch circle and wire loops of
vine together.

Fill in wreath with additional
branches and vines; wire all pieces
tightly together to secure. Allow the
wreath to dry and trim with ribbons,
if desired.

Miniature Pressed Flower Picture/Ornament

Shown on page 185.

MATERIALS

A selection of pressed flowers
   (such as pansy, primula, red
   geranium, pentstemon, phlox,
   Indian hawthorn, lantana,
   alyssum, delphinium, queen's
   wreath, lobelia, verbena, forget-
   me-not, Queen-Anne's-lace,
   tansy, honeysuckle, and fern)
Scraps of colored paper or
   cardboard
Small picture frames (available in
   crafts stores)
White glue
Clear adhesive vinyl
Narrow ribbon for hanging

INSTRUCTIONS

To press flowers and foliage: Select
newly blossomed flowers (dry, with
no dew) and place individual blossoms between folded sheets of plain
newsprint. Slip these sheets into a
botany press (if available) or between the pages of a thick book (a
telephone book or encyclopedia, for
example). Weigh the book down
with heavy objects (bricks or rocks).

Thin-petaled flowers will take six
days or less to dry; thick-petaled
flowers will take a bit longer. Remove flowers from newsprint and
store in transparent page protectors
(available in stationery stores).

Do not leave flowers in press or
books too long or they will become
overly dry and brittle.

Press small ferns and foliage in
the same manner. (*Note:* Although
most flowers tend to keep their colors if dried properly, ferns tend to
lose their green color. You may find
it necessary to spray each pressed
fern with a light coat of flat green
paint in order to preserve its color.)

MOUNTING THE FLORAL DE-
SIGN: Cut a piece of colored paper
or cardboard to match frame (back
lightweight paper with cardboard if
necessary).

Next, select one or two flowers
and a few sprigs of greenery to compose your picture. You may want to
use one or two larger blossoms and
a few sprays of more delicate blossoms to balance the composition.

When the arrangement is just like
you want it to be, attach each flower, bud, and fern with tiny dabs of
white glue (use toothpicks to distribute glue and tweezers, if available,
to position flowers).

Once pressed flowers are secure,
frame design as is or protect with a
layer of self-adhesive vinyl. Cut adhesive vinyl about ¼ inch larger all
around than background. Remove
paper backing and carefully apply
vinyl over the flower arrangement;
press firmly in place and trim away
excess vinyl.

To seal, "laminate" vinyl to picture by pressing for a few seconds
with a cool iron, using a press cloth.
Place laminated picture under a
heavy book for a few days so that
picture will lie flat. Insert picture in
frame and add loop of ribbon for
hanging, if desired.

Dried Flower Wreath

Shown on pages 186–187.

MATERIALS

10- to 12-inch-diameter straw
  wreath for base
Spanish moss to cover base
Selection of the following dried
  materials: gray and green for
  background (sage, lamb's-ears,
  lemon balm, German statice,
  wormwood, thyme, oats, and
  assorted grasses); gold (yarrow);
  blue (larkspur and blue sage);
  pink (larkspur, sweetheart rose,
  globe amaranth); coral
  (hydrangea flowers, sugar bush)
Florist's wire
Small wooden or plastic floral
  picks (3 to 4 inches long)
Narrow- and medium-width
  assorted ribbons for bows
White crafts glue
Florist's wire

INSTRUCTIONS

Wrap basic straw wreath in a layer
of Spanish moss (secure moss with
dabs of white glue). Fill out the basic
wreath with sprigs of dried sage,
lamb's-ears, lemon balm, statice,
wormwood, thyme, oats, and other
grasses. Attach sprigs to florist's
picks with twists of thin wire before
inserting into wreath. Secure with
dabs of glue.

If the materials you are working
with seem particularly dry or brittle,
mist the plants with a squirt of water from a spray bottle as you work
to make them more pliable.

When base is completed, add
dried flowers to the face of the
wreath, wiring each flower to a
wooden or plastic floral pick and securing each new addition to the
wreath with a dab of white glue as
you proceed. Pay particular attention to the balance of color and pro-
portion (small and large blossoms)
as you compose your design.

When the wreath is completed to
your satisfaction, trim with a bow of
mixed ribbons (satin, velvet, and/or
grosgrain) in assorted colors, twining the ends of the ribbons back into
the wreath as shown.

Corn-Husk Flowers

Shown on page 188.

MATERIALS

Corn husks
Fabric dye
Floral tape
Dried flowers (for flower centers)
Glue
Thread
Dowel

INSTRUCTIONS

Boil the corn husks in water with
dye to achieve the desired color.

To form the flower petals, tear the
wet corn husks into 3-inch-wide sections. Twist the corn husk in the
center 3 times and then bend the
corn husk in half with the twist
tucked inside the wide half of the
corn husk. Wrap thread around the
end of each "petal." When you get
about 16 petals, wrap the flower
centers and also the petals onto a
wire with thread to form the stem.

The curl in the leaves is achieved
by wrapping the wet corn husks
around a dowel and securing them
in place with thread. Let the corn
husks dry overnight and then tear
them into the desired widths.

Cover and secure the leaves onto
the wire with floral tape.

Corn-Husk Wreath

Shown on page 189.

MATERIALS

16-inch-diameter straw wreath
Supply of dried corn husks
Small gourds
Small ears of Indian corn and
  dried chili peppers
Hot-glue gun
Beige thread
Scissors

INSTRUCTIONS

Soak corn husks in hot, soapy water
until pliable (3 to 5 minutes).

Lay about five corn husks in a pile
on top of each other and trim them
to a point on each end. Next, wrap
several twists of thread around the
center of this set of "petals" to hold

them together; pull thread tight and
tie off. Separate petals so they stand
out individually. Make enough
groups of corn-husk petals to cover
the entire straw wreath.

Attach these bundles of corn-
husk petals to top and sides of the
straw wreath with a hot-glue gun.

To attach gourds to wreath, first
score one side of each gourd with a
large nail (this rough surface will allow the glue to grip the gourd much
better than if it were smooth). Attach gourds at intervals around surface of wreath using hot-glue gun.

Finally, use hot-glue gun to attach
the Indian corn and hot chili peppers at various points on the wreath.

Curved Centerpiece

Shown on pages 190–191.

MATERIALS

Large (26-inch-diameter) green
  plastic-foam wreath
30-inch square of green felt or
  plastic
3 dozen large, glossy lemon or
  magnolia leaves
Selection of red apples,
  pomegranates, pears, oranges (or
  fruits of your choice)
Assorted unshelled nuts
Small loops of dried apples or
  apricots strung on wire and tied
  with red ribbon
Approximately 24 medium-size
  pinecones
Small bunches of variegated holly
  (with berries)
Clippers, florist's wire
2 staple-shape floral pins
3- or 4-inch wooden or plastic
  floral picks

INSTRUCTIONS

Cut the plastic-foam wreath in half.
Flop one half and pin together with
floral pins to form S-shape base.

Next, cut a pair of plastic or felt
shapes 4 inches wider than the plastic-foam shapes and tape them together to form an S-shape. Insert
plastic or felt beneath plastic-foam
base and position on table for protection from scratches.

continued

continued from page 199
Nature's Bounty

Slip a few magnolia leaves partially under the plastic-foam base so they cover the plastic and form a background for the centerpiece.

Wire remaining magnolia leaves to 3- or 4-inch floral picks. Trim stems of holly on an angle to insert into the plastic foam.

Wire some of the pinecones to 3-inch picks and some to 4-inch picks. Pierce fruit with 3- and 4-inch picks.

Build the centerpiece by arranging the fruit symmetrically along the top of the S-shape foam base. Fill in gaps with leaves and holly. Add pinecones at strategic intervals. (Study photo, *pages 190–191*, for placement.)

For accents, string dried apricots or dried apple slices on wire and form into small (5-inch-diameter) "wreaths" to scatter across the centerpiece. Trim wreaths with bows.

Scatter assorted nuts along top and sides of the centerpiece for added texture. (*Note:* Nuts can be drilled and attached to floral picks or wrapped with florist's wire and secured to the plastic-foam base, if desired.)

Substitute or add other fruits, leaves, and nuts as desired (or as available) to sculpt your own version of this traditional centerpiece.

Holiday Fruit Pyramid
Shown on page 192.

MATERIALS
One 12-inch-high, cone-shape wooden form with nails (cone is approx. 5 inches wide at base tapering to 2½ inches wide at tip; see note below about making your own cone)
One 10- to 12-inch-diameter cutting board, plate, or circle of cardboard
15 to 18 shiny red apples
Small bunches of boxwood, holly, white pine, or other foliage

One small, fresh pineapple with leaves
12 to 15 lemon, magnolia, or rhododendron leaves
Clippers

INSTRUCTIONS
Note: The cone used is a traditional style. It has 2-inch-long finishing nails arranged in 9 vertical rows of 7 nails each, with 4 nails sticking up from the top to hold the pineapple. (See sketch, *below.* This ready-made cone can be purchased in two sizes from Country Manor, Dept. BH, Sperryville, VA 22740.)

Or, to make your own cone, whittle the approximate shape from an old log or a scrap piece of soft pine. Hammer 2-inch finishing nails into the cone in the pattern described above (9 rows of 7 nails each, 4 nails on top). Nails should stick out about 1 inch from base. Clip the head off each nail with a pair of nail nippers, leaving pointed spikes which can easily pierce the apples which are to be mounted on them.

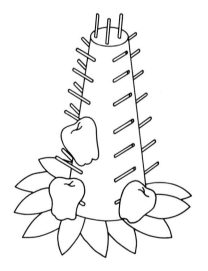

To make the centerpiece, trim stems and bases from bottoms of magnolia, lemon, or rhododendron leaves; arrange leaves on plate or cardboard base so that pointed ends extend beyond the outer edge of the base.

Center the wooden cone on top of the leaves and then stick 15 to 18 apples on the nail spikes in 5 or 6 rows of 3 to 4 apples each (refer to photo, *page 192,* for placement).

Next, tuck small sprays of boxwood or other bushy foliage in around apples so that the wooden cone base is completely hidden. Stick a small pineapple with abundant fresh foliage on top of the cone.

Note: Experiment with a variety of fruits and greens to create your own version of this traditional pyramid decoration.

Candle Ring
Shown on page 193.

MATERIALS
Crab apples
Picture-hanging wire
Narrow red ribbon
Assorted greenery

INSTRUCTIONS
Slice crab apples crosswise into ¼-inch-thick slices. String 36 slices on a length of picture-hanging wire. Stretch the wire straight and hang it in a dry place for one to two weeks.

When the slices are dry, form a circle with the wire and bend it together securely where it meets. Trim away any excess wire. Attach a bow of narrow red ribbon to the top.

Lay the wreath over the candlestick. Add holiday greenery.

Willow Plant Stand
Shown on page 10.
Finished size: 36 inches tall

MATERIALS
1- to 2-inch-diameter mature willow for frame
⅓- to ½-inch-diameter willow (straight) for curved and crossbar pieces
1½- to 2½-inch thin nails for frame
1-inch wire brads for attaching curved pieces
1- to 1½-inch thin nails for attaching shelf crossbars

INSTRUCTIONS

CUTTING THE PIECES: Cut the willow as follows:

Legs: Four 36-inch straight lengths of 1- to 2-inch diameter

Top shelf sides: Four 12-inch side-pieces of 1-inch diameter, and four 13-inch sidepieces of 1-inch diameter

Bottom shelf sides: Four 15-inch sidepieces of 1-inch diameter, and four 16-inch sidepieces of 1-inch diameter

Tabletop: Fourteen 13-inch pieces of ½-inch diameter

Bottom shelf: Ten 15½-inch pieces of ½-inch diameter

Curved designs: Twenty 30-inch pieces and thirty 6-inch pieces of ⅓-inch diameter

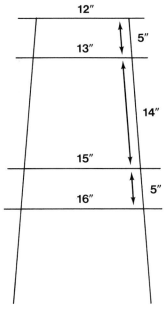

Diagram A

CONSTRUCTING THE STAND: Begin with the main frame. Nail the top and bottom shelf sides to two of the leg pieces, following Diagram A, *above*. Leave a ½-inch length on each piece to the outside of the leg. Repeat for the other two legs. You should now have two complete sides. To make the remaining two sides, add the top and bottom shelf sides to the original two sides and overlap the outside edges as you nail them in place.

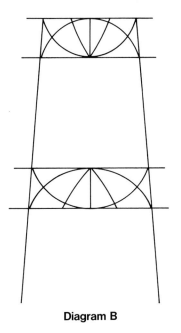

Diagram B

Because the size of each shelf varies, the legs will have a slight flare.

The thin willow used for the decorative, curved pieces should be fresh and pliable. Bend and nail the pieces in place following Diagram B, *above*.

The shelf is completed by evenly spacing and nailing the crossbars to the shelf sides. (Nail the bars approximately ½ to 1 inch apart.) You may also choose to nail the bars more closely together to form a solid shelf.

HELPFUL HINTS: Gather more willows than you will need. You may break a few.

Try to find willow pieces that are as straight as possible. Use the willow within a few days of cutting for best results.

Dried willow will contract slightly. Tap in any nailheads that loosen during the drying process.

Sources for Dried Flowers and Herbs

The following companies are possible sources for purchasing dried flowers and herbs if you choose not to dry your own:

Angelica's Herb and Spice Company
137 First Avenue
New York, NY 10003
212/677-1549

Aphrodisia
282 Bleecker Street
New York, NY 10014
212/989-6440

Caprilands Herb Farm
Silver Street
Coventry, CT 06238
203/742-7244

Ruby Mountain Everlastings
541 Judy Lane
Alder, MT 59710
406/842-5206

Note: Mail-order catalogs are available from the above suppliers.

Also keep in mind that your local florist or crafts shop may very well have the supplies you need.

VICTORIANA

◆

AN UNMATCHED ELEGANCE

While Victoria reigned in England, from 1837 to 1901, America experienced unprecedented geographic and economic growth. With rising prosperity came increased interest in the home and its decoration. Victorians embraced a range of styles that focused on the romantic, the exotic, and the ornate. The vivid embroidery in the matting, above, *is an excellent example.*

VICTORIANA

Quilts of the late 1800s illustrate the extravagance of Victorian styles.

A taste for exotica (probably sparked by exposure to Japanese culture at the Centennial Exhibition of 1876 in Philadelphia) led to increased emphasis on surface embellishment in all the decorative arts. As a result, quilts of this era were often far more pretty than practical.

The exquisite Japanese Fan quilt, *opposite,* is dated 1884. Pieced from an opulent selection of silks, satins, and velvets, it is lavishly embroidered with dozens of different stitches in a dizzying array of colors.

Floral motifs also flourished in the needle arts of the Victorian era.

As with most other motifs deemed suitable subjects for the "gentle arts" practiced by ladies, the rose was more than just a pretty flower.

According to Christian symbolism, the white rose is an emblem of purity, spirituality, and virginity, and the red rose betokens all the vanities of this world.

Given an undercurrent of symbolism, a filet crochet edging of white roses, *below,* would have been considered a charmingly appropriate embellishment for linens in a young girl's room or on a marriage bed.

VICTORIANA

Crochet was an immensely popular pastime among Victorian women of every station, and collectively they turned out yards of edgings and valances, heaps of pillow tops and bedspreads, and dozens of afghans and doilies.

Brought to America by Irish peasants fleeing the potato famine in the 1840s, crochet rapidly became a popular and decorous needlecraft. Mrs. Ann Stephens, influential author of an 1854 needlework manual, pointed to crochet as "one of those gentle means by which women are kept feminine and ladylike in this fast age."

By far the most popular patterns were for "crochet lace," or filet crochet designs, like the heart-pattern bedspread, *opposite*. Dozens of similar designs were printed in the fashionable ladies' magazines of the day, including *Godey's Lady's Book* and *The Modern Priscilla*.

Raised designs with novelty textures, such as the marguerite medallion adapted for the ruffled pillow and fringed coverlet, *left,* also met with great success among more adventuresome crochet enthusiasts of the late 19th century.

VICTORIANA

Grapes are another common motif in Victorian decorative arts and crafts. Whether molded in wax, carved in mahogany, or rendered in filet crochet or needlepoint, grapes were a familiar symbol of good cheer, good fellowship, fruitfulness, and generous hospitality.

Grapes also possessed the rounded forms, shapely leaves, and gracefully twining vines that so appealed to the Victorian penchant for intricate and ornate patterns.

Variations on the filet crochet insert on the linen dresser scarf, *below,* might be reworked along a valance or curtain border or assembled into panel inserts for a bedspread. A single block of the grape cluster motif, with a small selection of leaves and a few curly tendrils, would make a striking crocheted pillow-top for the down-filled parlor sofa.

The needlepoint grapevine wreath, *opposite,* set against a subtly striped background, is a perfect complement for the graceful curves of the Victorian chair for which it was designed.

The same wreath pattern also might be cross-stitched on a linen mat or tablecloth or stitched into a rug.

VICTORIANA

Berlin work was the term used for all types of needlework done on canvas during the Victorian Era. The name derives from the fact that the charted patterns and colored wools used for this type of work were originally imported only from Berlin, Germany.

As the technique gained currency in America and on the Continent, new sources for these materials sprang up, and this form of needlework is now more commonly known—at least in this country—by the less geographically specific name of "needlepoint."

By the end of the 19th century, the typical Victorian household contained a vast assortment of chairs, pillows, pictures, screens, and table mats in this popular technique. Perhaps the most typical period items of all are needlepoint stools, ranging in size from footstools to piano benches, with every size and shape in between.

As always, flowers, birds, and animals became the most popular design subjects, and they were almost always worked against a dark— usually black— background, as were the three lovely floral patterns pictured here.

Instructions for Victoriana

EMBROIDERED PICTURE MAT
Full-Size Pattern

COLOR KEY
A Pale Aqua
B Medium Gray-green
C Coral
D Gold
E Black
F Metallic Gold

STITCHES
1 Darning
2 Satin
3 Outline
4 Couched Filling
5 Couching

Embroidered Picture Mat

Shown on page 203.
Finished size is 8x10 inches

MATERIALS

12x14 inches of oatmeal-color linen
No. 5 pearl cotton in pale aqua
   (A), medium gray-green (B),
   coral (C), gold (D), and black (E)
Gold metallic thread
Acrylic or fabric paints in aqua,
   gray-green, coral, and gold
11x13 inches of lightweight foam
   core
Spray adhesive; white crafts glue

INSTRUCTIONS

The pattern, *opposite*, is full-size. Transfer the design to linen fabric.

Dilute acrylic paints with water (or follow manufacturer's instructions for fabric paints) and apply a *very light* wash of color to each section of the design. Refer to the color key, *below,* for guidance. Heat-set the color by ironing lightly on the wrong side of the fabric.

Embroider the paisley design, following the color and stitch chart, *opposite.* For additional assistance, see the stitch diagrams on *page 252.*

Begin by stitching around each section of the design with the outline stitch, using black pearl cotton. Complete each remaining portion of the designs using the appropriate colors and stitches.

Press the embroidered fabric on the wrong side.

Machine-stay-stitch around the oval opening to reinforce the fabric. Cut out the center of the oval to within ½ inch of the stay-stitching.

Position the paper pattern on an 11x13-inch piece of foam core and mark the oval opening. Cut out the oval shape. Coat the foam core lightly with spray adhesive; center and firmly press the embroidered mat in place.

Clip the edges of the fabric opening up to, but not through, the stay stitching. Pull the raw edges of the fabric to the back of the frame and secure the edges with dabs of white glue. Tape the picture of your choice in place.

Frame the embroidered matted picture as desired.

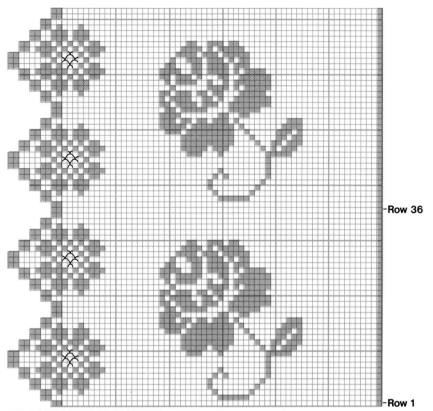

WIDE-SCALLOPED ROSE EDGING

Row 36

Row 1

Wide-Scalloped Rose Edging

Shown on page 204.

MATERIALS

DMC 6-cord Cordonnet Tatting &
   Crochet Cotton Size 70
No. 14 steel crochet hook

Gauge: With suggested materials, 7 spaces = 1 inch, 7 rows = 1 inch.
Size: Edging measures about 11 inches at widest point.

INSTRUCTIONS

Starting at narrow part make 189 sts, taking care not to work the sts too tightly.

Row 1: Dc in 4th ch from hook and in next 2 chs, (ch 2, sk 2 chs, dc in next ch) 59 times, dc in next 6 sts. Ch 8, turn.

Row 2: **Dc in 4th ch from hook and in each of next 4 chs, dc in first dc—2 blocks increased,** (ch 2, sk 2 dc, dc in next dc) twice, (ch 2, dc in next dc) 29 times, (2 dc in space, dc in next dc) 6 times, (ch 2, dc in next dc) 24 times, dc in last 2 dc and in top of turning-ch. Ch 3, turn.

continued

FAN WEDGE
Cut 7

A .... B

FAN CENTER
Cut 1

FAN CRAZY QUILT
Full-Size Patterns

continued from page 213
Victoriana

Row 3: Dc in next 3 dc, (ch 2, dc in next dc) 23 times, 2 dc in sp, dc in next dc, (ch 2, sk 2 dc, dc in next dc) 24 times, 2 dc in sp, dc in next dc, (ch 2, dc in next dc) 3 times, 2 dc in space, dc in next dc, ch 2, dc in last 6 dc and in top of turning-ch. Ch 8, turn.

Row 4: Increase 2 blocks as before and work across row in blocks and spaces as shown on chart on *page 213.*

Except for flower centers on scallops, all spaces will consist of 2 dc with ch-2 between, and all blocks are composed of 2 dc in place of the ch-2. The center of floral motif is made by using ch-5 loops on *Rows 7* through *10;* there will be one such loop on *Row 7,* 2 loops each on *Rows 8* and *10,* and 3 loops on *Row 9.* Repeat *Rows 1–36* for desired length.

Fan Crazy Quilt

Shown on page 205.
Finished size: Approximately 53x68 inches

MATERIALS
3 yards of black taffeta fabric
4 yards of red satin for borders
  and quilt back
Assorted scraps (totaling about 4 yards) of silk, satin, taffeta (old neckties are a good source of scraps)
4 yards of outing flannel
Assorted colors of embroidery floss and pearl cotton
Tracing paper
Cardboard or plastic for templates

INSTRUCTIONS
(*Note:* All patterns and measurements for patterns and borders *include* ¼-inch seam allowances.)

TO BEGIN: Trace and make templates for the full-size pattern pieces, *left.* The solid lines denote cutting lines; the dashed lines denote sewing lines or finished piece outlines. The dotted line is a fold line.

Draw an 8-inch square on graph paper and make a template for quilt blocks.

CUTTING INSTRUCTIONS: From the black taffeta fabric, cut 48 fan centers. Using the square template, cut 48 background squares.

Use the fan wedge pattern to cut seven wedges for each block (336 total) from the silk, satin, and taffeta fabric scraps.

From the red satin fabric, cut two 4½x63-inch borders; cut two 4½x56-inch borders. Reserve the remaining red satin for the quilt back.

TO MAKE ONE BLOCK: Fold one fan wedge in half lengthwise with *right* sides together, matching points A and B. Sew from the fold to the AB point, taking ¼-inch seam allowance. Turn the tip right side out, forming the pointed wedge tip. Repeat for the remaining fan wedges.

Sew seven prepared wedges together along the sides to form a fan. Pin the fan to a black taffeta square.

Baste under the curved edge of a fan center piece. Pin the fan center in the corner of a square, adjusting the position of the fan so the fan center covers the bottom raw edges of the fan wedges.

Baste the side edges of the fan to the black square just outside the seam line. Appliqué the curved edge of the fan center; remove the basting along this edge.

Embellish the seams between the wedges with a variety of embroidery stitches worked in assorted colors and types of embroidery thread. Study the stitch diagrams on *page 252* and the quilt photograph on *page 205* for ways to combine various stitches. Add simple motifs in the fan centers, if desired.

TO MAKE THE QUILT TOP: Make 48 fan blocks.

Referring to the color photograph, *page 205,* lay out the blocks in six rows with eight blocks in each row. The fans in the quilt shown, *page 205,* form a circle in the quilt center, surrounded by partial circles.

Join the blocks into rows; then, sew the rows together. Add decorative embroidery stitches along the block seams.

Sew the 4½x63-inch borders to the quilt sides; trim excess. Sew the remaining borders to the top and bottom; trim excess. Add decorative embroidery stitches along the border seams and simple embroidery motifs at the border corners.

TO FINISH THE QUILT: Piece together the red satin fabric into a rectangle about one inch larger on all sides than the quilt top. Piece together the flannel into a rectangle of the same size as the quilt back.

Lay out the flannel rectangle on a large surface with the *wrong* side up. Center the quilt back atop the flannel with the *right* side of the quilt back up. Center the quilt top, *wrong* side up, over the quilt back. Pin the layers together around the outer edges.

Sew around the perimeter of the quilt top, leaving an opening for turning. Trim the excess flannel and quilt back. Turn the quilt right side out; blindstitch the opening closed.

Tie the quilt to the quilt back at all the block corners, forming the knots on the quilt back. (See directions for tying a quilt, *page 35.*)

Crocheted Spread And Pillows

Shown on page 206.
Finished size: Each hexagon measures 14 inches across

MATERIALS
Coats & Clark's South Maid Mercerized Cotton (400-yard ball): 44 balls of white or ecru for Single-Size Spread; 55 balls for Double-Size Spread
Size 7 steel crochet hook

INSTRUCTIONS
Single-Size Spread—Make 38 Hexagon Motifs and 4 Half-Motifs.
Double-Size Spread—Make 53 Hexagon Motifs and 6 Half-Motifs.
Pillow top—Make one Hexagon.

HEXAGON MOTIF: Starting at center, ch 9. Join with sl st to form ring.

Rnd 1: Ch 1, 18 sc in ring. Join to first sc.

Rnd 2: Ch 3, 4 dc in back lp of next st, drop lp from hook, insert hook in top of ch-3 and draw dropped lp through—starting pc st made; * ch 2, skip 1 sc; *5 dc in back lp of next sc, drop lp from hook, insert hook in first dc of the 5-dc group and draw dropped lp through*—pc st made. Rep from * around, end with ch 2. Join to top of first pc st.

Rnd 3: Ch 5, * dc in next lp, ch 2, dc in next pc st, ch 2. Rep from * around, end with dc in last sp, ch 2. Join to 3rd ch of ch-5.

Rnd 4: Ch 1, sc in joining, * 3 sc in next sp, sc in next dc. Rep from * around, end with 3 sc in last sp. Join to first sc.

Rnd 5: Ch 1, sc in joining; working in *back* lp of each st only, sc in next sc; * *3 sc in next sc*—3-sc group made; sc in next 3 sc. Rep from *

around, end with sc in last sc. Join— 18 3-sc groups.

Rnds 6–16: Ch 1, sc in joining, working in *back* lp of each st only and making 3 sc in center sc of each 3-sc group, sc in each sc around. Join. At end of last rnd fasten off. Mark center st between each 3-sc group.

Rnd 17: Overlap the 5 sc following any marked sc over the 5 sc before same marked sc; make a lp on hook, working through both thicknesses sc in the 5 sc, ch 4, * overlap the 5 sc following next marked sc over the 5 sc before the same marked sc; working through both thicknesses sc in the 5 sc, ch 4. Rep from * around. Join to first sc.

Rnd 18: Working in *back* lp only, sc in first 2 sc, * 3 sc in next sc, sc in next 2 sc, sc in next 4 ch, (sc in 5 sc, sc in next 4 ch) twice; sc in 2 sc. Rep from * around, end with sc in last 4 ch. Join.

Rnds 19–23: Working in *back* lp only, sc in each sc around making 3 sc in center sc of each 3-sc group. Join. At end of last rnd fasten off.

Rnd 24: Join thread to center sc of any 3-sc group, working through *both* lps of sc, ch 4, dc in same place, * (ch 1, skip 1 sc, dc in next sc) 18 times; ch 1; in center sc of next 3-sc group make dc, ch 1 and dc. Rep from * around, end with ch 1. Join to 3rd ch of ch-4—120 sps.

Rnd 25: Sl st in sp, ch 4, dc in same sp, * (ch 1, dc in next sp) 19 times; ch 1; in next sp make dc, ch 1 and dc. Rep from * around, end with ch 1. Join to 3rd ch of ch-4—126 sps.

Rnd 26: Working in *back* lp only and counting each ch-1 as a st, * make 3 sc in next st, sc in next 41 sts. Rep from * around. Join—264 sc.

Rnd 27: Sl st in center sc of first 3-sc group, working in *back* lp only, * 3 sc in center sc, sc in 3 sc, (pc st in next sc, sc in 5 sc) 6 times; pc st in next sc, sc in 3 sc. Rep from * around. Join.

Rnd 28: Sl st in center sc of first 3-sc group, working in *back* lp only, 3
continued

continued from page 215
Victoriana

sc in center sc, sc in each st around making 3 sc in center sc of each 3-sc group. Join.

Rnd 29: Sl st in center sc of first 3-sc group, working in *back* lp only, * 3 sc in center sc, sc in next 2 sc, (pc st in next sc, sc in 5 sc) 7 times; pc st in next sc, sc in 2 sc. Rep from * around. Join.

Rnd 30: Rep *Rnd 28.*

Rnd 31: Working through *both* lps; in center sc make sl st, ch 4 and dc; * (ch 1, skip 1 sc, dc in next sc) 25 times; ch 1; in center sc of next 3-sc group make dc, ch 1 and dc. Rep from * around, end with ch 1. Join to 3rd ch of ch-4.

Rnd 32: Sl st in next sp, ch 4, dc in same sp, * (ch 1, dc in next sp) 26 times; ch 1; in next sp make dc, ch 1 and dc. Rep from * around, end with ch 1. Join to 3rd ch of ch-4.

Unless otherwise stated, work in back lps of sts only.

Rnd 33: * Make 3 sc in next st, sc in next 55 sts. Rep from * around. Join to first sc.

Rnd 34: Sl st in center sc, * 3 sc in center sc, sc in next 4 sc, (pc st in next sc, sc in 5 sc) 8 times; pc st in next sc, sc in 4 sc. Rep from * around. Join.

Rnd 35: Rep *Rnd 28.*

Rnd 36: Sl st in center sc, * 3 sc in center sc, sc in 3 sc, (pc st in next sc, sc in 5 sc) 9 times; pc st in next sc, sc in 3 sc. Rep from * around. Join.

Rnd 37: Rep *Rnd 28.*

Rnd 38: Sl st in center sc, * 3 sc in center sc, sc in next 2 sc, (pc st in next sc, sc in 5 sc) 10 times; pc st in next sc, sc in 2 sc. Rep from * around. Join.

Rnd 39: Rep *Rnd 28.*

Rnd 40: Working through *both* lps, sl st in center sc, ch 4, dc in same place, * (ch 1, skip 1 sc, dc in next sc) 34 times; ch 1; in center sc of next 3-sc group make dc, ch 1 and dc. Rep from * around, end with ch 1. Join.

Rnd 41: Sl st in sp, ch 4, dc in same sp, * (ch 1, dc in next sp) 35 times; ch 1; in next sp make dc, ch 1 and dc. Rep from * around, end with ch 1. Join. Fasten off.

HALF-MOTIF: Starting at center of long edge, ch 9. Join to form ring.

Row 1: Ch 1, 11 sc in ring, sl st in last 3 ch of ring. Join with sl st to first sc. *Do not turn.*

Row 2: Ch 5, (pc st in next sc, ch 2, skip 1 sc) 4 times; pc st in next sc, ch 2, dc in last sc. Fasten off. *Hereafter, fasten off at end of each row; join thread at beg of row as indicated.*

Row 3: Join thread to 3rd ch of ch-5, ch 4, dc in same place; * in next sp make (ch 1, dc) twice; ch 1; in next sp make (dc, ch 1) twice; in next pc st make dc, ch 1 and dc. Rep from * across, end with dc, ch 1 and dc in last dc.

Row 4: Join thread to top of ch-4, ch 4, dc in same place, * (ch 1, dc in next sp) 5 times; ch 1; in next sp make dc, ch 1 and dc. Rep from * across.

Row 5: Join thread to top of ch-4, ch 1, working in *back* lp only, make 2 sc in same place, * (sc in next dc, sc in next sp) 6 times; sc in next dc, 3 sc in next sp. Rep from * across, end with 2 sc in last sp.

Row 6: Working in *back* lp only, join thread to first sc, ch 1, 2 sc in same place, * sc in next 3 sc, (pc st in next sc, sc in 3 sc) 3 times; 3 sc in next sc. Rep from * across, end with 2 sc in last sc.

Row 7: Working in *back* lp only, join thread to first sc, ch 1, 2 sc in same place, * sc in each st to center sc of next 3-sc group, 3 sc in center sc. Rep from * across, end with 2 sc in last sc.

Row 8: Working in *back* lp only, join thread to first sc, ch 1, 2 sc in same place, * sc in next 3 sc, (pc st in next sc, sc in 3 sc) 4 times; 3 sc in next sc. Rep from * across, end with 2 sc in last sc.

Row 9: Rep *Row 7.*

Row 10: Working through *both* lps, join thread to first sc, ch 4, dc in same place, * (ch 1, skip next sc, dc in next sc) 11 times; ch 1; in center sc of next 3-sc group make dc, ch 1 and dc. Rep from * across, end with dc, ch 1 and dc in last sc.

Row 11: Join thread to top of ch-4, ch 4, dc in same place, * (ch 1, dc in next sp) 12 times; ch 1; in next sp make dc, ch 1 and dc. Rep from * across.

Row 12: Working in *back* lp only, join thread to top of ch-4, ch 1, 2 sc in same place, * skip next dc, (sc in next sp, sc in next dc) 12 times; sc in next sp, skip next dc, 3 sc in next ch-1 sp. Rep from * across, end with 2 sc in last sp.

Row 13: Working in *back* lp only, join thread to first sc, ch 1, 2 sc in same place, * sc in next 27 sc, 3 sc in next sc. Rep from * across, end with 2 sc in last sc.

Rows 14–17: Working in *back* lp only, join thread to first sc, ch 1, making 2 sc in first and last sc and 3 sc in center sc of the 3-sc group, sc in each sc across.

Row 18: Working through *both* lps, join thread to first sc, ch 4, dc in same place, * (ch 1, skip 1 sc, dc in next sc) 18 times; ch 1; in center sc of next 3-sc group make dc, ch 1 and dc. Rep from * across, end with dc, ch 1 and dc in last sc. Fasten off.

Beginning and ending rows on Half-Motif as established and starting with *Rnd 25* of Hexagon Motif, continue working in rows in same pat as for Hexagon Motif to within last 2 rnds. *Now work 2 rnds as follows:*

Rnd 1: Join thread to first sc, ch 4, dc in same sc, * (ch 1, skip 1 sc, dc in next sc) 34 times; ch 1; in center sc of next 3-sc group make dc, ch 1 and dc. Rep from * across 3 sides, end with dc, ch 1 and dc in last sc; continue making ch-1 sps evenly along remaining long edge, end with ch 1, sl st in 3rd ch of ch-4.

Rnd 2: Sl st in sp, ch 4, dc in same sp, * ch 1, dc in next sp. Rep from * around, making dc, ch 1 and dc in each corner sp. Join. Fasten off.

TO ASSEMBLE SPREAD: Refer to the photograph, *page 206,* for placement of Hexagon Motifs and Half-Motifs. Single Size requires 3 rows of 8 blocks and 2 rows of 7 blocks. Double Size requires 4 rows of 8 blocks and 3 rows of 7 blocks. Sew together on wrong side. Fill in spaces at top and bottom with Half-Blocks.

Fringe: Cut five strands of thread each 10 inches long. Double these strands to form a loop. Insert hook in sp on edge of spread and draw loop through. Draw loose ends through loop and pull up tightly to form a knot. Knot five strands as before in every other sp or every ½ inch around 3 sides, leaving one narrow edge free. Trim fringe.

TO ASSEMBLE PILLOW: Cut two hexagons slightly larger than the crocheted hexagon. Center and tack the crocheted top to the right side of one fabric hexagon, using matching thread. Sew fabric ruffle along sides of hexagon top.

With right sides facing, sew pillow front to back; leave one side open. Clip corners, turn, and stuff. Sew opening closed.

Filet Crochet Heart Bedspread

Shown on page 207.
Finished size: Directions are given for twin size bed; changes for double and queen size beds are given in parentheses. About 73 inches wide x 89 inches long (87 inches wide x 89 inches long; 93 inches wide x 89 inches long), including 6½-inch border all around

MATERIALS
J. & P. Coats "Knit-Cro-Sheen" (325 yds.), Art. A. 65: 60 (65-70) balls No. 1 White
Steel crochet hook No. 8, or size required to crochet to gauge
J. & P. Coats Dual Duty Plus sewing thread

Gauge: 5 mesh [[dc, ch 1) 5 times] = 1 inch; 1 filet motif (25 rows) = 5½ inches long.

INSTRUCTIONS
CLUSTER (cl): (Yo and draw up a loop, yo and draw through 2 loops on hook) 2 times in same st, yo and draw through 3 loops on hook.

LACET STITCH: *Row 1:* Dc in dc, skip 3 ch, ch 3, dc in dc.
Row 2: Dc in dc (ch 2, sc in ch-3 space, ch 2), dc in next dc. Repeat *Rows 1* and *2* for lacet throughout. Note that lacet is always preceded

FILET CROCHET HEART BEDSPREAD

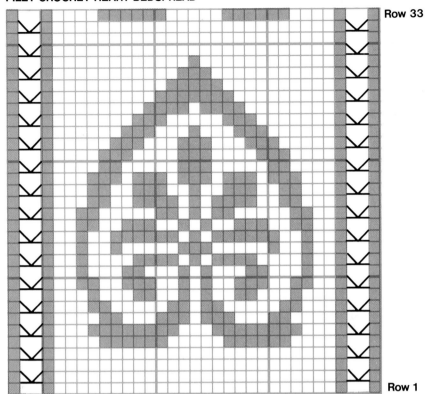

CHART 1 (HEART PANEL)

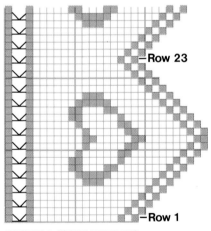

CHART 2 (SIDE BORDER)   CHART 3 (BORDER CORNER)

and followed by a filled mesh; the dc before and after is a portion of that mesh.

Note: Unless otherwise noted, ch 3 to turn on each row counts as first dc of next row.

MOTIF PANEL: (Chart 1): Make 4 (5, 6). Ch 68.
Row 1: Work in 3rd ch from hook, dc in next ch, ch 3, skip 3 ch, dc in

next ch, work cl in next ch, dc in next ch, (ch 1, skip 1 ch, dc in next ch) 25 times; cl in next ch, dc in next ch, ch 3, skip 3 chs, dc in next ch, cl in next ch, dc in next ch. Ch 3, turn.
Row 2: Work cl in cl, dc in next dc, ch 2, sc in ch-3 loop, ch 2, dc in next dc, cl in cl, dc in next dc, (ch 1, dc in next dc) 25 times, cl in cl, dc in next dc, ch 2, sc in ch-3 loop, ch 2, dc in next dc, cl in cl, dc in top of ch-3. Ch 3, turn. *continued*

continued from page 217
Victoriana

Rows 3 and 4: Keeping to lacet pat as established, repeat *Row 2*.

Row 5: Work cl in cl, dc in next dc, ch 3, dc in next dc, cl in cl, dc in next dc, (ch 1, dc in next dc) 4 times, (cl in ch-1 space, dc in next dc) 6 times, (ch 1, dc in next dc) 5 times, (cl in ch-1 sp, dc in next dc) 6 times, (ch 1, dc in next dc) 4 times, cl in cl, dc in next dc, ch 3, dc in next dc, cl in cl, dc in last dc. Ch 3, turn.

Row 6: Work cl in cl, dc in dc, ch 3, dc in dc, cl in cl, dc in dc, (ch 1, dc in next dc) 3 times, cl in ch-1 space, (dc in dc, cl in cl) 6 times, dc in dc, cl in ch-1 space, (dc in dc, ch 1) 3 times, dc in dc, cl in ch-1 space, dc in dc; following chart 1, complete row.

Repeat *Rows 5–32* until 12 motifs are complete. Then work one more row with 25 open mesh across.

SIDE PANEL: *Note: Side panels are worked along one long side of the 3-motif (4, 5) panels and on both sides of the remaining motif panel. If you want to make any adjustments in the width of the bedspread, work more or fewer rows as needed in these panels (keep in mind that any adjustment must be made equally on **all** side panels). When working, note that point of motif is toward bottom of bed and take care that the side panel is worked accordingly for all pieces.*

Row 1: With one motif panel turned to work across one long edge, join thread in upper right-hand corner; ch 4 for first dc and ch 1, * dc in top of post of next dc, ch 1; repeat from * across entire side edge, end with dc in top of last dc post. Ch 4, turn.

Row 2: * Dc in next dc, ch 1; repeat from * across, end with dc in 3rd ch of starting ch–4. Repeat *Row 2* until the width of the entire piece (including the motif panel) measures 13½ (13½, 12½) inches.

Work side panel on all remaining strips the same. Then select one strip to work the side panel on opposite long side.

ASSEMBLING THE SPREAD: Using sewing thread, sew 4 (5–6) panel strips together. Referring to photo on *page 207*, the side panels are on the outside edges of the spread and alternate with the motif panels.

SIDE BORDER (Chart 2): *Note: Border is made in four separate pieces, one for each side of bedspread.* Ch 40.

Row 1: Work cl in 3rd ch from hook, dc in next ch, ch 2, skip 1 ch, sc in next ch, ch 2, skip 1 ch, dc in next ch, cl in next ch, dc in next ch, (ch 1, skip 1 ch, dc in next ch) 12 times, cl in next ch, dc in next ch, ch 1, skip 1 ch, dc in next ch, cl in next ch, dc in next ch. Ch 4, turn.

Row 2: Work cl in 4th ch from hook *(increase made)*, dc in next dc, ch 1, skip cl, dc in dc after cl, cl in next ch-1 space, dc in next dc, ch 1, skip cl, dc in next dc, (ch 1, dc in next dc) 12 times, cl in cl, dc in dc, ch 3, dc in dc, cl in cl, dc in top of turning ch. Ch 3, turn.

Row 3: Cl in cl, dc in dc, ch 3, dc in dc, cl in cl, dc in dc, (ch 1, dc in next dc) 13 times, ch 1, skip cl, dc in next dc, cl in ch-1 space, dc in dc, ch 1 skip cl, in last dc work dc, cl, and dc *(increase made)*. Ch 4, turn.

Rows 4 through 11: Continue to follow chart, work increase on even-numbered rows the same as *Row 2;* increase on odd-numbered rows the same as *Row 3*. At end of *Row 11*, ch 3 and turn.

Row 12: Work cl in cl, dc in dc, cl in ch-1 space, dc in dc, ch 1, skip cl, dc in dc, complete row following chart. *Row 12 of chart 2 completed.* Ch 3, turn.

Row 13: Following chart, work row with no increases. Ch 3, turn.

Row 14: Yo and draw up a loop in cl, yo and through 2 loops on hook, yo and draw up a loop in dc, yo and through 2 loops on hook, yo and through all loops on hook *(decrease made)*, cl in ch-1 space, complete row following chart.

Row 15: Following chart, work row to last dc, yo and draw up a loop in dc, yo and through 2 loops on hook, yo and draw up a loop in cl, yo and through 2 loops on hook, yo and through all loops on hook *(decrease made)*. Ch 3, turn.

Rows 16 through 23: Following chart, work as established decreasing as on *Rows 14 and 15*.

Repeat Rows 2–23 until border fits one long edge of assembled strips. The border must fit from corner to corner (the border corners are made separately) and may be eased slightly to fit. End border strip at Row 21, 22, or 23. With sewing thread, sew border to side of assembled strips. Make another border strip the same for opposite side of bedspread. Sew in place as before.

Remaining 2 border strips: Work as before, but work strips long enough so that the top of the straight edge sections overlap at corners. Sew border strips to remaining 2 sides of assembled strips.

BORDER CORNERS (Chart 3): Make 4. Ch 31.

Row 1: Work cl in 3rd ch from hook, dc in next ch, ch 1, skip 1 ch, dc in next ch, cl in next ch, dc in next ch, (ch 1, skip 1 ch, dc in next ch) 12 times. Turn.

Row 2: Ch 4 for first dc and ch 1, following chart complete row. Continue working to top of chart; work increases and decreases (as indicated on chart) the same as on side border. At top of chart, fasten off.

Grape Runner

Shown on page 208.
Finished size: 20x54 inches

MATERIALS

DMC 6-cord Cordonnet crochet
    cotton Size 100
No. 14 steel crochet hook
Firmly woven linen or cotton
    fabric, 2 strips each 6 inches
    wide and slightly longer than
    finished length desired for
    runner

Gauge: With suggested materials, 8
squares = 1 inch, 8 rows = 1 inch.

Adjusting the size: Grape motif
strip measures about 8 inches wide,
edging around outside of runner is 1
inch across at widest point. Runner
shown measures 20 inches wide and
about 1½ yards long, but any required length can be made by working necessary number of repeats
from chart. Width can be varied according to size of fabric strips used.

INSTRUCTIONS

Make a chain of approximately 200
sts, being careful not to work too
tightly.

Foundation Row: Dc in 8th ch
from hook, make (ch 2, skip 2 ch, dc
in next ch) across until a total of 62
spaces has been made. Ch 5, turn.

Row 1: Dc in 2nd dc (ch 2, dc in
next dc) across until a total of 24
spaces has been made. Work (2 dc
in next space, dc in next dc) twice,
(ch 2, dc in next dc) 8 times, (2 dc in
next space, dc in next dc) twice, (ch
2, dc in next dc) twice, (2 dc in next
space, dc in next dc) 3 times, (ch 2,
dc in next dc) 21 times, making last
dc in top of turning ch. Ch 5, turn.

Row 2: Dc in 2nd dc, (ch 2, dc in
next dc) for a total of 21 spaces, (ch
2, skip 2 dc, dc in next dc) 3 times, ch
2, dc in next dc, 2 dc in space, dc in
each of next 7 dc, 2 dc in space, (dc
in next dc, ch 2) 6 times, dc in next

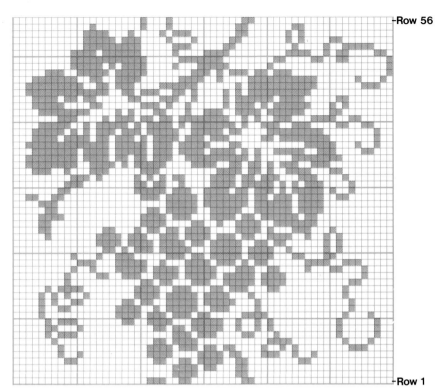

GRAPE RUNNER

dc, 2 dc in space, dc in next 4 dc, ch
2, skip 2 dc, dc in next dc. Work
across in spaces to end of row. Ch 5,
turn.

Continue working filet design as
shown on chart, *above,* having all
spaces consist of 2 dc with ch-2 between, and blocks composed of 2 dc
in place of the ch-2. Repeat Rows 1–
56 for length desired. After last row
of strip is made work ch 3, turn and
work a row of solid dc across end,
making 5 dc in opposite corner. Continue with solid dc across other 3
sides, having 5 dc in each corner.
Join in top of ch-3 and fasten off.

Joining crochet to fabric: Wash
and steam-press both crochet and
fabric to remove shrinkage. Hem
fabric neatly by hand or machine so
strips are same length as crochet.
Sew fabric carefully by hand along
each long side of crocheted strip.

Edging: Row 1: Ch 26, dc in 8th ch
from hook, (ch 2, skip 2 ch, dc in next
ch) 6 times. Ch 7, turn.

Row 2: Dc in last dc made (1
space increased), (ch 2, dc in next

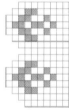

EDGING

dc) 6 times, ch 2, skip 2 chs, dc in 3rd
ch. Ch 5, turn.

Row 3: Dc in 2nd dc, (ch 2, dc in
next dc) 4 times, (2 dc in next space,
dc in next dc) twice, ch 2, skip 2 chs,
dc in next ch, ch 2, dtr (3 times over
hook) same as last dc. Ch 7, turn.

Row 4: Increase 1 space, follow
chart across.

Rows 5 and 6: Follow chart,
above, across, ch 5 to turn at end of
both rows.

continued

continued from page 219
Victoriana

Row 7: Work 5 spaces and 2 blocks as shown, ch 2, skip 2 dc, dc in next dc, dtr in next dc. Ch 5, turn.

Repeat *Rows 1–8* on chart until edging is long enough to go completely around runner, plus 8 inches to allow for fullness in corners and for shrinkage. Wash and press edging; sew first and last rows together. Sew edging by hand to outside of runner, gathering equal amounts of fullness in each corner.

Wreath of Grapes Needlepoint Chair

Shown on page 209.
Finished size: Design measures 13x13 inches on 14-count canvas

MATERIALS

14-count needlepoint canvas
3-ply Paternayan Persian wool
   yarn in the following colors: *(for grape design)* 690 dark leaf green, 691 leaf green, 692 medium leaf green, 650 dark olive, 652 medium olive, 480 rust, 430 dark brown, 310 dark grape, 311 grape, 312 medium grape, and 313 light grape; *(for background)* 321 plum, and 442 golden brown
Tapestry needle
Graph paper
Colored pencils or markers
Masking tape

INSTRUCTIONS

(*Note:* Dimensions of needlepoint canvas are determined by existing chair seat cover. Remove cover from chair and lay out flat. Measure height and width of cover. Add two inches along each side; purchase canvas accordingly.)

The wreath pattern, *page 221,* is one-fourth of the design. The entire design covers an area 188 stitches wide and is approximately square. The motif, when worked over 14-count canvas as shown on *page 209,* measures 13x13 inches. If dimensions do not fit your chair seat, adjust canvas size. Use canvas with a smaller thread count to make motif larger, and a canvas with a larger thread count to make motif smaller.

TO MAKE THE GRAPH: Referring to quadrant pattern, *page 221,* chart one repeat of motif on left-hand side of graph paper. Using partial elements of adjacent motifs as indicated on pattern (outlines of adjacent grapes), chart adjacent motifs at right angles to original motif. Fill in remaining motif on right-hand side of graph paper (which is an upside-down mirror image of first motif charted). Mark center of graph as indicated on chart.

STITCHING THE DESIGN: With sewing thread, baste center lines on piece of needlepoint canvas. Using completed graph as a stitch guide, work design in continental and basket-weave stitches, using 2 plies of Persian yarn. When complete wreath motif is stitched, fill in background of canvas with alternating vertical stripes of 321 plum and 442 golden brown, making each stripe one stitch wide.

Block needlepoint and upholster chair seat.

Needlepoint Footstools

Shown on page 210.
Finished size: Excluding the solid border, the small design measures 4¾ inches square; the larger design measures 7½x8 inches

MATERIALS

10-count canvas to measure 5
   inches wider on all sides than
   the stool you intend to cover
Persian yarn in the colors listed on
   the color key
Colored pencils
Graph paper
Masking tape
Tapestry needle
Needlepoint frame
Footstool

INSTRUCTIONS

Measure the top of the footstool, chair seat, or whatever you wish to cover in needlepoint. Allow an additional 5 inches of canvas on all four sides for mounting. Fold the canvas around the surface that will be covered to determine exactly how much background you will need to stitch in yarn. (*Note:* The more padded the top is, the more background will be needed to completely cover the curve.)

Use colored pencils to transfer the patterns, *page 222 or 223,* to graph paper, or work directly from our patterns. If your surface is small, use the smaller pattern.

Use strips of masking tape on all raw edges of the canvas to prevent raveling.

Find the middle of the pattern and the middle of the canvas. Begin working here.

Separate the Persian yarn into single strands. Use 3 strands on 10-count canvas.

The basic stitches of needlepoint are continental and basket weave (see diagrams, *page 252*). Both stitches slant from lower left to upper right across one intersection of needlepoint canvas. They look identical from the top of the canvas. Continental is worked in straight rows, usually from left to right. Continental tends to pull the canvas out of shape, and should be used in small areas or as an outline stitch. Basket weave is worked in diagonal rows and is designed to fill in larger areas.

Work the entire design in the continental stitch. Using a needlepoint frame will eliminate much of the distortion that occurs when stitching.

Fill in the background with the basket-weave stitch and black yarn.

Steam-press or block the needlepoint to return the canvas to its original shape. Mount the needlepoint as desired.

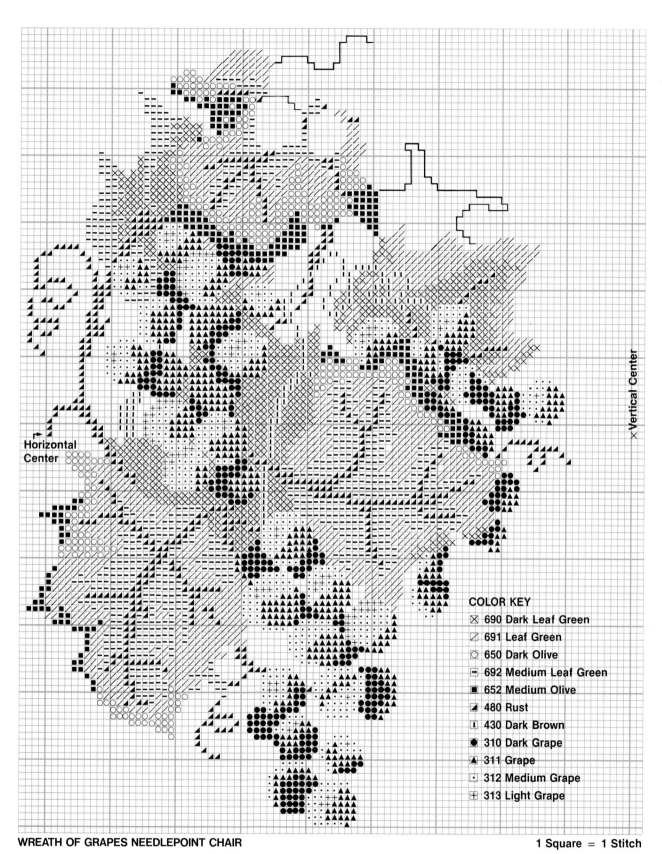

Horizontal Center

× Vertical Center

COLOR KEY

⊠ 690 Dark Leaf Green
⊘ 691 Leaf Green
◎ 650 Dark Olive
⊟ 692 Medium Leaf Green
▪ 652 Medium Olive
◪ 480 Rust
⊡ 430 Dark Brown
● 310 Dark Grape
▲ 311 Grape
⊡ 312 Medium Grape
⊞ 313 Light Grape

WREATH OF GRAPES NEEDLEPOINT CHAIR

1 Square = 1 Stitch

continued from page 220
Victoriana

Needlepoint Bench

Shown on page 211.
Finished size: 12½x34 inches, excluding solid border

MATERIALS

10-count canvas large enough to
   cover the bench chosen

Paternayan persian yarn in the
   colors listed on the color key
Colored pencils
Graph paper
Masking tape
Tapestry needle
Needlepoint frame
Bench

INSTRUCTIONS

Because of the large numbers of
floss colors used, both symbols and
colors were required for chart on
pages 223, 224, and 225. Use colored
pencils to transfer design to graph
paper. It was necessary to divide
chart into three parts. Realign carefully when transferring.

Use general stitching instructions
for footstools, *page 220,* to complete
design and to finish bench cover.

LARGE NEEDLEPOINT FOOTSTOOL

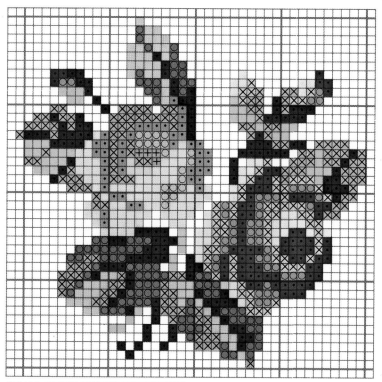

SMALL NEEDLEPOINT FOOTSTOOL

**COLOR KEY FOR LARGE AND
SMALL NEEDLEPOINT FOOTSTOOLS**

DMC FLOSS	PATERNAYAN YARN
Blue-Greens	
■ 500	520
◎ 502	522
☒ 503	523
☐ 504	525
Greens	
■ 935	601
☒ 470	693
☐ 472	694
Pinks	
■ 3685	910
◎ 3687	912
☒ 3354	906
☐ 761	934
Corals	
▨ 3328	931
◎ 356	871
☒ 758	933
☐ 754	491
Yellow	
▨ 676	753

FOR LARGE CHART ONLY

DMC FLOSS	PATERNAYAN YARN
▨ 301	880
◎ 436	731
☒ 738	735

FOR SMALL CHART ONLY

DMC FLOSS	PATERNAYAN YARN
▩ 680	751

COLOR KEY FOR NEEDLEPOINT BENCH

- ⊡ White (263)
- ⊞ Light Beige (465)
- ☒ Beige (464)
- ■ Dark Beige (462)
- ☐ Light Pink (946)
- ⊡ Pink (945)
- ☒ Rose (943)
- ▤ Red (941)
- ■ Maroon (940)
- ☐ Light Lavender (325)
- ☒ Medium Lavender (324)
- ■ Purple (322)
- ☐ Yellow (715)
- ⊡ Dark Yellow (713)
- ☒ Orange (802)
- ▭ Old Gold (753)
- ◎ Dark Old Gold (750)
- ■ Rust (722)
- ⊡ Light Tan (494)
- ☒ Brown (490)
- ■ Dark Brown (483)
- ■ Black (220)
- ☐ Light Green (654)
- ⊡ Medium Green (653)
- ☒ Avocado (651)
- ▭ Light Blue-Green (605)
- ◎ Blue-Green (604)

NEEDLEPOINT BENCH

NEEDLEPOINT BENCH

COLOR KEY FOR NEEDLEPOINT BENCH

⊡ White (263)	▨ Light Pink (946)	■ Maroon (940)
⊞ Light Beige (465)	▣ Pink (945)	▨ Light Lavender (325)
⊠ Beige (464)	⊠ Rose (943)	⊠ Medium Lavender (324)
■ Dark Beige (462)	▨ Red (941)	■ Purple (322)

Yellow (715)	◎ Dark Old Gold (750)	■ Dark Brown (483)	⊠ Avocado (651)
⊡ Dark Yellow (713)	▨ Rust (722)	■ Black (220)	⊟ Light Blue-Green (605)
⊠ Orange (802)	⊡ Light Tan (494)	▨ Light Green (654)	◎ Blue-Green (604)
⊟ Old Gold (753)	⊠ Brown (490)	⊡ Medium Green (653)	

THE FLOWERING OF AMERICAN PATCHWORK

◆

FLORAL-PATTERN QUILTS

Patchwork is perhaps the most distinctive of American crafts, and floral motifs—both pieced and appliquéd—are among the oldest and most perennially popular of all patchwork designs.

THE
FLOWERING OF
AMERICAN
PATCHWORK

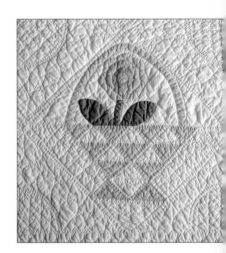

In the true folk-art tradition, American quilters based many of their most beautiful designs on natural motifs.

A few floral-inspired patterns were pieced geometrics, like the familiar Grandmother's Flower Garden design on pages 226–227. Many more were executed entirely in appliqué, like the Peony Quilt on page 227. But, some of the loveliest floral patterns required a mastery of *both* patchwork techniques.

The Flower Basket Quilt pictured here has pieced baskets and border, while the handles and flowers are appliquéd. The quilting on this coverlet is exceptionally fine.

Instructions for quilts in this section begin on page 238.

THE FLOWERING OF AMERICAN PATCHWORK

Tulips, with their graceful shapes and brilliant colors, are a favorite with quilt makers. Among the more than two dozen traditional designs based on this blossom are the Tulip Garden pattern, *opposite,* and the more stylized Dutch Tulip design, *below*. The Tulip Garden pattern is probably an adaptation of a mid-19th-century design, and the Dutch Tulip dates from the 1930s.

THE FLOWERING OF AMERICAN PATCHWORK

Red and green appliqué designs on a white or muslin ground were popular quilts in the early 19th century. Many of these quilts were made with nine rose blocks set on the diagonal and encircled by vines or swag borders, like the Tea Rose quilt shown *below*.

Other common names for this design were Whig or Democrat Rose, California Rose, and Rose of Sharon. Quilters often personalized this familiar pattern by rearranging design elements to suit individual tastes.

At the turn of the century, the simpler field flowers became popular as quilt motifs. Often, flowers and foliage were appliquéd in an overall garland design (rather than in blocks) as in the Daisy Chain quilt, *opposite*.

THE FLOWERING OF AMERICAN PATCHWORK

From the Golden Age of Greece and Rome through the running of the latest local marathon, the wreath has been a symbol of honor, respect, and achievement. It is hardly surprising, therefore, that wreaths of flowers and foliage should appear as common elements in the traditional design vocabulary of quilting.

Floral wreaths were especially popular motifs for album, presentation, and other special occasion quilts, and a wreath pattern quilt was almost always counted among the 12 coverlets in every young girl's dowry chest.

A quick survey of traditional patchwork patterns turns up wreath designs of bluebells, carnations, dahlias, geraniums, pansies, violets, hollyhocks, dogwood, moonflowers, columbine, and—of course—the ever-favorite rose. It is often difficult to distinguish among the motifs, since the stylized flowers and buds in one pattern often resemble those in others.

In the quilt pictured here—a variation on the Rose of Sharon wreath—the fine stitching and intricately pieced teardrop border mark it as an especially elegant example of the genre.

235

THE FLOWERING OF AMERICAN PATCHWORK

Rose designs of every description have been popular throughout the history of American quilt making, and the origins of the various pattern names are as intriguing as the designs themselves.

Some names are strictly descriptive (Moss Rose, Tudor Rose, and Prairie Rose, for example); others honor a region (Ohio, Virginia, and Topeka Rose are but three).

A few pattern names are fiercely political (a splendid Radical Rose design dates from the Civil War era), but most are totally idiosyncratic. Pictured here, for example, is a handsome quilt in the Seth Thomas Rose pattern—apparently so named in honor of a 19th-century Connecticut clockmaker.

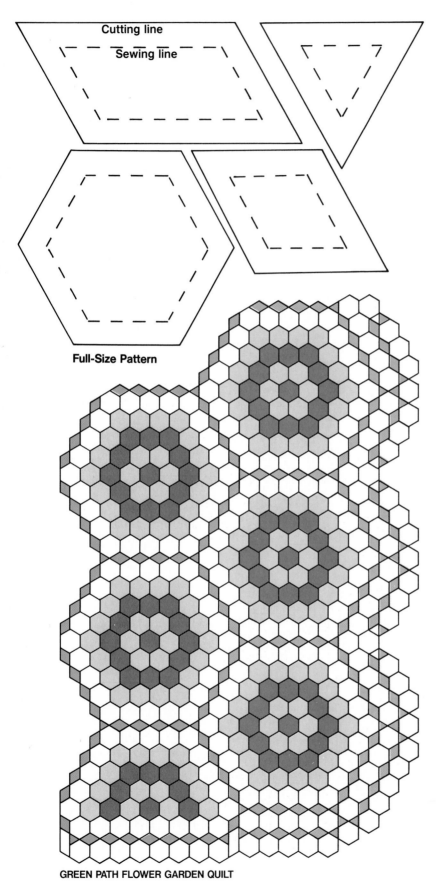

Cutting line

Sewing line

Full-Size Pattern

GREEN PATH FLOWER GARDEN QUILT

Green Path Flower Garden Quilt

Shown on pages 226–227.
Finished size: 82x92 inches

MATERIALS

½ yard of solid yellow 44-inch-wide fabric for flower centers and second rows of flower petals

¼ yard *each* of solid pastel 44-inch-wide fabrics in the following colors: green, pink, lavender, peach, orange, blue, and rose for second row of flower petals

Scraps of assorted print pastel fabrics to coordinate with solid pastel fabric for first and third row of flower petals (enough of one fabric to cut 24 hexagons)

4¾ yards of white cotton fabric for hexagons, triangles, and parallelograms

3½ yards of light green fabric for paths and bias binding

6 yards of white cotton fabric for backing

Cardboard or plastic for templates

Quilt batting

INSTRUCTIONS

The center of pieced top consists of 46 flower blocks. Each *block* is made by joining 61 individual hexagons as follows: one yellow for center, 24 pastel print hexagons for first and third rows of flower petals, 12 solid pastel hexagons for second row of petals, and 24 white hexagons for borders around flowers.

Along short sides of quilt are six partial flowers that consist of one center hexagon, 14 pastel print hexagons for first and third rows of petals, seven solid-color hexagons for second row of petals, and 13 white hexagons for borders.

A single row of green diamonds circle flowers like a path, and a double row of green paths complete quilt border.

TO BEGIN: To make templates, trace *cutting line* of hexagon, triangle, diamond, and parallelogram patterns, *opposite,* onto cardboard or a plastic lid; cut out. Next, trace *seam line* of shapes and cut templates for marking stitching lines. (To ensure accurate piecing, replace templates as they become worn.)

CUTTING INSTRUCTIONS: Beginning with cutting line template, trace hexagons on wrong side of each fabric. Place templates on fabric so that two parallel sides of hexagon are aligned along horizontal or vertical grain line of fabric. Center seam line template inside each larger hexagon and trace around it.

Cut hexagons from fabrics as follows: 52 hexagons from yellow for centers. Cut 594 assorted solid-color hexagons for second row of petals. Cut in multiples of 12 (same color) for each of 46 center flowers and in multiples of seven for six border flowers.

Cut 1,188 assorted print fabric hexagons for first and third rows of petals. Cut in multiples of 24 for center flowers and in multiples of 14 for border flowers. When cutting from print fabrics, you may want to center a flower on some hexagons. This is an effective use of fabric.

From white fabric, trace and cut 12 parallelograms and 24 triangles. Cut 1,608 white hexagons for paths on 52 center blocks. (Additional white hexagons will be needed for border after center blocks and partial flowers are sewn together.)

From green, cut 834 diamonds and 222 triangles.

For ease in assembly, stack hexagons for *each* of the flowers and string them together on a knotted strand of thread.

BLOCK PIECING: Referring to diagram, *opposite,* piece flower blocks as follows: Sew one of print hexagon sides to yellow center hexagon, right sides together. Stitch from seam line to seam line, leaving seam allowances free. Continue to add hexagons until first row of petals is complete. Press seams *around* circle to one side and seams at *top* of yellow hexagon toward center of flower. Add second and third rows of petals pressing seams when each

row is completed. Then add 24 white hexagons to outer edge of each flower following the diagram, *opposite.*

Piece partial flower blocks together in same manner, referring to diagram, *opposite.*

ASSEMBLY: Join 46 blocks by adding green diamonds and triangles between flower blocks. There will be four rows with seven blocks and three rows with six blocks. Then add three partial flowers to *each* of top and bottom edges. Follow piecing diagram, *opposite,* to add border. Note position of parallelograms and small triangles as you add border to partial flower sides.

FINISHING: Cut backing and batting materials 2 inches larger than quilt top. Sandwich batting between top and backing, and baste together. Quilt ¼ inch inside seam lines of each hexagon shape.

Trim backing and batting even with quilt top. Make bias binding from green fabric and bind quilt. Sew binding to follow quilt edges to shape scallops.

Peony Quilt

Shown on page 227.
Finished quilt: Approximate size is 67⅝x90¼ inches.

MATERIALS

3½ yards of yellow fabric
4½ yards of medium green fabric
1¼ yards of hot pink fabric
5½ yards of backing fabric
Tracing paper; graph paper
Cardboard or plastic for templates
Water-erasable marking pen
Pink embroidery floss
Quilt batting

Block Diagram

INSTRUCTIONS

All patterns are *finished* size; add ¼-inch seam allowances when cutting pieces from fabric unless directed otherwise.

TO BEGIN: Draw a 16-inch square on graph paper for pattern piece X. Draw a diagonal line through square to make two triangles; one triangle is pattern piece Y. Draw another diagonal line to divide second triangle into two smaller triangles; small triangle is pattern piece Z. Make templates for X, Y, and Z.

To make template for triangular base of peony block, draw a 5½-inch square on graph paper. Draw a diagonal line through square to make 2 triangles. Make a template for triangle.

Trace and make templates for flower and leaf patterns, *page 240.*

Use block drawing, *above,* as a placement guide for appliqué.

CUTTING INSTRUCTIONS: From yellow fabric, cut 10 squares using template X. From remaining yellow fabric, cut approximately nine yards of 1½-inch-wide bias strips for quilt binding.

From green fabric, use template Y to cut 26 triangles with *long* side of triangles on straight of fabric grain. Use template Z to cut four triangles with triangle legs on straight of fabric grain. Use triangular base template to cut 10 triangles with triangle legs on straight of grain.

continued from page 239
**The Flowering of
American Patchwork**

Use leaf template to cut 20 leaves. From remaining green fabric, cut approximately 7 yards of ¾-inch-wide bias strips for stems. Press bias in thirds lengthwise to about ¼-inch finished width, concealing bottom raw edge under top fold.

From pink fabric, cut 30 star-shape peony flowers. (Note: Flowers on quilt shown were appliquéd with embroidery floss in a buttonhole stitch. If you plan to appliqué using a buttonhole stitch, *do not add seam allowances when cutting.*)

BLOCK PIECING: Using a water-erasable marking pen, lightly trace block drawing onto a yellow square as a placement guide for appliqué pieces.

Baste stems in place, cutting green bias to length as you work. Baste under seam allowance, around leaves, and along long edge of triangular base. Pin leaves and triangular base in position. Pin flowers in place.

Using embroidery floss, buttonhole-stitch around each flower. Keep stitches closely spaced to prevent fraying. Blindstitch stems, leaves, and top of base. Remove basting threads.

ASSEMBLY: Appliqué 10 of the peony blocks.

Peony blocks are set in a zigzag set. Referring to assembly diagram, *below,* sew blocks and triangles into three rows. Join rows to complete quilt top.

FINISHING: Mark quilt top in a diagonal grid of 1¼-inch squares. Piece quilt back from backing fabric. Layer and baste quilt top, batting, and quilt back together; quilt.

When quilting is complete, trim excess batting and quilt back even with quilt top. Bind outer edges of quilt with yellow bias binding.

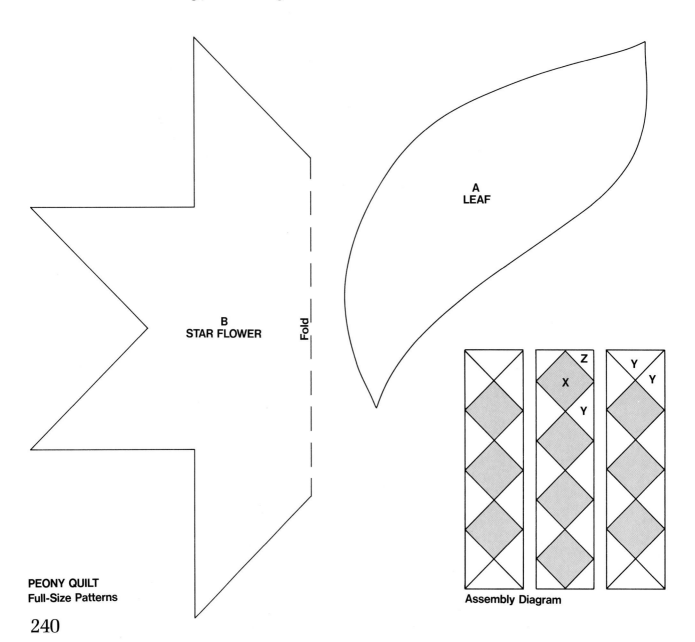

**A
LEAF**

**B
STAR FLOWER**

Fold

PEONY QUILT
Full-Size Patterns

Assembly Diagram

FLOWER BASKET QUILT

continued from page 241
**The Flowering of
American Patchwork**

Flower Basket
Quilt

Shown on pages 228–229.
Finished size: 74¼x88½ inches

MATERIALS
1¼ yards of yellow cotton
  fabric (for baskets)
11 yards of muslin (for front
  and backing)
Fabric scraps (¼ to ½ yard
  each) in light, medium, and dark
  reds, blues, purples, greens, and
  oranges (for flowers, stems,
  and leaves)
Embroidery floss in assorted
  colors
Yellow bias binding
Quilt batting
Plastic lids or cardboard (for
  templates)

INSTRUCTIONS
The quilt shown consists of 20 basket blocks, each 10½ inches square, set on diagonal (with muslin blocks between) to form five horizontal rows, each with four pattern blocks. A multicolored sawtooth border (pieced from fabrics used for flowers joined to muslin triangles) set between muslin strips surrounds the blocks. Edges are finished with yellow binding.

CUTTING INSTRUCTIONS: Cut two 44x95-inch pieces of muslin for quilt backing. Border measurements that follow include ¼-inch seam allowances. From each length, cut a strip 3½ inches wide (for outermost border). Set backing and strips aside.

From remaining muslin, cut two 3½x70½-inch strips (for outermost border), plus two 3x59¾-inch strips, and two 3¼x79½-inch strips (for inner border). Set strips aside.

Next, draw a 10½-inch square on paper; cut it in half diagonally. Use one triangle as a pattern for half-blocks that are (1) set together with baskets to make complete pattern

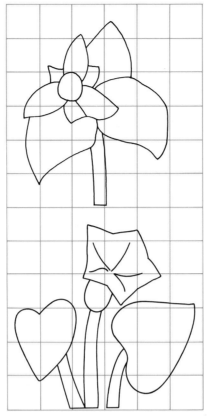

1 Square = 1 Inch

blocks and (2) set into ends of rows along edges of quilt. Adding ¼-inch seam allowances all around, cut 34 large triangles—20 with legs of triangle on straight of fabric grain (for pattern blocks), and 14 with long side of triangle on straight of fabric grain (for edges of quilt). Set aside and label stacks of triangles.

Cut remaining paper triangle (see above) in half again, to make a small triangle equal to one-fourth

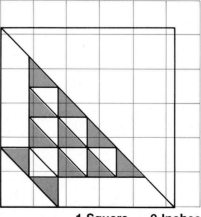

1 Square = 2 Inches

size of block. Adding ¼-inch seam allowances, cut four quarter-blocks for four corners of quilt. Set aside.

BLOCK PIECING: Enlarge basket pattern, *below*. (To make patterns for small triangles, draw a 1¾-inch square. Cut square in half diagonally; trace one triangle onto plastic lid or cardboard for template. For triangle at base of basket, cut a 3½-inch square in half diagonally; trace triangle onto template and cut out.)

Adding ¼-inch seam allowances, cut pieces for 20 baskets from muslin and yellow fabric. Stitch pieces together, referring to pattern and photograph. Note that baskets form half of each 10½-inch-square pattern block.

For basket handle, cut a yellow 1½x15-inch bias strip. Fold strip in thirds lengthwise and press. Appliqué basket handle to top portion of block (see photograph).

Flowers in baskets are simple shapes cut from solid-color fabrics and appliquéd onto large muslin triangles that form top half of each pattern block.

Enlarge flower patterns, *page 241* and *left,* and use these patterns to add flowers to basket blocks. On quilt shown, several blocks are the same. Repeat your favorites from designs given.

Cut pattern pieces from a variety of solid-color fabrics, adding ¼-inch seam allowances. Turn under seam allowances, baste, and appliqué designs to top halves of basket blocks.

Then, embellish motifs with simple embroidery stitches using contrasting floss.

To assemble block, pin together pieced basket and appliquéd triangle; stitch, using ¼-inch seams. Press seams. Make 20 blocks.

ASSEMBLY: Working from upper left to lower right, seam appliquéd pattern, and plain blocks and triangles together in eight rows (from upper left to lower right) as follows. *Row 1:* Join long side of quarter-block to upper left side of basket block, then stitch muslin half-blocks (triangles) to lower left and upper right sides of basket block.

Note: Stitch half-blocks in place so long side will fall along perimeter of quilt top before adding borders.

Row 2: Join muslin triangle to basket block, add a muslin block, a basket block, and a second muslin triangle.

Row 3: Stitch two plain blocks between three basket blocks; add muslin triangles to ends. *Row 4:* Sew three plain blocks between four basket blocks; add muslin triangle to lower left end and muslin quarter-block to upper right end.

Row 5: Assemble same as Row 4, except sew half-block to upper right end of row and quarter-block to lower left end.

Rows 6-8: Assemble same as Rows 3-5, except reverse position of triangles at ends.

Next, sew 3x59¾ muslin inner border strips to quilt top and bottom, easing quilt to fit as needed. Sew 3¼x79½-inch borders to sides.

Cut and piece sufficient triangles from colored fabrics and muslin for sawtooth border, using small triangle used for basket as a pattern. Join pieces into squares by stitching a colored triangle to a muslin one along long edges, then sew squares together into strips. Use 37 combined triangles for top and bottom borders. Use 47 combined triangles for side borders. Sew borders to top and bottom, then to sides of quilt.

Add muslin outermost border strips to top and bottom of quilt top, then to sides.

FINISHING: Finally, sandwich batting between quilt top and backing. Baste all layers together and quilt as desired. Finish quilt by binding edges with yellow bias binding.

TULIP QUILT Block Diagram

Tulip Quilt
Shown on page 230.
Finished quilt: 73x83½ inches

MATERIALS
5¾ yards of muslin
2¼ yards of light red fabric
1 yard of gold fabric
2¼ yards of light teal fabric
5½ yards of backing fabric
Teal embroidery floss
Cardboard; tracing paper
Quilt batting

INSTRUCTIONS
TO BEGIN: Trace patterns, *right;* make templates from cardboard. For center ring design, draw 4¼-inch-diameter circle; draw 3¾-inch-diameter circle within first circle. Make template for ring. Patterns are finished size; add ¼-inch seam allowances when cutting fabric.

CUTTING INSTRUCTIONS: From muslin, cut two 4x79-inch borders

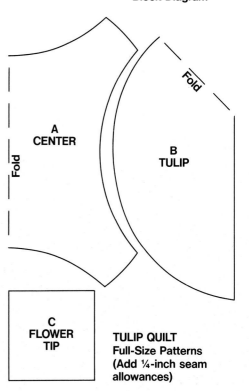

A CENTER
Fold
Fold

B TULIP

C FLOWER TIP

TULIP QUILT
Full-Size Patterns
(Add ¼-inch seam allowances)

243

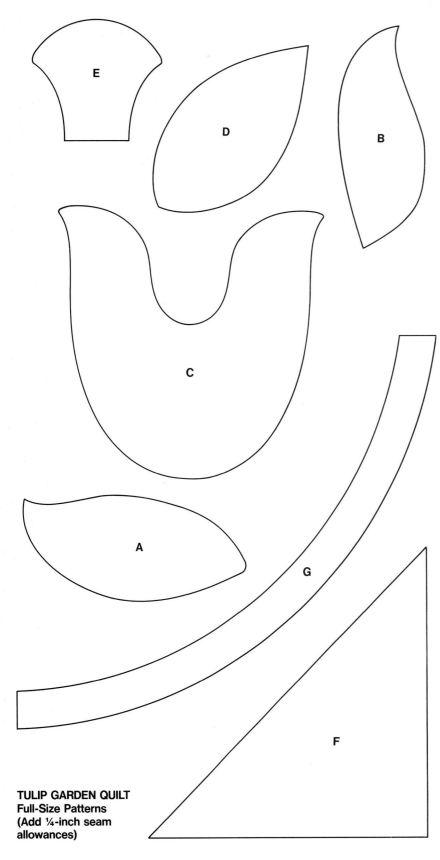

continued from page 243
**The Flowering of
American Patchwork**

and two 4x76-inch borders. Next, cut forty-two 11-inch squares. Measurements for borders and squares include ¼-inch seam allowances.

From gold fabric, cut 42 center pieces and 168 flower tips.

From red fabric, cut 168 tulips.

From light teal fabric, cut 42 rings; cut two 2x68-inch borders and two 2x76-inch borders. From remaining teal fabric, cut 9 yards of 1½-inch-wide bias for binding.

ASSEMBLY: Baste under edges of appliqué pieces, clipping where necessary. Referring to placement diagram, *page 243,* pin shapes to muslin squares; appliqué in place. Using three strands of floss, make five small blanket stitches at inner corner of each tulip.

Stitch squares into six long strips of seven blocks each. Join strips together. Quilt top without borders measures approximately 63½x74 inches, with seam allowances.

Sew 2x76-inch teal borders to sides; trim excess. Sew 2x68-inch teal borders to top and bottom; trim.

Sew 4x79-inch muslin borders to sides of quilt and 4x76-inch borders to top and bottom; trim excess.

FINISHING: Piece together quilt back. Layer and baste top, batting, and back together; quilt as desired. When quilting is complete, trim batting and back even with quilt top. Bind edges with teal bias.

Tulip Garden Quilt
Shown on page 231.
Finished size: 84½x100½ inches

MATERIALS
7 yards of white cotton fabric
3 yards of green cotton fabric
2 yards of pink cotton fabric
¼ yard pink of print cotton fabric
6 yards of backing fabric

**TULIP GARDEN QUILT
Full-Size Patterns
(Add ¼-inch seam
allowances)**

INSTRUCTIONS

Quilt is made up of 20 tulip blocks (11½ inches square, finished), set 4 blocks by 5 blocks alternated with white squares.

CUTTING INSTRUCTIONS: Make templates from plastic or heavy paper for patterns A–G, *opposite*. Because patterns are finished size, add ¼-inch seam allowances when cutting. Measurements for borders include ¼-inch seam allowances, and borders will be trimmed to length when added to quilt top.

From white fabric, cut four borders, each 3¾x104 inches. Make a template for an 11½-inch square. Adding ¼-inch seam allowances, cut 32 squares. Divide square template into two triangles. Divide one triangle into two small triangles. For blocks, cut 14 large triangles with long side of triangle on straight of fabric grain, adding seam allowances for corners. Cut four small triangles with legs of triangles on straight of fabric grain, adding seam allowances when cutting.

From remaining white fabric, cut 11 yards of 1¼-inch-wide bias for quilt binding.

From green fabric, cut four borders, each 3¾x104 inches. Cut 40 of pattern piece A, 20 of F, 60 of D, and 120 of B. From remaining green fabric, cut 8 yards of 1-inch-wide bias. Fold in thirds to ⅜ inch wide; press.

From pink fabric, cut eight borders, *each* measuring 3¾x52½ inches. Cut 60 D tulips.

From pink print, cut 60 of E.

BLOCK PIECING: Fold a white square diagonally each way and press lightly to form creases across diagonal of block. Cut a 6-inch length of green bias for main stem and a 7-inch length for cross stem. Center and baste 6½-inch bias strip on one fold with center of strip at center of block. Position template G 1¾ inches from bottom of stem and mark around template with a water-erasable pen. Baste 6½-inch bias strip inside marked outline running strip under main stem. Appliqué an A leaf to each side of main stem up 1¾ inches from point where main

TULIP APPLIQUÉ QUILT

stem and G meet. Appliqué an F triangle to bottom of stem.

Referring to photograph, *page 231,* position a C tulip at end of each stem. Slip two B leaves, one to each side, under each tulip. Tuck an E under top edge of each tulip. Center a D piece over each tulip. Appliqué all pieces in place.

ASSEMBLY: Sew 20 tulip appliqué blocks. Referring to photograph, lay appliqué blocks and plain blocks into five rows of four blocks each. Fill in outer edges with large triangles; place small triangles at corners. Sew together in diagonal rows.

To make borders, sew pairs of pink border strips together to form four 3¾x104-inch strips. Sew border strips into four borders, each with a white strip between a pink and green strip. Fold each border unit in half lengthwise to determine center. Matching center of a border unit to center of a quilt side, sew borders to sides of quilt top. Miter corners and trim off excess borders.

Mark each plain square with a 10- or 11-inch-diameter feathered circle. Mark outer setting triangles with portions of circle. Mark border with a feathered cable; fill in unmarked areas of border with a diagonal grid of 1-inch squares. Mark appliqué blocks with a diagonal grid of 1-inch squares. Piece backing fabric to size. Layer quilt top, batting, and backing; baste. Quilt on marked designs and outline-quilt ⅛ inch from all appliquéd pieces. Trim excess batting and backing; round off corners slightly; bind outer edges.

Daisy Chain Quilt

Shown on page 232.
Finished size: 86x100 inches

MATERIALS

5 yards of yellow cotton fabric
5 yards of white cotton fabric
1¼ yards of green cotton fabric
9 yards of backing fabric
Batting
Water-erasable pen

INSTRUCTIONS

Make templates for patterns A–D on *page 246.* Patterns are finished size; add ¼-inch seam allowances before cutting from fabric. Cutting dimensions for borders and center panels include seam allowances.

CUTTING INSTRUCTIONS: From yellow fabric, cut two 14½x100½-inch borders, two 14½x58½-inch borders, two 12x60½-inch borders, and two 8x22½-inch borders. From remaining yellow fabric, cut petals for 10 flowers; cut 70 of B and 40 of A. Each flower is made of seven B petals and four A petals arranged in random order. Cut 26 of C for centers of white daisies.

From white fabric, cut four pieces, each 17½x24½ inches. Cut two 6½x74-inch borders and two 6½x60-inch borders. Borders will be trimmed to length when added to quilt. Cut 11½ yards of 1-inch-wide bias for quilt binding. From remaining white fabric, cut 182 of B and 104 of A for 26 daisies. Cut 10 of C for centers of yellow daisies.

From green fabric, cut 64 of D. From green fabric, cut 17 yards of 1-inch-wide bias. Fold bias in thirds to a width of about ⅜ inch and press.

ASSEMBLY: Sew 8x22½-inch borders to 12½x60½-inch borders to form an open-centered 46½x60½-inch yellow rectangle.

Sew four 17½x24½-inch panels into a 34½x48½-inch rectangle for quilt center. Round off four corners starting about 6 inches from corner (a dinner plate is a good guide).

Position and baste rectangle over yellow frame so that 6½ inches of *continued*

245

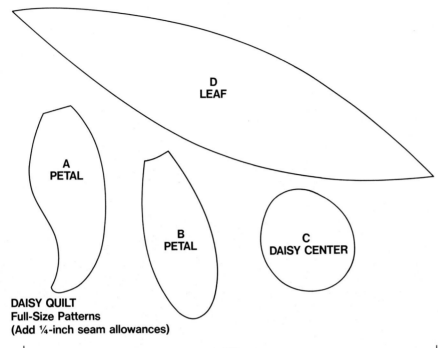

D
LEAF

A
PETAL

B
PETAL

C
DAISY CENTER

DAISY QUILT
Full-Size Patterns
(Add ¼-inch seam allowances)

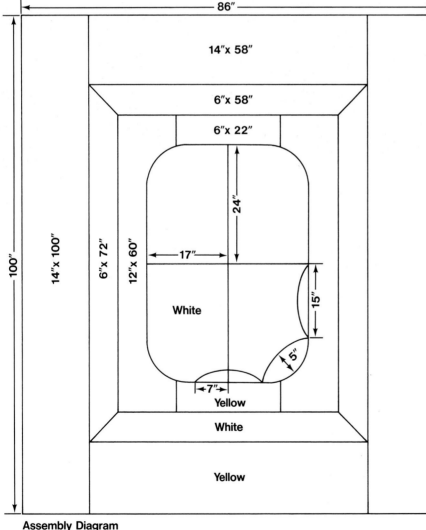

86"

14"x 58"

6"x 58"

6"x 22"

24"

17"

15"

White

5"

7"

Yellow

White

Yellow

14"x 100"

6"x 72"

12"x 60"

100"

Assembly Diagram

continued from page 245
The Flowering of
American Patchwork

yellow quilt border extends evenly around frame except at corners. It is not necessary to turn under raw edges of rectangle.

Mark vine positions on white rectangle 15 inches above and below each side seam. Mark vine positions 7 inches to each side of vertical seam at top and bottom of panel. Baste green bias in gentle curves that return to edge at marked positions. Corner curves are 5 inches from outer edge at widest point; other curves are 2½ inches from outer edge at widest point.

Mark positions for daisy centers at middle of each curve. Center daisies are 4–5 inches in from vine curves. White daisies are centered in yellow border. In quilt center, baste 4–5 inches of long bias stems in soft curves from curved bias toward daisy centers. Baste bias stems out toward daisies in yellow border. Referring to photograph, *page 232,* appliqué four D leaves to center sides and three leaves at end of each curve, with one leaf toward center and two leaves in yellow border (32 total of D).

Arrange yellow A and B daisy petals to form 10 daisies for quilt center. Each flower is made of four A and seven B petals. Appliqué petals in place covering bias stem ends. Appliqué a white center C in middle of each flower. Repeat for 10 white daisies in yellow border.

Position and baste green bias around edge of white rectangle to cover all raw edges. Appliqué all bias pieces. Complete all appliqué for quilt top; trim excess yellow fabric from quilt back, leaving ¼-inch seam allowance.

Sew white borders to quilt top; miter corners and trim off excess borders. Quilt top should measure about 58½x72½ inches, including seam allowances. Sew 14½x58½-inch borders to top and bottom; sew 14½x100½-inch borders to sides.

To complete one corner, appliqué design, then position and appliqué a 36-inch length of green bias 6 inches from border seam with 18 inches extending to each side from corner. Appliqué four D leaves at vine corner; appliqué a D leaf to each side of vine 5 inches in from *each* end of vine. Appliqué a white daisy on each portion of vine with daisy center 7 inches from corner. Appliqué a daisy at each end of vine. Repeat for remaining three corners (total of 32 D and 16 white daisies).

Mark top for quilting as desired. Quilt on *page 232* features spider web quilting in center panel, and daisy and leaf shapes in border.

Piece quilt back. Layer top, batting, and backing; baste. Quilt as desired. Bind outer edges.

Tea Rose Appliqué Quilt

Shown on page 233.
Finished size: 88¾x92¾ inches

MATERIALS

14½ yards of white cotton for top, borders, and back
6½ yards of green cotton
1¾ yards of red fabric
¾ yard of yellow fabric
½ yard of pink fabric
Quilt batting

INSTRUCTIONS

Refer to rose block, *right,* for placement of pattern pieces.

Make patterns from templates A–H on *page 248.* Patterns are finished size; add ¼-inch seam allowances to pieces before cutting from fabric.

CUTTING INSTRUCTIONS: From white fabric, cut three pieces, *each* 44x94 inches, for quilt back and borders. From one piece, cut a center back panel 8x94 inches and three borders, *each* 4½x94 inches. Border measurements include ¼-inch seam allowances and will be trimmed to exact length when added to quilt top. Sew 8x94-inch panel between two 44x94-inch panels for back.

To cut squares and triangles for top, make a 20-inch square template. Template and triangles made from it *are finished size. Be sure to add ¼-*

TEA ROSE APPLIQUÉ QUILT

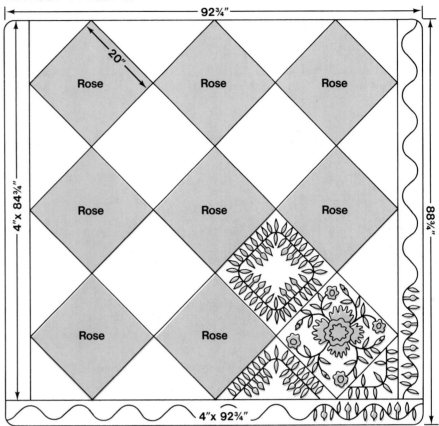

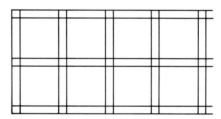

Quilting is double line grid of 1½" squares with second line ¼" from first line. Grid is set square.

TEA ROSE APPLIQUÉ QUILT

Block Diagram

inch seam allowances before cutting pieces from fabric.

From remaining white fabric, use 20-inch square template to mark and cut 13 squares. Divide template diagonally into two triangles. Use a triangle to cut eight triangles with straight of fabric grain along long side of triangle. Divide triangle template into two smaller triangles. With small triangle, cut four triangles with short sides on fabric grain.

From red, cut nine of B; 36 of G; 126 of H. From pink, cut 36 of D. From yellow, cut nine of C; 36 of E.

From green fabric, cut 650 of F (small leaves) for appliqué blocks. Cut about 84 additional leaves for borders. Cut 36 of A (large leaves) for rose blocks. Cut approximately 50 yards of 1-inch-wide bias. Reserve 10½ yards of bias for binding. Fold and press remaining bias in thirds to a finished width of ⅜ inch.

BLOCK PIECING: Appliqué four A leaves in place. Cut off four 9-inch
continued

F

B

C

D

E

G

A

H

TEA ROSE APPLIQUÉ QUILT
Full-Size Patterns
(Add ¼-inch seam allowances)

248

continued from page 247
**The Flowering of
American Patchwork**

and four 6-inch pieces of vine from ⅜-inch green bias. Appliqué vine pieces. Sew 22 F leaves in indicated positions along vine. Add an F leaf to end of each 6-inch vine (4 total). Appliqué a G bud over each end leaf. Appliqué a B flower, then a C flower in center. Appliqué a D flower, then an E flower at end of each 9-inch vine. Make nine blocks.

BLOCK PIECING: Draw a 13-inch square on heavy paper, rounding off corners slightly. Use square to draw placement guides for vine.

Center and baste vine over placement line. Approximately 52 inches of ⅜-inch vine is needed for each square, 26 inches of vine for *each* large ½-block triangle, and 16 inches of vine for each corner block.

Forty-eight F leaves and 12 H buds are used for each full vine block. Refer to photograph, *page 233,* for leaf placement. Appliqué buds, leaves, and vine in place. Repeat for four blocks.

Appliqué eight half-block triangles with one-half of full block design. Twenty-two F leaves and six H buds are needed for each half-block.

Appliqué four corner blocks with corner portion of vine design. Each corner uses 12 F leaves.

ASSEMBLY: Refer to diagram, *page 247,* to lay out completed blocks. Alternate rose blocks and vine blocks. Add corner block at each corner and half blocks to fill in side edges. Sew units together in diagonal rows.

Trim two 4x90-inch borders to 85¼ inches long for side borders. Trim remaining border piece to 93¼ inches long for bottom border.

To make each side border, position and baste approximately 3 yards of vine along border so it has 13 curves (spacing between peaks on curves is about 13 inches). Twenty-six F leaves and 13 H buds are used on each side border. Appliqué H bud at center of each curve; appliqué F leaf 1 to 1½ inches to each side of each bud. Appliqué vine.

Bottom border is similar to side. Position and baste about 3 yards of vine so it has 16 curves. Thirty-four F leaves and 16 buds are used on bottom border. Sew side borders to opposite sides of the quilt. Sew the bottom border along quilt bottom.

FINISHING: Layer and baste top, backing, and batting. Quilt with double-line grid of squares, spacing lines ¼ inch and 1¼ inches apart. Trim batting and backing, rounding corners. Bind.

Posy Wreath Quilt

Shown on pages 234–235.
Finished size: 83½x85½ inches.

MATERIALS

7 yards of white fabric
4 yards of red fabric
4 yards of teal fabric
⅛ yard of yellow print fabric
5 yards of backing fabric
Water-erasable pen
Quilt batting

INSTRUCTIONS

Transfer full-size pattern pieces on *page 248* onto paper. Make cardboard or plastic templates for patterns. Draw a 16-inch square on graph paper. Make a template for this square without adding seam allowances on template.

CUTTING INSTRUCTIONS: From white fabric, cut top border 6½x71½ inches. Use 16-inch square template to cut 13 squares; add ¼-inch seam allowances.

Divide square template into two large triangles. Use one triangle template to mark and cut eight triangles from white fabric with long side of triangle on straight of fabric grain, adding ¼-inch seam allowances.

Divide one triangle template into two smaller triangles. Use small triangle template to mark and cut four triangles from white fabric with legs of triangle on straight of fabric grain; add ¼-inch seam allowances. From white fabric, cut 81 wedge pieces for pieced border. Save remaining white fabric for bias binding.

From red fabric, cut two borders,

each 1¼x71½ inches, and two borders, *each* 1¼x73 inches. (Dimensions for borders and sashing pieces include ¼-inch seam allowances.) Cut sashing as follows: 18 pieces *each* measuring 1¼x16½ inches, two *each* 1¼x17½ inches, two *each* 1¼x51½ inches, and two *each* 1¼x85 inches.

continued

POSY WREATH QUILT

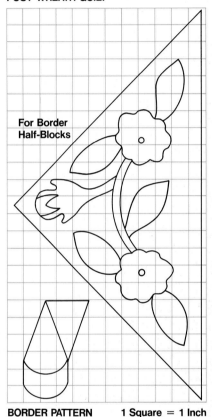

**For Border
Half-Blocks**

BORDER PATTERN   **1 Square = 1 Inch**

POSY WREATH QUILT

Block Diagram

249

continued from page 249
**The Flowering of
American Patchwork**

Cut 72 red posies and eight buds. Cut 84 red scallops for borders.

From teal blue fabric, cut eight bud stems, 64 large leaves, and 196 small leaves. Cut 84 cone shapes for borders. From remaining teal, cut 60 *bias* strips *each* 1¼x7 inches. Fold and press in thirds *lengthwise* to finish about ⅜ inch wide.

Cut 72 circles about 1 inch in diameter for posy centers.

BLOCK PIECING: To make a posy, snip a ⅛-inch-diameter circle in position indicated for center.

To reverse-appliqué a center, baste yellow print circle under hole with *right* side of yellow fabric toward *wrong* side of posy. Turn under center hole about ⅛ inch and appliqué it to yellow fabric. Make 72.

With a water-erasable pen, mark appliqué design on white squares and triangle pieces. Curve prepared bias strips along curves on design and appliqué in place. Pin prepared posies and other design elements in place and appliqué.

Appliqué 13 squares, eight large triangles, and four corner triangles.

ASSEMBLY: Referring to photograph on *pages 234–235,* lay out blocks and triangles. Sew blocks into diagonal rows with 1¼x16½-inch sashing strips between blocks. Sew diagonal rows together, fitting remaining sashing strips between appropriate rows.

Center and sew a 1¼x71½-inch border to opposite sides of quilt top. Center and sew a 1¼x73-inch border to remaining sides. Trim sashing strips even with borders.

FINISHING: Sew a red scallop to the curved edge of *each* teal cone piece. Sew three borders, alternating 28 colored cones with 27 white wedges, beginning and ending each border with a colored cone.

Center and sew a pieced border to opposite sides of quilt top. Center and sew a pieced border to bottom

of quilt. Borders will extend at both ends to allow for mitering bottom corners and adding top border. Miter corners of pieced borders at bottom two corners of quilt top. Sew white border to top of quilt. Trim off excess pieced borders.

Piece back; layer and baste together top, batting, and back. Outline-quilt around appliqué shapes. Quilt white areas in parallel lines spaced ½ inch apart. From remaining white fabric, make 1-inch-wide bias binding. Trim batting and back even with top; bind.

Seth Thomas Quilt

Shown on page 237.
Finished size: 89¾x113 inches.

MATERIALS
10½ yards of white fabric
3¼ yards of green fabric
¾ yard of red fabric
¼ yard of orange fabric
8 yards for quilt back
Quilt batting

INSTRUCTIONS
From plastic or heavy paper, make templates for patterns A–M on *page 251.* Make template for 16½-inch square to cut background pieces. Patterns are finished size; add ¼-inch seam allowances to all pieces when cutting from fabric.

CUTTING INSTRUCTIONS: Cut off a 3¼-yard-long piece from white fabric. Cut four 10½-inch-wide borders from this fabric. (Measurement includes seam allowances, and borders will be trimmed to length when added to quilt top.)

Use 16½-inch square template to cut 18 squares from remaining white fabric, adding ¼-inch seam allowances. Cut square template into two triangles. Cut one triangle into two smaller triangles. With long side of large triangle template on straight of fabric grain, cut 10 triangles, adding ¼-inch seam allowances. Cut four small triangles with legs of triangle on straight of fabric grain, again adding seam allowances.

From remaining white fabric, cut 12 yards of 1½-inch-wide bias for binding. Cut appliqué pieces from colored fabrics. The number to cut for one block is stated first, with total number for quilt in parentheses.

From green fabric, cut pieces as follows: 8 (96) of B, 4 (48) of E, 2 (24) of G, 6 (72) of H, 1 (12) of K, 1 (12) of L, and 3 (36) of M. Cut an additional 40 of M for borders. From remaining green, cut 11½ yards of 1⅜-inch-wide bias. Fold bias in thirds to finished width of ½ inch; press.

From red fabric, cut 2 (24) of B, 8 (96) of C, 1 (12) of D, and 2 (24) of I.

From orange fabric, cut 1 (12) of C, 2 (24) of F, and 2 (24) of J.

From pink fabric, cut 1 (12) of A.

BLOCK PIECING: Fold white square in half diagonally and press in a crease lightly. Position bottom of vase (piece L) on diagonal axis, 4½ inches up from corner of block. Refer to photograph, *page 237,* to lay out pieces to complete design. Pin or baste and appliqué pieces to block. Make 12 blocks.

ASSEMBLY: Lay out 12 appliqué blocks and six plain blocks in four rows of three blocks each. Blocks are "set on point" with plain blocks between rows of pattern blocks. Fill in outer edges with triangles. Sew together in diagonal rows.

Sew borders to quilt top, matching center of borders to center of quilt top sides. Miter corners; trim off excess border fabric.

Referring to photograph on *page 237,* appliqué about 110 inches of green bias for a vine along *each* quilt side, forming 12 gentle curves. Appliqué 12 M leaves along curves on each side to alternate sides of vine. At top use two 48-inch-long bias strips to form four curves each with vines crossing at top center. Repeat for bottom. Appliqué eight leaves to alternate sides of top and bottom vines along curves.

Mark plain blocks with 15-inch-diameter feathered circles. Mark triangles with portions of circles. Mark other white areas and vases with a diagonal grid of ¾-inch squares. Quilt; finish quilt as desired.

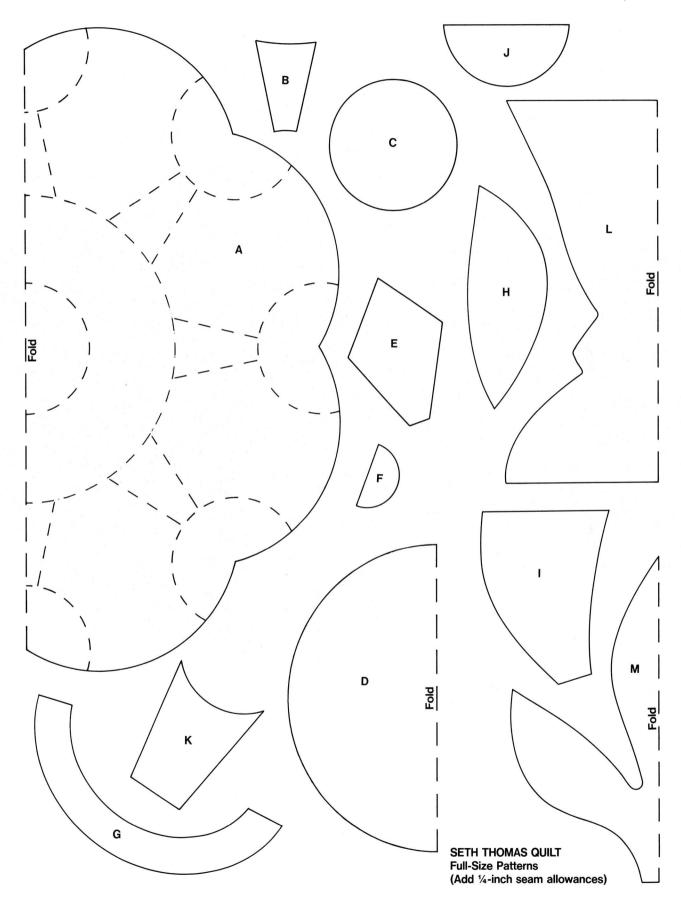

SETH THOMAS QUILT
Full-Size Patterns
(Add ¼-inch seam allowances)

BASIC STITCHES

Embroidery Stitches

Buttonhole Stitch

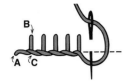

Chain Stitch

Couched Filling Stitch

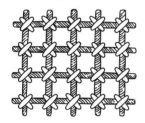

Couching Stitch

Darning Stitch

Featherstitch

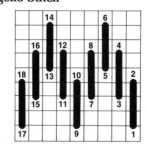

French Knot

Long-and-Short Stitch

Outline (or Stem) Stitch

Parallel Featherstitch

Satin Stitch

Needlepoint Stitches

Bargello Stitch

Basket-Weave Stitch

Continental Stitch

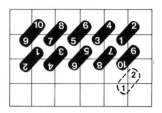

Cross-Stitch

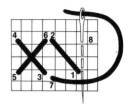

Crocheting Abbreviations

beg	begin(ning)
ch	chain
cl	cluster
dc	double crochet
lp(s)	loop(s)
pc	popcorn
rep	repeat
sc	single crochet
sk	skip
sl st	slip stitch
sp	space
st(s)	stitch(es)
*	repeat from * as indicated

Knitting Abbreviations

dec	decrease
inc	increase
k	knit
p	purl
pat	pattern
rem	remaining
rep	repeat
rnd	round
sk	skip
sl st	slip stitch
st(s)	stitch(es)
tog	together
yo	yarn over
*	repeat from * as indicated

ACKNOWLEDGMENTS

We would like to express our gratitude and appreciation to the many people who helped us with this book.

Designers

Ivan Barnett—frame, 12–13
Ruth Bousman—pressed flower frame, 185
Marlene Burrell—herb wreaths and nests, 184–185
Sue Cleaver—floorcloth, 74–75
Coats and Clark—pillows, fringed spread, 206
Pam Dennis and Rick Weiss—willow furniture, 10–11
Joel Doss—spice drawers, 169
Ann Doyle—rosebud wreath and box, 184–185
Linda Emmerson—silhouettes, 52
Barbara Forbes—apple wreath, 183; table decorations, 190–193
Jim Forbes—onion box, 168–169
Jill Fitzhenry and Nancy Jefferson—painted pieces, 14–15
Meryl Griffiths—fraktur birth sampler and house blessing, 48–49
Jan Hollebrands—doll, 117; flowers and wreath, 188–189
Eileen Hoover—sampler, 142–143
Victoria Justmann—stenciling, 96–99
Living History Farms—quilt, 18–19
Christine Noah-Cooper—cut-paper lampshade, 30–31; heart, 50–51
Beverly Rivers—blocks, 116–117
Mary Rust—place mats, 8–9
Rosa Snyder—background faux finishes, 94–95; boxes and frames, 103
Stearns and Foster—quilt, 232
Judie Tasch—doll, 16–17
Valley Hill Herbs and Everlastings—floral wreath, 186–187
Barbara Vassler—bandboxes, 162–163
Jack Vessels—doll cupboard, 123
Jerry Vis—marbled floors, 100–101

Jim Williams—fire screen and crewel pillow, 27; towels, 28; mirror frame and doily, 30–31; rose-hip wreath, 184–185; needlepoint chair seat, 209

Photographers

Sean Fitzgerald—12, 22–23, 24–25, 27, 28–29, 30–31, 47 (center), 52 (top and lower left), 53 (lower left), 71, 75, 95 (center), 102 (top), 104–105, 120–121, 122, 124–125, 141 (center), 162–163, 164–165, 169, 203 (center), 206–207, 208, 210, 230–231, 232, 234–235, 236–237
Susan Gilmore—7, 15
Hedrich-Blessing—184–185
William Hopkins, Sr.—19, 69 (center), 76, 80, 166–167, 168 (lower left), 182–183, 188
Michael Jensen—6–7, 8, 10, 17 (bottom), 20–21, 26, 46–47, 48–49, 50–51, 52 (lower right), 53 (top), 54–55, 68–69, 70, 72–73, 74, 77, 78–79, 81, 94–95, 103, 104–105, 116–117, 118–119, 123, 142–143, 144–145, 146–147, 148–149, 161 (center), 168 (top and lower right), 183 (center), 186–187, 189, 190–191, 192–193, 202–203, 204–205, 209, 211, 226–227, 228–229, 233
Maris/Semel—9, 13, 100–101, 102 (bottom)
Perry Struse—11, 18, 53 (lower right), 96–97, 98–99, 140–141, 160–161
Al Tenfer—16, 17 (top)

Credits

Laura Ashley, 714 Madison Ave., New York, NY 10021
Jim Borcherding
Mr. and Mrs. Doug Burns
The Margaret Cavigga Quilt Collection, 8648 Melrose Ave., Los Angeles, CA 90069
The Century Shoppe, 333 Fifth St., West Des Moines, IA 50265
The Christopher Inn, 201 Mill St., Excelsior, MN 55331

Mr. and Mrs. George Cleaver and Annie
Ruth DeCook
Dot's Frame Shop, 4717 Fleur Dr., Des Moines, IA 50321
Elinor's Antiques, 102 Fifth St., West Des Moines, IA 50265
Kathy Engle
The Evergreen Press, P.O. Box 4971, Walnut Creek, CA 94596
Mr. and Mrs. Jim Forbes
Jim Gentry, Director, Southern Highland Handicraft Guild, Asheville, NC 28815
Louise German
Ginny's Antiques, 333 Fifth St., West Des Moines, IA 50265
Harry and David Orchards, Medford, OR 97501
Ron Hawbaker
Heart of Country Antiques Show, Opryland Hotel, Nashville, TN 37214
Fred Hudson
Imperial Wallcovering, 23645 Mercantile Rd., Cleveland, OH 44122
Karastan Rug Mills, 919 Third Ave., New York, NY 10022
The community of Lewes, Delaware
Living History Farms, 2600 NW. 111th St., Urbandale, IA 50322
Dr. and Mrs. James E. Marvil
Mr. and Mrs. Robert Meehan
Jane Mollenhoff
Joan Moshimer, Craftsman Hooked Rugs, Kennebunkport, ME 04046
Murphy's Landing, 2187 E. Highway 101, Shakopee, MN 55379
Pella Lace Curtains/Heritage Imports, P.O. Box 328, Pella, IA 50219
Mr. and Mrs. John Raymond
Schumaker's Inn, 212 W. Main St., New Prague, MN 56071
Sam and Becky Senti
Darrell Shull
Don Sires
St. James Hotel, 406 Main St., Red Wing, MN 55066
Tom Thompson
Mr. and Mrs. Jack Vessels
Jack West
Don Wipperman
Linda Youngquist

For photographs, see pages noted in **bold** type; remaining numbers refer to instructions pages.

S–T

U–Z

Have BETTER HOMES AND
GARDENS® magazine delivered to
your door. For information,
write to: MR. ROBERT AUSTIN
P.O. BOX 4536
DES MOINES, IA 50336